Springer Proceedings in Business and Economics

More information about this series at http://www.springer.com/series/11960

Sebastian A. Văduva · Randolph Wilt
Ioan Fotea · Lois P. Văduva
Editors

Civil Society: The Engine for Economic and Social Well-Being

The 2017 Griffiths School of Management and IT Annual Conference on Business, Entrepreneurship and Ethics (GMSAC)

EMANUEL UNIVERSITY OF ORADEA
INTEGRITY, EXCELLENCE & PASSION

Springer

Editors
Sebastian A. Văduva
Griffiths School of Management
Emanuel University of Oradea
Oradea, Romania

Ioan Fotea
Griffiths School of Management
Emanuel University of Oradea
Oradea, Romania

Randolph Wilt
College of Business
and Communications
Concordia University Texas
Austin, TX, USA

Lois P. Văduva
Emanuel University of Oradea
Oradea, Romania

ISSN 2198-7246 ISSN 2198-7254 (electronic)
Springer Proceedings in Business and Economics
ISBN 978-3-030-07883-6 ISBN 978-3-319-89872-8 (eBook)
https://doi.org/10.1007/978-3-319-89872-8

Printed on acid-free paper

This Springer imprint is published by the registered company Springer International Publishing AG part of Springer Nature
The registered company address is: Gewerbestrasse 11, 6330 Cham, Switzerland

Preface

The GSMAC 2017 Conference, organized by the Griffiths School of Management and IT within Emanuel University of Oradea, explores the theme of the civil society as the engine for economic and social well-being.

While this subject has been heavily debated at a global level, the perspective of civil society contributing to this process is much less deliberated. Research and practice have proven that there is a great potential for civil society organizations to directly and indirectly support socioeconomic well-being. Nevertheless, active societies and growing economies can, in turn, contribute to strengthening the role of non-state actors. As a result, the interplay between civil society economic and social well-being is a highly relevant subject to research and discuss by both academics and practitioners in government, business, and the nonprofit sector.

This volume brings together different perspectives and studies that are crucial in understanding emerging trends that influence the concurrence between Civil Society, economy, and social well-being. The authors of *A Cross-Generational Perspective on Green Loyalty in Romanian Retail* argue that in last years, the Civil Society has increased the demand for environmentally friendly, green products, thus putting pressure on retailers to come up with new solutions to secure green loyalty. *Linking Business with Civil Society: The Bridging Role of CSR* highlights the role of Corporate Social Responsibility as a mediator between business and civil society, offering a survey-based research that proves the link between the attitude of the manager regarding business in society and their social responsibility actions.

An interesting point of view is brought by the authors of *Comparative Study Regarding Organizational Culture: Nonprofit Organization and Profit-Oriented Organization*, through a case study that illustrates the differences in facilitating local socioeconomic development.

The issues of consumer behavior and social values impact the civil society, the research *Investigating the Different Roles of the Factors Affecting Ethically Questionable Consumer Behavior* being of value in demonstrating that influencing factors of ethically questionable behavior change their importance depending on the type of the behavior.

Politicized Economy and Its Effects on Business Sustainability: A Case Study on Romania investigates the way in which the politicization of the economy could impact both the Romanian economy and the local businesses. The authors argue that business sustainability contributes but also depends on the sustainability of its economical and social environment.

The study *Developing a Culture of Service Utilizing the Civil Society in Romania: Needs Assessment and Training Preparation for the Hospitality Industry* fulfills a void in Romanian research, as the hospitality sector is one of the most important categories of economic growth despite the limitations of research in this area. This study aims to provide answers and solutions to the emerging hospitality industry in Romania by focusing on the principal traits that can be found in more developed countries and how those traits can be adjusted to the Romanian culture.

Semiotics and the Entrepreneurial Creation's Myths reveal the relationship between rational approaches and relational ones, as two complementary perspectives in a new interdisciplinary paradigm.

The current global climate has produced many social problems, which demand creative solutions. *The Role of the Civil Sector in Contribution to Social Well-Being and in Shaping Active Citizenship* argues the importance of civil society in creating social welfare by producing services and jobs. The premises of this theory are strengthened by a study conducted in Hungary that focuses on the way in which organizations can contribute to active citizenship.

Quo vadis Romanian Marketing: The Future and Contribution of the Romanian Community? is a study that marks the main directions in the fundamental research and in the applied marketing research, while demonstrating that civil society, through its requirements, including the field of marketing communication, plays a significant role in solving the problem regarding the benefits and costs of marketing.

The authors of the article *Online Research and Learning Environment to Facilitate the Elaboration of Bachelor's/Master's Theses in Multidisciplinary Teams* argue that research is a key component in the development of the civil society and the first step toward developing the practice of research is in the University setting. To facilitate research, this research proposes the development of a national or even international electronic research and learning environment, meant to facilitate the connection between all possible stakeholders in the elaboration of bachelor's/master's theses.

Global Governance and the Role of Non-state Actors in Improving the Social and Economic Development of Growing Economies: A Conceptual Approach Using a Global Public Health Framework on Violence Prevention presents a comprehensive study on the problem of violence and its impact on economy. The study aims to highlight the different approaches that can create a broad understanding of the issue. The authors argue the fact that the public health approach to violence offers a unique view that can determine the principal factors related to violence. Also, societies would benefit from a better collaboration regarding the dissemination of valuable data and information that could, in turn, provide better solutions for the prevention of violence.

Developing Prosperity in Romania's Second-Tier Cities Through STEM Education is a study that demonstrates the importance of changing the curriculum in schools with the purpose of promoting science, technology, engineering, and mathematics. The authors argue that a focus on stem education would bring significant developments on multiple levels in society, as jobs related to these subjects are considered to be some of the fastest growing pursuits in the twenty-first century. Moreover, putting a focus on stem education in Romania's second-tier cities would mean local economic growth, which would in turn positively affect the national economy.

The article *Romanian Hospitality Degree Graduates: Perceptions and Attitudes Among Industry Professionals* argues the fact that proper training would develop the hospitality sector in Romania that, in turn, would have a significant impact on the overall economy. The authors present the current situation in the Romanian hospitality industry, noting the fact that despite the drop in GDP and employment, there has been an increase in service education, which is a positive trend with a promising future.

We trust that you will find this useful.

Oradea, Romania Sebastian A. Văduva
Austin, USA Randolph Wilt
Oradea, Romania Ioan Fotea
Oradea, Romania Lois P. Văduva

Contents

Chapter 1
A Cross-Generational Perspective on Green Loyalty in Romanian Retail

Dan-Cristian Dabija and Brîndușa Mariana Bejan

Abstract In the century of social media, mobile technologies and online communication, retailers are faced with more and more complex challenges in their attempt to satisfy and maintain current consumers, and attract new customers. Faced with increasing challenges in the development of attractive offers for target groups, and with the need to implement sustainable business strategies, retailers choose to widen their appeal with environmentally friendly, green products and to approach customers according to their values, motivations, preferences and attitudes. In order to establish the extent to which food and non-food retailers in Romania are capable of building green loyalty among various generations of consumers (Baby Boomers, Gen Xers, Millennials and Gen Zers) against the background of consumers' green values, green propensity and green reuse motivation, the authors conducted a survey-based empirical exploratory study. By means of structural equation modelling, it is shown that consumers' green loyalty varies between generations, Millennials, Generation Z being a lot more oriented towards green loyalty than their parents or grandparents.

Keywords Green loyalty · Green consumer values · Romanian retail
Structural equation modelling

Clasificare JEL Q01 · Q55

1.1 Introduction

In today's society, the available resources and the way in which these are used have become a growing concern, due to people's increased access to information

---

D.-C. Dabija (✉) · B. M. Bejan
Faculty of Economics and Business Administration, Department of Marketing, Babeș-Bolyai University Cluj-Napoca, Cluj-Napoca, Romania
e-mail: cristian.dabija@econ.ubbcluj.ro

B. M. Bejan
e-mail: brandusa.bejan@econ.ubbcluj.ro

S. A. Văduva et al. (eds.), *Civil Society: The Engine for Economic and Social Well-Being*, Springer Proceedings in Business and Economics,
https://doi.org/10.1007/978-3-319-89872-8_1

(Viswanathan et al. 2013) and the huge role of social media in the spread of online communication (Young 2015; Dabija and Grant 2016). Companies, as well as specialists, constantly seek new ways to address and satisfy people's needs and adapt to their ever-changing and evolving expectations and demands (Dabija and Pop 2008). Therefore, the identification of alternative, sustainable, green, environmentally friendly products, allowing mankind to preserve the planet's resources, reduce pollution, protect the environment and improve the population's health is as important and timely for companies as is the use of new production technologies, process innovation, the streamlining of activities and decision-making transparency and correctness (Pop and Dabija 2013; Postelnicu and Dabija 2015). Marketers constantly seek new solutions and techniques to change and adapt 'ordinary' products and brands by means of new technologies in the production of recyclable materials and components, and organic ingredients, which protect the environment and do not in any way undermine their integrity (Hamid 2014).

Many retailers view sustainable products as a niche variety, which cannot be widely marketed in stores or be part of their offers, due to low demand and the higher per unit production, transportation and storage costs, as a consequence of the smaller quantity of articles produced. The higher the visibility and degree of acceptance of such products, the lower the costs of maintaining such varieties, and the better the image of retailers among consumers, by focusing on sustainability strategies, which also brings them higher profits. Certainly, the promotion of a strong image plays an extremely important role in supporting such brands (Collins et al. 2007). Being aware of the behavioural patterns adopted when purchasing sustainable products, and of the fact that such purchasing is very likely to be repeated in the future, as the consumer again chooses green products in a new shopping context, retailers often expand their offers to include such products, even if they currently do not generate enough revenue.

To introduce and keep selling sustainable, green products, it is important for retailers to be aware of and understand the various antecedents (prerequisites) setting off consumers' behaviour and reactions, regardless of their age, in determining their preference for such products. At the same time, retailers have to discover the means whereby they can generate customer loyalty towards green products, be it in terms of recommending and re-purchasing environmentally friendly products or revisiting retailers which implement and support sustainability strategies and measures. The literature highlights that young people are more willing than their parents and grandparents to adopt green behaviour and choose retailers implementing green strategies (Singh 2013; Lan 2014; Young 2015).

The measures and tactics employed by retailers to attract consumers and earn their loyalty may vary considerably depending on the kind of goods marketed (food versus non-food), and the frequency with which such goods are purchased (Pop et al. 2011; Swoboda et al. 2014). The loyalty displayed in revisiting, re-purchasing from and recommending a retailer that implements a green strategy may be determined by a number of behavioural antecedents, which enhance the individual's preference for the store concerned. An individual's environmental protection-oriented personal and social values, his/her propensity to search for and prefer green, sustainable products, the desire to make a small contribution to the preservation of resources and the motivation to buy environmentally friendly products represent important factors behind young, adult or elderly people's choice of a particular retailer and its products. Starting with the generational theory (Williams and Page 2009) based on the segmentation of individuals into generations according to their year of birth, the authors investigate, within a quantitative research study, the factors generating 'green' loyalty to food and non-food retail stores among four generations of consumers. These factors are the green values, green propensity and green reuse motivation of the consumers.

Following the literature review on the behavioural antecedents (the green values, green propensity and green reuse motivation of the consumers) shaping consumers' green loyalty, the authors highlight the different degrees of green awareness among different generations. The quantitative empirical study conducted by the authors among older (Baby Boomers), adult (Generation X) and young (Millennials and Generation Z) people shows how the third group (young people) are more willing to develop green loyalty to retail stores by revisiting and recommending the retailer to other people. Conclusions and directions for future research are presented at the end of the paper.

1.2 Green Loyalty and Its Antecedents

It is not only the need to produce sustainable products that retailers are faced with but also the challenge of attracting and satisfying consumers, gaining their loyalty, having them re-purchase brands or products, and revisit and recommend the store. Endowing a product with environmentally friendly or organic elements does not necessarily modify its appearance nor make it more user-friendly or attractive to consumers. Cowan and Kinley (2014) point out that people do not change their preference, do not buy products and do not become more loyal to supplying companies merely because their products are made of 'green' components or ingredients. An important role in the building of customer loyalty to products made of environmentally friendly components is certainly played by word-of-mouth, brand trust and brand effect, as well as people's willingness to pay a higher price for their favourite product. Loyalty blends the attitudinal dimension with the cognitive dimension, prompting consumers to pay a higher price for the characteristics of a product, as well as for the brand fame, sometimes to the detriment of the quality/price ratio (Garcia de los Salmones et al. 2005).

Customer loyalty to a retail format, company, product or brand may be regarded as the highest reward on the part of the customer when his/her wishes have been fulfilled and expectations have been satisfied or even exceeded (Pop and Dabija 2014). Even if the slightly higher price and the relatively recent entry in the market of green products might be thought of as barriers to their purchase, recent studies show that consumers' personal values and sustainable orientation, together with their desire to have a share in protecting the environment and preserving resources, will not only make them prefer such products but also command their loyalty (Lin et al. 2017).

Consumers across continents show increased willingness to pay a premium price for sustainable, organic or green products (Davari and Strutton 2014; Pop and Dabija 2014), and they often decide to buy on the basis of positive experiences and feelings towards such products and the intrinsic and extrinsic advantages gained by purchasing them. The benefits of customer loyalty are evident not only in the form of repeat purchasing and the preference for a store or retailer but also in the form of consumers' positive advertising (word-of-mouth recommendation) of the store/retailer to other people and increased attachment to the brand (Pop and Dabija 2014).

Customer loyalty may also be engendered by retailers undertaking campaigns to promote social responsibility and raise awareness about the need to protect the environment (Singh et al. 2008). People usually show positive appreciation when a company is actively involved in the preservation of resources, provides support to the disadvantaged or devotes time, effort, staff and resources to solve environmental problems. Their appreciation will translate into revisiting, re-purchasing, word-of-mouth recommendation and preference for the same brands, stores or retailer. Meeting consumers' expectations assures retailers that they will return to their favourite stores (Pop and Dabija 2014). Conversely, falling short of expectations might encourage consumers to defect to the competition or spread negative word-of-mouth comments.

Each retailer wishes its customers were immune to the marketing efforts of its competitors, to the effect that they only buy from its stores and prefer only its brands which they re-purchase and recommend products (Dabija and Băbuț 2014). Despite retailers' increasing offers of green, organic or environmentally friendly products, such varieties are still for a niche only market, which makes their mass marketing and purchase by a greater number of consumers less feasible, particularly as they are marketed at a price higher than that of similar traditional products. The major challenge for any company trying to promote sustainable products and launch green brands in the market lies in building green consumer loyalty among its target segments (Dabija and Bejan 2017). This loyalty is based on a specific mindset (Pop and Dabija 2013) which prefers almost exclusively products made of sustainable, organic, green elements or ingredients contributing to environmental protection, and is the result of three essential antecedents: green consumer values, green consumer propensity and green reuse motivation (Garcia de los Salmones et al. 2005; Dabija and Bejan 2017).

Green Consumer Values. An individual's values represent principles learned over time, experience and circumstance. The importance of one's own values differs between individuals, being specific indicators used to assess a situation or decision. Consumer values influence the social norms guiding an individual in his/her actions (Solomon 2014), which in turn influence their beliefs and behaviour (Collins et al. 2007).

The literature has shown that there is a direct link between an individual's values, beliefs and behaviour displayed in connection with sustainability and his/her green orientation (Karp 1996; Schultz and Zelezny 1999; Stern et al. 1999). In fact, collectivism-oriented people show greater concern for sustainability and willingness to participate in environmental protection actions than individualism-oriented people. Likewise, people advocating universalism and feeling close to other people as well as to the environment show a proactive attitude by championing the protection of nature, and by supporting companies' sustainable strategies and actions. At the opposite end are people driven by their own self-interests and exhibiting a conservative attitude. Such people resist change and do not pursue the welfare of society, as they reject everything related to sustainability and green products (Collins et al. 2007).

Green Consumer Propensity. It is important for retailers pursuing a sustainability strategy to properly understand not only the values of their customers but also how these values can be used to influence their preference and propensity for green products (Hamid 2014). Retailers attempt to persuade green-oriented customers into making known the monetary and psychological advantages gained from purchasing and consuming the products offered among their friends, acquaintances and the target groups they identify with. The customers of retail stores often express environmental concern with respect to the products they buy, and this is a reflection of their green attitude and desire to adopt sustainable products (Cohn and Vaccaro 2015). Environmental concern has a positive effect and a major impact on consumers' attitude to green products, a good predictor thereof being the individual's collectivist orientation (Kirmani and Khan 2016). Environmental concern assumes the existence of a proactive attitude on the part of consumers and a desire to share in solving environmental problems, preserving resources, etc. Further, modern consumers tend to adopt green products due to social influence from the relevant reference groups they identify with or belong to. Membership of strong reference groups can lead to a change in consumers' opinions and attitudes, as they may search, prefer or buy green products with increased vigour (Varshneya et al. 2017).

Consumers generally resist change to the effect that any change in the characteristics of a product may lead to a short- or long-term drop in sales (Zentes et al. 2012; Foscht and Swoboda 2017). Therefore, marketers are tasked with persuading consumers to prefer and buy sustainable, green, environmentally friendly products. They also have to take on the difficult task of getting consumers to use/exploit the purchased articles/products for a longer period, and reuse or recycle them (Dabija et al. 2016; Dabija et al. 2017). However, an individual's green orientation may be the needed catalyst for generating a favourable attitude translated into the preference of not only sustainable products but also products meeting sustainability requirements.

Green Reuse Motivation. An individual's care and attachment to nature conservation may foster the adoption of sustainable products and spark the intention to buy green products (Bisschoff and Liebenberg 2015). It is the collectivism-oriented individuals who support environmental protection and conservation campaigns, as they are more willing to recycle, reuse or extend the lifespan of the products they buy (do Paço et al. 2013). Individuals' knowledge of the environment, their affinity for environmental protection activities, green values and proactive attitudes underlying their past actions often serve as good predictors of future green behaviour (Cowan and Kinley 2014). Individuals who recycle products are thought of as innovators when adopting green products (Haws et al. 2014) because they achieve maximum effect from existing resources by reusing old products in a creative way, in accordance with environmental protection norms. Product recycling and reusing is a form of sustainable consumption behaviour (Joshi and Rahman 2016). The adoption of green products and the support given to companies for environmental protection actions are major parts of sustainable behaviour, while recycling is a complementary element.

People's penchant for recycling is generally caused by their positive attitude to environmental protection and the individual's set of fundamental values (Roberts and Bacon 1997). A passive attitude to environmental problems and challenges, together with lack of convenience and other disruptions, may inhibit an individual's desire to recycle products. However, for many people, recycling behaviour is a moral norm (Tanner and Kast 2003).

In light of the previously mentioned aspects, we put forward the following hypothesis:

H_1, the incidence of green consumers' values, green consumers' propensity and green reuse motivation in building consumer loyalty to the retail formats considered varies.

1.3 Green Consciousness of Consumer Generations

The adoption of sustainable behaviour, looking diligently for organic or green products and taking part in environmental protection campaigns are behaviours shaped by individuals' value systems, attitudes, lifestyles, preferences, experience (Euromonitor International 2015a) and socio-demographic characteristics. Namkung and Soocheong (Shawn) (2014) conclude that age is an important element which might influence an individual's willingness to pay a higher price for green products. In fact, older people aged over 55 (Baby Boomers) consume more sustainable products than their younger peers because they have adequate financial resources and pay greater attention to their health (Hur et al. 2015). Baby Boomers' education and life experience (Gurău 2012; Young 2015) accounts for their greater concern for global warming and healthy diet as part of their effort to lower man's impact on nature and resources (DiPietro et al. 2013; Euromonitor International 2015a). However, typical of this generation is their loyalty to brands and products they have been familiar with since their youth. Older people are very reluctant to change consumption habits and buy new products, even if such products make a better contribution to environmental protection and conservation of resources (Hur et al. 2015). Many Baby Boomers now regret the choices they have made in life, as well as the fact that they may have contributed to excessive use of resources through the products they have bought or preferred. With this reality in mind, some Baby Boomers re-think their past choices, being at present more concerned with the issue of sustainability and environmental protection (Venn et al. 2017). In light of their values and attitudes, we believe that, H_2, Baby Boomers pay greater attention to green propensity than the younger generations.

Green products are keenly preferred, sought and bought by other generations as well: Gen Xers (born between 1965 and 1980), Millennials (1981–1994) and Generation Z (born after 1995) (Taken Smith 2011; Gurău 2012; Doster 2013; Eastman et al. 2014; Young 2015). Gen Xers are relatively well-educated, despite the hostile living conditions they have been through, especially in Eastern countries and the former communist bloc (Euromonitor 2009). They place great emphasis on family and social relationships, are flexible and pragmatic, and pursue spiritual values and intellectual development (Hernaus and Pološki Vokic 2014). On the other hand, Millennials are a lot more anxious to achieve their objectives (Howe and Strauss 2003) using, just like the next generation (Z), social media, mobile technology, smartphones, etc., to communicate and always keep abreast of the latest news (Shaw et al. 2008). Displaying an antagonistic attitude to Baby Boomers, Millennials and Generation Z members are a lot more straightforward and communicative, and concerned with ethnic and multicultural issues, but also loyal to the communities they belong to or identify with. Therefore, the problems and ideals of their friends and acquaintances are also their own problems and ideals (Bucic et al. 2012). Young people are aware of environmental problems and of their duty to diminish the human impact on nature, and, for this reason, they are willing to seek and buy green, organic products, contributing to the preservation of resources (Dunmore 2013; Singh 2013; Lan 2014). As they are concerned with their own future, they are willing to accept and pay a higher price for eco-friendly products/articles (Lu et al. 2013).

These aspects encourage companies to use green products as the main lever to earn the loyalty of Millennials, Generation Z and Baby Boomers. Capturing the attention of these customers and drawing them to the retailer's stores will result in their serving as opinion leaders and endorsers, influencing and persuading others into buying green, organic products which preserve resources (Singh et al. 2008).

1.4 Methodology of Research

A survey-based empirical exploratory study has been conducted to highlight the extent to which the members of the four generations considered (Baby Boomers, Gen Xers, Millennials and Generation Z) are able to build up their 'green' loyalty to the retail stores selling food, electronic and household appliances, DIY, furniture, interior design as well as fashion, footwear and sportswear items, driven by behavioural factors determining their green orientation (green values, green propensity and green reuse motivation). The investigated model is presented in Fig. 1.1.

During the research, over 100 interviewers (students of the authors) asked respondents for their opinions on the themes investigated. The data collected through questionnaires were systematically compiled, centralized and then interpreted with research-specific statistical software—SPSS and AMOS (for structural equation modelling) (Churchill 1991). To develop the questionnaire and its themes, each question was operationalized in accordance with the guidelines in the literature, while the statements were tailored to the context of the generations investigated and the various types of retail (Table 1.1). In fact, the scales used in the present research were also used in the context of food retail (Nasir and Karakaya 2014), concerning the factors affecting and determining green consumer behaviour (Lastovicka et al. 1999; Haws et al. 2014), and in the context of socially responsible consumption (Antil and Bennett 1979; Antil 1984).

Out of almost 3,500 interviews carried out in 2016, 3,382 were validated. The socio-demographic sample representativeness was ensured by the prior training of interviewees who had to select respondents by using the quota sampling method according to age and gender (Churchill 1991). These quotas were established for each interviewee according to the distribution of Romania's population in the Statistical Yearbook (2014). The interviewees had to conduct face-to-face interviews in public places, at the respondents' homes or workplaces and in the neighbourhood of different retail stores. Each interviewee was instructed to conduct ten interviews in these places. Only respondents having recent experience (last three months) of the stores concerned (fashion, footwear, food, electronic and household appliances, DIY, furniture and interior design) were invited to interview. The randomness of answers was ensured by each respondent having to name three stores in a category. The first respondent was asked to analyse the statements in Table 1.1 in relation to the first spontaneously named store, the second respondent analysed the second store, etc. In drawing the sample, efforts were made to ensure the territorial representativeness of answers, as interviews were carried out in rural areas (about 15% of questionnaires) as well as in urban municipalities of different population levels: small cities (less than 20,000 inhabitants), medium-sized cities (20,000–75,000 inhabitants) and large cities (over 75,000 inhabitants). Respondents expressed their level of agreement with respect to the statements in Table 1.1 on a five-point Likert scale. Questionnaires with more than 5% of missing answers were later excluded from the analysis.

After the data were collected, they were statistically tested to determine their correctness, reliability and internal consistency by means of Cronbach's α coefficient ($\alpha > 0.7$), the 'item-to-total' correlation, the KMO criterion (>0.7), Bartlett's test of sphericity (exploratory factor analysis) (SPSS) and structural equation modelling (AMOS) (Churchill 1991). The values of the tests exceeding the minimum acceptable thresholds are presented in Table 1.2.

Due to the high internal consistency of the dimensions of green consumers orientation (green consumer values, green consumer propensity, and green reuse motivation), these were integrated into a factor analysis (Walsh and Beatty 2007). The results (Table 1.3) confirm that the dimensions were clearly defined by respondents. The

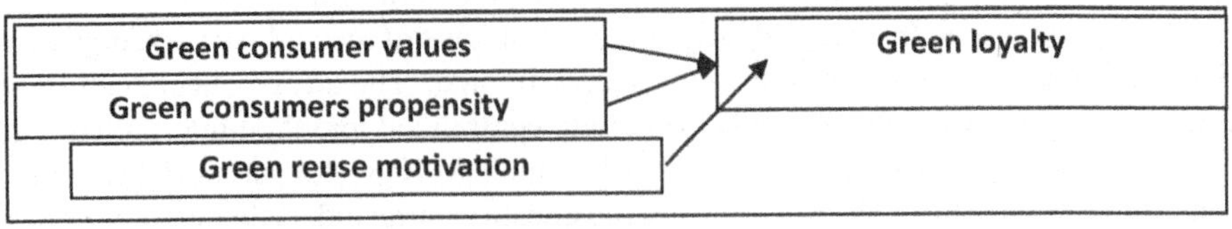

Fig. 1.1 The investigated general model *Source own research*

Table 1.1 Operationalization of investigated concepts

Construct	Items
Green consumer values (Lastovicka et al. 1999)	When I make a decision, I also consider the impact of my actions on the environment
	My shopping/buying habits are influenced by my care for the environment
	I describe myself as an environmentally responsible person
	It is important to me that fashion, sportswear and footwear articles should not harm the environment
	I am deeply worried by the waste of the planet's resources
Green consumer propensity (Antil and Bennett 1979; Antil 1984; Dabija et al. 2016)	I am concerned about compliance with environmental protection rules in the…. industry and trade
	I am concerned about the negative effect on the environment of the…. industry and trade
	The…. articles that I purchase must always have a low impact on the environment
	I always try to find out as much information as possible about the… articles that I purchase
Green reuse motivation (Lastovicka et al. 1999; Haws et al. 2014)	I am interested in recycling my products after I no longer use them
	Although they are still useful, many good fashion, sportswear and footwear articles are thrown away
	Optimizing the use of my resources makes me feel good
	If one takes care of one's own… articles, one will certainly make savings
	If I can reuse one of my … articles, then there is no point in buying a new one
Green loyalty (Nasir and Karakaya 2014)	In the next three months I intend to buy 'green' (organic) … articles
	I will recommend the 'green' … articles (organic fibres, etc.) to my friends and acquaintances
	I will buy more 'green' … articles in the future
	In the near future I will try out other 'green' … articles which I have not bought before
	If the 'green' … articles I need are not available, I will seek them in other stores, even if they are very far away from my home

Table 1.2 Results of testing validity and reliability of collected data

Dimension	No. of items	$\alpha^1 > 0.7$	$KMO^2 > 0.7$	χ^2; df; p^3	Eigenvalue	% variance
Green consumer values	5	0.883	0.857	8,801.13; 101; ****	3.409	68.174
Green consumers propensity	6	0.813	0.808	5,496.14; 123; ****	2.825	56.505
	5	0.842				
Green reuse motivation	4	0.788	0.742	2,074.39; 26; ****	2.078	51.96
Green loyalty	5	0.897	0.873	10,142.811; 10; ****	3.564	71.28

[1]—Cronbach's α coefficient (checking data reliability)
[2]—Kaiser–Meyer–Olkin criterion (exploratory factor analysis) for each dimension
[3]—Bartlett's test of sphericity (χ^2—hi square, df—degrees of freedom, p—probability
****$p<0.001$; *** $p<0.01$; ** $p<0.05$; * $p<0.1$)
Source own research

fit indices exceed the minimum thresholds considered (Churchill 1991; Forza and Filippini 1998; Ju et al. 2006): $KMO = 0.911 > 0.7$, $\chi^2 = 19{,}801.815$****; $df = 910$).

The validation of the model proposed by the authors (Fig. 1.1) was achieved through structural equation modelling (AMOS) applied to all respondents, as well as to each of the four generations. In each case, the fit indices exceed the minimum acceptable thresholds (>0.8; ≤ 0.08) recommended by the literature (Forza and Filippini 1998; Ju et al. 2006). This allows the proper interpretation of results (Table 1.7).

Sample structure by retail formats
The breakdown of respondents by generations was based on their year of birth, according to the guidelines in the literature: Baby Boomers 1945–1964; Generation X 1965–1979; Millennials 1980–1994 and Generation Z 1995–2000 (Gurău 2012; Doster 2013; Eastman et al. 2014; Lan 2014; Young 2015; Dabija et al. 2017). The interviewees were instructed not to approach people under 15, due to the belief that they did not have proper experience in buying food, household appliances or DIY products. Respondents had to have some experience with the types of goods considered (clothing articles, including shoes; electronic and household appliances, IT and accessories; DIY, furniture and interior design; and food products); otherwise, they were eliminated from the sample (filter question).

Socio-demographic characteristics of the sample
As can be seen in Table 1.4, most respondents were Millennials (1,215 persons) divided into almost equal groups of men (638 persons) and women (577 persons). Gen Xers and Generation Z represent the next two groups in terms of sample size (862 Gen Xers and 868 Zs), while Baby Boomers were the smallest group of respondents in the sample (222 women and 215 men). The number of Baby Boomers in the

Table 1.3 Factor analysis of the investigated dimensions

Items factors	1	2	3
When I make a decision I also consider the impact of my actions on the environment	0.860		
My shopping/buying habits are influenced by my care for the environment	0.809		
I describe myself as an environmentally responsible person	0.755		
It is important to me that fashion, sportswear and footwear articles should not harm the environment	0.748		
I am deeply worried by the waste of the planet's resources	0.692		
I am concerned about compliance with environmental protection rules in the…. industry and trade		0.801	
I am concerned about the negative effect on the environment of the…. industry and trade		0.728	
The…. articles that I purchase must always have a low impact on the environment		0.650	
I always try to find out as much information as possible about the… articles that I purchase		0.599	
I am interested in recycling my products after I no longer use them		0.527	
Although they are still useful, many good… articles are thrown away			0.601
Optimizing the use of my resources makes me feel good			0.593
If one takes care of one's own… articles, one will certainly make savings			0.552
If I can reuse some of my goods, then there is no point in buying new ones			0.425
Eigenvalues	5.662	1.689	1.265
% of Variance	40.44	12,0	9.03

Extraction Method: Principal Axis Factoring; Rotation Method: Oblimin with Kaiser Normalization

Source own research

sample is relatively small because it was rather difficult for interviewees to contact them, and because they were reluctant to answer all the questions in the questionnaire. The analysis of respondents' income reveals that most of them earned between the minimum (205 EUR) and average (460 EUR) wage being paid at the time of data collection. Obviously, younger people, notably members of Generation Z, had an income below the minimum wage (234 persons), followed by Millennials (73 persons), while Gen Xers and Baby Boomers had higher incomes (wages) due to their experience and years of service. Most Gen Xers (75 persons—2.2% of the sample) and Millennials (50 persons—1.5% of the sample) had an income exceeding two national average wages (920 EUR). 18.5% of respondents refused to reveal their income.

The number of rural respondents broken down by generations is almost equal Gen Xers (130 persons), Millennials (149 persons) and Generation Z (157 persons), but strikingly less small in the case of Baby Boomers (81 persons). This is due to the manner in which respondents were approached, preferably in public places, at their workplace and in the proximity of stores (Table 1.5).

Over half of respondents (55.8%) lived in three- or four-person households. This is the case with about 550 respondents from each of the generations Z, Y and X (Table 1.5). It is expected, therefore, that they had a rich experience in purchasing food and non-food products and in visiting these retail chains. Such products were also purchased by people living in one-person households: 52 Baby Boomers (1.5% of the sample), 72 Gen Xers (2.1% of the sample), 208 Millennials (6.2%) and 134 Generation Z members (4.0%). These were periodically faced with the decision to buy food, clothing, shoes, electronic and household products, and were likely to be more critical of retailers due to their previous experience with them.

The share of net income allotted by the members of the four generations to spending on green or sustainable products was variable (Table 1.6). It has been noticed that, for the sample as a whole, more than half of respondents (1,743 persons—51.5% of the sample) allocated up to 20% of their available income to the purchase of various green food and non-food products, while one-third of them (1,016 persons—30% of the sample) used between 21% and 40% of their income to buy their favourite green products. This supports our belief that respondents had proper shopping experience and, therefore, a good knowledge of retail brands and formats, being able to build a proper image of the market approach strategies and measures implemented. A relatively small number of consumers (168 persons—4.9% of the sample) allocated over 61% of their available net income to the purchase of different food and non-food sustainable products.

A research study conducted in eight European countries has identified significant differences in the fulfilment of consumers' intentions to buy organic food when the organic food market is booming, with lots of offers from retailers and producers. As a matter of fact, a strong and significant correlation has been noticed in these countries between consumers' intentions to buy organic food and their actual buying behaviour. At the opposite end are the countries in which the development of the organic food market is at an early stage, and the correlation between buying intention and buying behaviour is weak, as either intention is lacking or behaviour is lacking

Table 1.4 The four generations by gender and income

Generations	Baby boomers		(X)		Millennials		Z		Total	
	n	%	n	%	n	%	n	%	n	%
Gen										
Male	215	6.4	350	10.3	638	18.9	388	11.5	**1,591**	**47.0**
Female	222	6.6	512	15.1	577	17.1	480	14.2	**1,791**	**53.0**
Total	**437**	**12.9**	**862**	**25.5**	**1,215**	**35.9**	**868**	**25.7**	**3,382**	**100.0**
Net monthly income (lei)										
Below minimum wage*	25	0.7	24	0.7	73	2.2	234	6.9	**356**	**10.5**
Minimum*—average** wage	222	6.6	376	11.1	569	16.8	248	7.3	**1,415**	**41.8**
Between 1 and 2 average wages**	116	3.4	310	9.2	354	10.5	37	1.1	**817**	**24.2**
Over 2 average wages**	38	1.1	75	2.2	50	1.5	6	0.2	**169**	**4.9**
Undisclosed wage	36	1.1	77	2.2	169	5.0	342	10.2	**625**	**18.5**
Total	**437**	**12.9**	**862**	**25.5**	**1,215**	**35.9**	**868**	**25.7**	**3,382**	**100.0**

Note Net minimum wage and net average wage at the time of research were 925 RON (205 EUR) and 2,065 RON (460 EUR), respectively
Source own research

Table 1.5 Residence and household size of respondents

Generations	Baby boomers		X		Millennials		Z		Total	
	n	%	n	%	n	%	n	%	n	%
Residence										
Urban	356	10.5	732	21.6	1,066	31.5	711	21.0	**2,865**	**84.7**
Rural	81	2.4	130	3.8	149	4.4	157	4.6	**517**	**15.3**
Total	**437**	**12.9**	**862**	**25.5**	**1,215**	**35.9**	**868**	**25.7**	**3,382**	**100.0**
Household size (number of persons)										
One	52	1.5	72	2.1	208	6.2	134	4.0	**466**	**13.8**
Two	155	4.6	170	5.0	335	9.9	102	3.0	**762**	**22.5**
Three–Four	197	5.8	549	16.2	600	17.8	538	15.9	**1,884**	**55.8**
Five and over	33	1.0	71	2.1	72	2.1	84	2.8	**270**	**8.0**
Total	**437**	**12.9**	**862**	**25.5**	**1,215**	**35.9**	**868**	**25.7**	**3,382**	**100.0**

Source own research

Table 1.6 Percentage of shopping expenses and the categories of goods purchased by members of the generations considered

Generations	Baby Boomers		X		Millennials		Z		Total	
	n	%	n	%	n	%	n	%	n	%
% shopping expenses										
Below 20%	252	7.5	469	13.9	637	18.9	385	11.4	**1,743**	**51.5**
21-40%	118	3.5	243	7.2	405	12.0	250	7.4	**1,016**	**30.0**
41-60%	52	1.5	108	3.2	132	3.9	163	4.8	**455**	**13.5**
Over 61%	15	0.4	42	1.2	41	1.2	70	2.0	**168**	**4.9**
Total	**437**	**12.9**	**862**	**25.5**	**1,215**	**35.9**	**868**	**25.7**	**3,382**	**100.0**
Category of goods										
DIY, furniture, interior design	104	3.1	195	5.8	291	8.6	154	4.6	744	22.0
Electronic, household appliances, IT	97	2.9	198	5.9	306	9.0	162	4.8	763	22.6
Food	93	2.7	191	5.6	217	6.4	306	9.0	807	23.9
Fashion, sportswear, footwear	143	4.2	278	8.2	401	11.9	246	7.3	1.068	31.6
Total	**437**	**12.9**	**862**	**25.5**	**1,215**	**35.9**	**868**	**25.7**	**3,382**	**100.0**

Source own research

or both (Thøgersen and Zhou 2012). Kirmani and Khan (2016) also conclude that consumers in the European markets where the offer of green products is beginning to take shape (Serbia) are willing to pay a higher price for organic, environmentally friendly products. Hence, consumers want to have a share in the protection of the environment.

Most respondents made purchases from stores carrying green or sustainable clothing, sportswear and footwear products (1,068 persons—31.6% of the sample), and an almost equal percentage of them from stores selling food (23.9%), electronic products, household appliances and accessories (22.6%) and DIY, furniture and interior design articles (22.0%). It is interesting that Generation Z members visited to a greater extent the food stores (306 persons) with which they seemed to have the richest experience, while the other three generations visited more the clothing, sportswear and footwear stores (Table 1.6). Certainly, the available net income allocated to shopping was smaller in the case of young people, but larger in the case of the older generations who were working, and thus able to make a living and allot greater amounts of money to the purchase of non-essential products.

1.5 Research Findings

The objective of the research, that is, highlighting the extent to which various behavioural factors (green consumer values, green consumer propensity, green reuse motivation) contribute to building the 'green' loyalty of the members of the four generations considered (Baby Boomers, Xers, Millennials and Z) in Romanian retail (Fig. 1.1) was the starting point for the calculation of the model using structural equation modelling. As the model was found to be stable and the fit indices (Table 1.7) exceed the minimum acceptable thresholds (CFI, AGFI, NFI, TLI, GFI >0.8; SRMR, RMSEA ≤ 0.08) specified in the literature (Forza and Filippini 1998, pp. 1–20; Ju et al. 2006, pp. 373–393), the authors proceeded with the interpretation of results.

One finding is that *green consumers' propensity* for all generations generally had the strongest and most significant influence on building customer loyalty to the analysed retail formats. Naturally, this impact was stronger in intensity in the case of young consumers, members of Generation Z (0.510****), than in the case of Gen Xers (0.486****) and Baby Boomers (0.472***), which is a sign that young people are more aware of the need to protect the environment than older people, since they are the ones who will be confronted in the future with the problems and challenges raised by the lack of sufficient environmental protection. Therefore, young people seemed concerned to a greater extent with the impact on the environment of the food and other products they buy, and always try to buy those goods with the lowest impact on nature. Respondents were willing to re-purchase organic, environmentally friendly products with 'green' components or ingredients, recommend their consumption to other people or buy them in larger quantities in the future. Loyalty to these retail formats translated into preference for retailers adopting a green strategy over those which do not and visiting them even when one has to cover a longer distance.

Table 1.7 Behaviour incidence of consumers' green orientation in enhancing their loyalty towards the retail formats, broken down by consumer generations

Effects		Model fit	
Generation Z (1995-present)	n = 868	χ^2	2,235.342
Green reuse motivation → Green Loyalty	0.263****	df	629
Green consumers values → Green Loyalty	0.250****	χ^2/df	3.554
Green consumers propensity → Green Loyalty	0.510****	GFI	0.932
Generation Y (1980–1994)	n = 1,215	AGFI	0.918
Green reuse motivation → Green Loyalty	0.200****	NFI	0.928
Green consumers values → Green Loyalty	0.251****	CFI	0.947
Green consumers propensity → Green Loyalty	0.508****	TLI	0.943
Generation X (1965–1979)	n = 862	*p < 0.1	**p < 0.05
Green reuse motivation → Green Loyalty	$0.103^{n.s.}$	***p < 0.01	
Green consumers values → Green Loyalty	0.170***	****p < 0.001	
Green consumers propensity → Green Loyalty	0.486****	$^{n.s.}$—insignificant	
Baby Boomers (1945–1964)	n = 437	RMSEA (≤0.08)	
Green reuse motivation → Green Loyalty	$0.058^{n.s.}$	0.0270	
Green consumers values → Green Loyalty	0.194**	SRMR (≤0.08)	
Green consumers propensity → Green Loyalty	0.472***	0.0443	

Source own research

The values of the green consumer, i.e. the intrinsic drivers simultaneously shaping and influencing his/her attitudes, perceptions, thinking, buying behaviour and consumption habits, fostered by his/her green, organic orientation, exerted an influence of average intensity and had different significance across the generations considered. Therefore, their impact was almost identical in terms of intensity and significance for the members of Generation Z (0.250****) and Millennials (0.251****) (Table 1.7). In other words, young people had already cultivated a strong attitude about sustainable consumption and the impact of their actions on the environment, making attempts, whenever they use food and non-food products, to contribute to the preservation of natural resources. In this way, they exhibited environmentally responsible behaviour. On the other hand, green values contributed to a lesser extent to building green loyalty in the case of Gen Xers (0.170***) and Baby Boomers (0.194**). This is probably because they grew up in a time when less emphasis was put on sustainability, social responsibility, environmental protection, reduction in the consumption of packaged and raw materials, etc., as other research studies also confirm (Namkung and Soocheong (Shawn) 2014). However, it has been noticed that, in the case of the two generations, green values contributed to strengthening and/or building loyal behaviour towards the retail formats that manage to attain 'green' status and those that adopt a 'green' strategy or implement proper measures to diminish consumption of resources worldwide.

Unlike Gen Xers ($0.103^{n.s.}$) and Baby Boomers ($0.058^{n.s.}$), young people—Generation Z (0.263****) and Millennials (0.200****)—were motivated to avoid discarding and excessive consumption of products, and to reuse or recycle food, clothing and electronic products, household appliances and furniture, etc. The insignificance of influence in the case of adult people as compared to the impact of average intensity and great significance in the case of young people leads to the conclusion that young people are motivated not only to make financial savings and help companies reduce the consumption of resources, but also prefer the retailers, and develop loyal behaviour towards the store chains that promote recycling, reusing, reduction of consumption of raw materials and resources, etc., within their market-approaching green actions and sustainability strategies (Table 1.7).

1.6 Conclusions

The results clearly show that an individual's own green values and motivation to buy environmentally friendly products are much stronger among Millennials and Generation Z members. They are more willing to display loyal behaviour towards the retailers implementing a sustainability strategy than are their parents and grandparents. At the same time, young people buy green products more frequently because they want to contribute to the protection of the environment. Consequently, the hypothesis H_1 is confirmed, according to which *the incidence of green consumers' values, green consumers' propensity and green reuse motivation in building consumer loyalty to the retail formats considered varies*.

Sustainability and green products are obviously important to all consumers, regardless of age. Consumers are able to build their green loyalty and re-purchase from their favourite retailer, or recommend it to others based on their green orientation, their personal values fostering the search and consumption of organic products and their motivation to buy them. However, the results obtained disprove the hypothesis H_2 according to which *Baby Boomers pay greater attention to green propensity than the younger generations*. The results actually show that young people (Millennials and Generation Z) are more likely to exhibit green behaviour than Baby Boomers.

The results also reveal that young people are more motivated to contribute to reducing the consumption of products than the older generations. The insignificance of the relationship between the motivation to reuse products and the loyalty (Table 1.7) felt towards the analysed retail formats is accounted for by the fact that adult people were not brought up in a spirit of recycling and reusing and, as such, they are more likely to consume products without thinking about the impact of their own actions on the environment. Therefore, companies are charged with the demanding task of identifying appropriate ways to educate consumers in the spirit of consumption reduction and environmental protection.

The system of sustainability and environmental protection-oriented personal values underlies consumers' favourable attitude to organic, environmentally friendly products. Once the attitude is firmly established, the individual will prefer and purchase those products. Repeating the purchase will develop trust in the products and create a positive image of them. In the end, the individual will display loyal behaviour, purchasing more frequently the products which best satisfy his/her needs, comply with their values and make them happier and more content. Sustainability still remains a concept whose facets and implications are not fully understood by some retailers. They use sustainability to improve their reputation and image among the target groups, and less to provide added value, and effectively contribute to the protection of the environment through the products sold as sustainable.

The literature (Silva Braga Junior et al. 2015) points to situations in which articles not made according to sustainability norms, even if not harmful to health or the environment, are marketed as green products. They may have an attractive design contrasting with that of similar traditional products and are beautifully packaged to draw customers' attention but they do not contribute in any way to the protection or the preservation of the environment. The 'rush' for a sustainable image to attract customers preferring and purchasing such products may sometimes outweigh the actual implementation of such principles. In other words, sustainability is viewed by some retailers as a life and business principle, while to others it is only a marketing or PR 'tool' used to draw customers, sell products and make profits.

Future research will have to highlight the extent to which consumers' perception of retailers varies when the purchase is made from food versus non-food stores, and from electronics and household appliances versus fashion and footwear stores. The retail format may also be a major driver of loyal behaviour. Last but not least, another aspect calling for further analysis is the situation of notable differences between men and women in exhibiting green loyal behaviour towards the retailers considered.

Acknowledgements This work was supported by a grant of the Romanian National Authority for Scientific Research and Innovation, CNCS—UEFISCDI, project number PN-II-RU-TE-2014-4-0312.

References

Antil, J. A., & Bennett, P. D. (1979). Construction and validation of a scale to measure socially responsible consumption behaviour. In K. H. Henion II & T. C. Konnear (Eds.), *The Conserver Society* (pp. 51–68). Chicago: American Marketing Association.

Antil, J. A. (1984). Socially responsible consumers: profile and implications for public policy. *Journal of Macromarketing, 4*(2), 18–39. https://doi.org/10.1177/027614678400400203.

Bisschoff, C. A., & Liebenberg, P. (2015). *Identifying factors that influence green purchasing behavior.* Masters thesis. Potchefstroom Campus of the North-West University. https://dspace.nwu.ac.za/bitstream/handle/10394/19927/Liebenberg_P_2015.pdf?sequence=1&isAllowed=y.

Braga Jr., S. S., da Silva, D., Gabriel, M. L., & de Oliveira, Braga, W. R. (2015). the effects of environmental concern on purchase of green products in retail. *Procedia—Social and Behavioral Sciences, 170*, 99–108. https://doi.org/10.1016/j.sbspro.2015.01.019.

Bucic, T., Harris, J., & Arli, D. (2012). Ethical consumers among the millennials: A cross-national study. *Journal of Business Ethics, 110*(1), 113–131. https://doi.org/10.1007/s10551-011-1151-z.

Churchill, G. A. (1991). *Marketing research: Methodological foundation* (5th ed.). Fort Worth: The Dryden Press.

Cohn, D. Y., & Vaccaro, V. L. (2015). The influence of global consumer values and perceived risk factors on green vehicle adoption. *Journal of International Business and Economics, 15*(3), 35–52. https://doi.org/10.18374/jibe-15-3.3.

Collins, C. M., Steg, L., & Koning, M. A. (2007). Customers's values, beliefs on sustainable corporate performance, and buying behavior. *Psychology and Marketing, 24*(6), 555–577. https://doi.org/10.1002/mar.20173.

Cowan, K., & Kinley, T. (2014). Green spirit: Consumer empathies for green apparel. *International Journal of Consumer Studies, 38*(5), 493–499. https://doi.org/10.1111/ijcs.12125.

Dabija, D. C., & Băbuț, R. (2014). Enhancing consumers' satisfaction and loyalty of retailers in romania through store ambiance and communication. *Procedia Economics and Finance, 15*, 371–382.

Dabija, D. C., Băbuţ, R., Dinu, V., & Lugojan, M. (2017). Cross-Generational analysis of information search based on social media in Romania. *Transformations in Business & Economics* (under review).

Dabija, D. C., & Bejan, B. (2017). Behavioral antecedents for enhancing green customer loyalty in retail. In C. Vasiliu & M. Olariu (Eds.), *BASIQ 2017—New trends in sustainable business and consumption*. Editura ASE: Bucharest-Graz.

Dabija, D. C., & Grant, D. (2016). Investigating shopping experience and fulfillment in omnichannel retailing: a proposed comparative study in Romanian and UK of generation Y consumers. In D. Menachof (Ed.), *Doing the right things. Ethical issues in logistics and supply chair*. Abstracts of the 21st annual logistics research network conference. Corby, Northamptonshire: The Logistics Institute, 53.

Dabija, D. C., & Pop, N. A. (2008). typological aspects of retailers on the background of market concentration. *Management & Marketing, 3*(5/9), 43–60.

Dabija, D. C., Pop, N. A., & Postelnicu, C. (2016). Ethics of the garment retail within the context of globalization and sustainable development. *Industria Textilă, 67*(4), 270–279.

Dabija, D. C., Postelnicu, C., & Dinu, V. (2017). Cross-generational analysis of ethics and sustainability. Insights from Romanian retailing. In S. O Idowu, C. Sitnikov, D. Simion, C. Bocean, C., (Eds.), *Current issues in corporate social responsibility*. Thur: Springer International Publishing.

Davari, A., & Strutton, D. (2014). Marketing mix strategies for closing the gap between green consumers' pro-environmental beliefs and behaviors. *Journal of Strategic Marketing, 22*(7), 563–586. https://doi.org/10.1080/0965254x.2014.914059.

DiPietro, R. B., Gregory, S., & Jackson, A. (2013). Going green in quick-service restaurants: customer perceptions and intentions. *International Journal of Contemporary Hospitality Tourism Administration, 14*, 139–156.

do Paço, A., Alves, H., Shiel, C., & Filho, W.L. (2013). Development of a green consumer behaviour model. *International Journal of Consumer Studies, 37* (4), 414–421. https://doi.org/10.1111/ijcs.12009.

Doster, L. (2013). Millennial teens design and redesign themselves in online social networks. *Journal of Consumer Behaviour, 12*(4), 267–279. https://doi.org/10.1002/cb.1407.

Dunmore, D. (2013). *Has technology become a need? A qualitative study exploring three generational cohorts' perception of technology in regards to Maslow's hierarchy of needs*. (Ph.D., Capella University). Retrieved from ProQuest Dissertations and Theses.

Eastman, J. K., Iyer, R., Liao-Troth, S., Williams, D. F., & Griffin, M. (2014). The role of involvement on Millennials' mobile technology behaviors: The moderating impact of status consumption, innovation, and opinion leadership. *Journal of Marketing Theory and Practice, 22*(4), 455–470. https://doi.org/10.2753/mtp1069-6679220407.

Euromonitor. (2009). *The World's Gen Xers: Latchkey kids (29-44s) come into their own*. Available at http://www.euromonitor.com/the-worlds-gen-xers-latchkey-kids-29-44s-come-into-their-own/report. Referred on June 7, 2016.

Euromonitor International. (2015a). *Eco worriers: global green behaviour and market impact*. Retrieved May 5, 2016, from http://www.euromonitor.com/eco-worriers-global-green-behaviour-and-market-impact/report.

Forza, C., & Filippini, R. (1998). TQM impact on quality conformance and customer satisfaction: A causal model. *International Journal of Production Economics, 55*(1), 1–20. https://doi.org/10.1016/s0925-5273(98)00007-3.

Foscht, T., & Swoboda, B. (2017). *Käuferverhalten: Grundlagen-Perspektiven-Anwendungen* (6th ed.). Wiesbaden: Springer-Gabler.

Garcia de los Salmones, M. D., Crespo, A. H., & Rodriguez del Bosque, I. (2005). Influence of corporate social responsablity on loyalty and valuation of services. *Journal of Business Ethics, 61*(4), 369–385. https://doi.org/10.1007/s10551-005-5841-2.

Gurău, C. (2012). A life-stage analysis of consumer loyalty profile: Comparing generation X and millennial consumers. *Journal of Consumer Marketing, 29*(2), 103–113. https://doi.org/10.1108/07363761211206357.

Hamid, A. R. (2014). A study on the relationship between consumer attitude, perceived value and green products. *Iranian Journal of Management Studies (IJMS), 7*(2), 315–328.

Haws, K. L., Winterich, K. P., & Naylor, R., W. (2014). Seeing the world through GREEN-tinted glasses: Green consumption values and responses to environmentally friendly products. *Journal of Consumer Psychology*, 24(3), 336–354. https://doi.org/10.1016/j.jcps.2013.11.002.

Hernaus, T., & Pološki, Vokic, N. (2014). work design for different generational cohorts. *Journal of Organizational Change Management*, *27*(4), 615–641.

Howe, N., & Strauss, W. (2003). *Millennials go to college: strategies for a new generation on campus: recruiting and admissions, campus life, and the classroom*. Washington, DC: American Association of Collegiate Registrars and Admissions Officers.

Hur, W. M., Woo, J., & Kim, Y. (2015). The role of consumer values and socio-demographics in green product satisfaction: The case of hybrid cars. *Psychological Reports: Employment Psychology & Marketing, 117*(2), 406–427. https://doi.org/10.2466/01.pr0.117c19z1.

Joshi, Y., & Rahman, Z. (2016). Predictors of young consumer's green purchase behaviour. *Management of Environmental Quality: An International Journal, 27*(4), 452–472. https://doi.org/10.1108/meq-05-2015-0091.

Ju, T. L., Lin, B., Lin, C., & Kuo, H. J. (2006). TQM critical factors and KM value chain activities. *Total Quality Management & Business Excellence, 17*(3), 373–393. https://doi.org/10.1080/14783360500451614.

Karp, D. (1996). Values and their effect on pro-environmental behavior. *Environment and Behavior, 28*(1), 111–133. https://doi.org/10.1177/0013916596281006.

Kirmani, M. D., & Khan, M. N. (2016). Environmental concern to attitude towards green products: Evidences from india. *Serbian Journal of Management, 11*(2), 159–179. https://doi.org/10.5937/sjm11-9241.

Lan, S. (2014). *An importance-performance analysis of multigenerational preferences in guestroom technology* (2014). *UNLV theses, dssertations, Professional Papers, and Capstones*. Paper 2620.

Lastovicka, J., Bettencourt, L., Hughner, R., & Kuntze, R. (1999). Lifestyle of the tight and frugal. *Journal of Consumer Research, 26*(1), 85–98. https://doi.org/10.1086/209552.

Lin, J., Lobo, A., & Leckie, C. (2017). The role of benefits and transparency in shaping consumers' green perceived value, self-brand connection and brand loyalty. *Journal of Retailing and Consumer Services, 35*, 133–141. https://doi.org/10.1016/j.jretconser.2016.12.011.

Lu, L., Bock, D., & Joseph, M. (2013). Green marketing: What the Millennials buy. *Journal of Business Strategy, 34*(6), 3–10. https://doi.org/10.1108/JBS-05-2013-0036.

Namkung, Y., & Soocheong (Shawn), J. (2014). Are consumers willing to pay more for green practices at restaurants? *Journal of Hospitality & Tourism Research, 20*(10), 1–28.

Nasir, V. A., & Karakaya, F. (2014). Underlying motivations of organic food purchase intentions. *Agribusiness, 30*(3), 290–308. https://doi.org/10.1002/agr.21363.

Pop, N. A., & Dabija, D. C. (2013). Development of an organic food mentality in romania. In A. R. Thomas, N. A. Pop, & C. Brătianu (Eds.), *The changing business landscape of romania: lessons for and from transition economies* (pp. 45–60). New York: Springer Publishing House.

Pop, N. A., Dabija, D. C, Dumitru, I., Pelău, C., Petrescu, & E. C. (Eds.). (2011). *Marketing internaţional—teorie şi practică*. Bucureşti: Uranus.

Pop, N. A., & Dabija, D. C. (2014). fostering loyalty through social responsability actions in Romanian retail. *Romanian Journal of Marketing, 9*(4), 11–32.

Postelnicu, C., & Dabija, D. C. (2015). Transfer and diffusion of new technologies within the supply chain of multinational companies with operations in developing economies—a contemporary approach. In S. Văduva & A. R. Thomas (Eds.), *Geopolitics, Development, and National Security—Romania and Moldova at the Crossroads* (pp. 53–66). New York: Springer Publishing House.

Roberts, J. A., & Bacon, D. R. (1997). Exploring the Subtle relationship between environmental concern and ecologically conscious consumer behavior. *Journal of Business Research, 40*(1), 79–89. https://doi.org/10.1016/s0148-2963(96)00280-9.

Schultz, P., & Zelezny, L. (1999). Values as predictors of environmental attitudes: Evidence for consistency across 14 countries. *Journal of Environmental Psychology, 19*(3), 255–265. https://doi.org/10.1006/jevp.1999.0129.

Shaw, S., & Fairhurst, D. (2008). Engaging a new generation of graduates. *Education Training, 50*(5), 366–378.

Singh, S. (2013). *Generation Z: Rules to reach the multinational consumer*. Sapient. Retrieved June 15, 2016, from http://www.sapient.com/content/dam/sapient/sapientnitro/pdfs/insights/TR1_GenZ.pdf.

Singh, J., Garcia de los Salmones Sanchez, M. D., & Rodriguez del Bosque, I. (2008). Understanding corporate social responsibility and product perceptions in consumer markets: A Cross-cultural evaluation. *Journal of Business Ethics, 80*(3), 597–611. https://doi.org/10.1007/s10551-007-9457-6.

Solomon, M. R. (2014). *Consumer behavior: Buying, having and being* (11th ed.). Prentice Hall: Pearson Education.

Stern, P., Dietz, T., Abel, T., Guagnano, G., & Kalof, L. (1999). A value belief norm theory of support for social movements: The case of environmental concern. *Human Ecology Review, 6*(2), 81–97.

Swoboda, B., Berg, B., & Dabija, D. C. (2014). International transfer and perception of retail formats: a comparison study in germany and romania. *International Marketing Review, 31*(2), 155–180.

Taken, Smith, K. (2011). Digital marketing strategies that millennials find appealing, motivating, or just annoying. *Journal of Strategic Marketing*, 19 (6), 489–499.

Tanner, C., & Kast, S. W. (2003). Promoting sustainable consumption: Determinants of green purchases by swiss consumers. *Psychology and Marketing, 20*(10), 883–902. https://doi.org/10.1002/mar.10101.

Thøgersen, J., & Zhou, Y. (2012). Chinese consumers' adoption of a "green" innovation—The case of organic food. *Journal of Marketing Management, 28*(3–4), 313–333. https://doi.org/10.1080/0267257x.2012x658834.
Varshneya, G., Pandey, S. K., & Das, G. (2017). Impact of social influence and green consumption values on purchase intention of organic clothing: a study on collectivist developing economy. *Global Business Review, 18*(2), 1–16. https://doi.org/10.1177/0972150916668620.
Venn, S., Burningham, K., Christie, I., & Jackson, T. (2017). Consumption junkies or sustainable consumers: Considering the grocery shopping practices of those transitioning to retirement. *Ageing & Society, 37*(01), 14–38. https://doi.org/10.1017/s0144686x15000975.
Viswanathan, V., & Jain, V. (2013). A Dual-system approach to understanding "Generation Y" decision making. *Journal of Consumer Marketing, 30*(6), 484–492.
Walsh, G., & Beatty, S. E. (2007). Customer based corporate reputation of a service firm: Scale development and validation. *Journal of the Academy of Marketing Science, 35*(1), 127–143. https://doi.org/10.1007/s11747-007-0015-7.
Williams, K., & Page, R. (2011). Marketing to the generations. *Journal of Behavioral Studies in Business, 3,* 1–17.
Young, E. (2015). *How millenials get news: Inside the habits of america´s first digital generation.* Chicago: Associated Press-NORC Center for Public Affairs Research & American Press Institute.
Zentes, J., Swoboda, B., & Foscht, T. (2012). *Handelsmanagement* (3rd ed.). München: Vahlen.

Chapter 2
Linking Business with Civil Society: The Bridging Role of CSR

Tomina Săveanu, Daniel Bădulescu and Florin Filip

Abstract The role and the importance of business within our societies are topics of great interest for both academics and practitioners, but the current understanding of this topic is far from being clear or undisputable at the moment. The classic principle that businesses act legally and ethically is a real blessing for the society, denoting that businesses should not get involved in achieving major social or environmental objectives, is at present questionable. For years now, corporate social responsibility (CSR) has become a key element in shaping the relation between businesses, public policy, and civil society. In this paper, we are presenting the results of a survey-based research conducted among 109 small- and medium-sized enterprises (SMEs) located in the northwestern region of Romania. The paper addresses the role of CSR as a mediator between businesses and civil society and analyzes the attitude of SMEs' managers toward CSR activities, as well as the role of businesses in communities and the relation between the intention to conduct CSR activities and their actual implementation. The results show a clear interest of SMEs in CSR and a strong link between the understandings that managers have regarding the role of businesses in society and their social responsibility actions. The most important factor explaining the level of involvement in social activities is related to the attitude of firms' managers regarding what extent a company should set social welfare as a priority. The implications of these findings show that businesses are socially responsible and civically involved as long as their managers perceive CSR to be essential among for competing individual responsibilities, in other words, they manifest active citizenship (also) in the economic area.

Keywords Business and civil society · CSR · SMEs

T. Săveanu · D. Bădulescu (✉) · F. Filip
Faculty of Economic Sciences, University of Oradea, Oradea, Romania
e-mail: dbadulescu@uoradea.ro

T. Săveanu
e-mail: tsaveanu@uoradea.ro

F. Filip
e-mail: ffe17@yahoo.com

S. A. Văduva et al. (eds.), *Civil Society: The Engine for Economic and Social Well-Being*, Springer Proceedings in Business and Economics,
https://doi.org/10.1007/978-3-319-89872-8_2

2.1 Introduction

Corporate social responsibility (CSR) is a heterogeneous and multi-dimensional organizational phenomenon. It is an essential aspect in the life of a company and consists of the impacts of its actions on all interested parties, on society and the environment by means of showing evidence of a transparent and ethical behavior. In addition to being part of the internal changes and reorientation of a company's commercial strategies, CSR represents a visible answer of business adaption to customers' expectations, and more largely, to the needs of a society. The European Commission in its *Green Paper on Corporate Social Responsibility: A Business Contribution to Sustainable Development* states that CSR is "a concept whereby companies integrate social and environmental concerns in their business operations and in their interaction with their stakeholders on a voluntary basis" (European Commission 2002: 5). The Organisation for Economic Cooperation and Development (OECD) notes that "corporate responsibility involves the search for an effective 'fit' between businesses and the societies in which they operate" (Organisation for Economic Cooperation and Development (OECD) 2016).

In this paper, we explore the issue of the bridging role of CSR between business and civil society, through a number of key elements such as the attitude and the role of managers concerning business involvement in CSR, the role of business in the community, and the relation between intention and effective implementation of CSR projects.

The paper is organized as follows: after some introductory consideration, we review several theoretical considerations on the corporate social responsibility's role, starting from business involvement in the community through charity work to improving social cohesion policy, competitiveness, civil engagement, social and environmental sustainability, the role of managers in managing CSR activities, and their manifestation in diverse and socioeconomic and cultural contexts. In the second part of the paper, we approach the survey-based research performed, presenting and discussing the results on the link between the managers' understanding regarding the role of business in society and their social responsibility actions. In the final part, we draw conclusions and discuss the implications derived from the empirical findings of our research.

2.2 The Relation Between CSR, Business Community, and Civil Society

Over the past decades, CSR has become an important element in shaping a new model of sustainable corporate governance, regardless of the size of companies. CSR is said to add to a more traditional understanding of business management (such as focusing on the bottom line) through taking into consideration broader social issues. According to Blowfield and Frynas (2005) or Rahim (2013: 44), the responsibility of a business toward society starts from the responsibilities of each company for their impact on society and the natural environment, going beyond legal compliance and the liability of individuals. It then involves a responsibility toward the behavior of those with whom a company does business with, and it ends with the relationship between the company and the society at large. The latter is achieved through improving business performance and through adding some sort of value to the society at large (Blowfield and Frynas 2005: 503). The European Commission (2011) itself emphasizes this new role of businesses:

> *it is time for a much broader definition of the role and responsibility of business in the globalised world, where growing responsibility should go hand in hand with growing influence. Many business leaders are aware of this need and their increasing engagement in dialogue with academics, stakeholders and policy makers demonstrates their readiness to face societal expectations* (European Commission 2011: 5).

Sastry (2011) makes an inspired synthesis, assigning a series of civic and social arguments to each role of business in society, as follows: (a) business should make profit—economically, politically, ideologically, managers as agents of shareholders need to be honest to their main task and by doing so they can contribute to social good; (b) business needs to be socially responsible—they need to address current social and environmental concerns; (c) businesses are actively involved in society—businesses need to act in harmony with society, to come back to basic moral principles; (d) businesses are not in contradiction with the common good—consumers will positively respond to those companies that are involved in charitable activities or solve social and environmental problems, etc.; and (e) businesses generate social value—a win-win relation, for business and society by creating greater value (Sastry 2011: 248).

Companies are assuming a growing role in governing societies, not only by means of the market but also through networks, thus engaging with the nonprofit sector through CSR projects (Moon and Vogel 2008: 309). For Beck (1997), companies have assumed a sub-political role in those areas in which governments have failed—such as environmental concerns, the use of resources, global warming, or crises associated with certain investments or new products, which were reluctantly received by the public.

There are many situations in which CSR occupies a key place within the business–public governance–civil society nexus. Nonetheless, CSR is a highly contextual phenomenon, depending on the specific features of a country, on its forms of governance, on the development of a given society, or a certain historical time period. This makes CSR, the actors involved in CSR, and their responsibilities to be very dynamic, undergoing ongoing transformation and adaptation.

Thus, from activities such as community-based charitable work in which companies/employees were involved, especially in education, social care, and local development (Matten and Moon 2008), CSR has gradually been credited with a positive role in improving policies in areas such as social cohesion, competitiveness, or social and environmental sustainability (Moon and Vogel 2008). CSR becomes a key element in the governance mechanism, making the transition from business to civil society, by means of a mix of policy and administrative instruments though what Deakin and Wash (1996) call "the enabling state".

The critics of CSR come from two different positions. On the one hand, they are the defenders of free markets based on the well-known statement of Milton Friedman "*The discussions of the 'social responsibilities of business' are notable for their analytical looseness and lack of rigor. What does it mean to say that 'business" has responsibilities'? Only people can have responsibilities. A corporation is an artificial person and in this sense may have artificial responsibilities, but 'business' as a whole cannot be said to have responsibilities, even in this vague sense*" (Friedman 1970). According to this position, the only social responsibility of business is to increase profits, accusing world business leaders they have abandoned the principle of efficiency in favor of the so-called "political correctness" (Badulescu and Petria 2013).

On the other hand, there is the position of the moral reformers and leftist political activists for whom CSR is a dangerous diversion that undermines democracy. Thus, a company "cannot be socially responsible, or at least not to a significant extent, and governments is primarily responsible in setting standards and norms, in order to avoid companies to act against the interest of society" (Reich 2007: 170). Moreover "the notion of a socially responsible corporation is potentially an oxymoron, because of the naturally conflicted nature of the corporation" (Devinney 2009: 44). In this view, CSR promotes a change in values, that "creates a deeply dysfunctional world" in which falsity and moral degradation are rewarded instead of being sanctioned—a world in which CSR is used by managers to maximize their own profits, provocatively invoking generosity and care for society. "Thus, a poison is being injected into our spiritual bloodstream. Think for a moment how the parable of the Good Samaritan (…) would read if a CSR manager had happened upon the robber's victim before the Samaritan" (Hastings 2016: 286).

Other radical commentators talk about a *community economy, or taking back* the economy through ethical action, going beyond the capitalist perspective, "individuals and communities across the globe are taking economic matters into their own hands to help create worlds that are socially and environmentally just" (Gibson-Graham et al. 2013: xiii) or about the *responsibility to socialize corporations* (RSC), "establishing a socially responsible economy and society from a managerial into a broader social and political question" (Sandoval 2015: 620).

2.3 Managers' Involvement in CSR Activities: Values, Organizational Culture and Management Style

The new responsibilities of CSR toward civil society are challenging and sometimes difficult for business managers. First of all, they need to pay attention to the new tasks of CSR, where the roles, rules, and boundaries are not as clear as in the business management. Second, they need to recognize that many of these new roles are placed outside of their own sphere of responsibility and many of the effects of CSR are discontinuous, patchy, and more difficult to be managerially influenced. Furthermore, the participation in networks, partnerships and in the new societal governance generates "a certain clouding of accountability"—a significant risk in a field in which managers are used to having clear, precise, and essential information (Moon and Vogel 2008: 319–320). Likewise, European Commission's reports note a considerable difference between managers' vision and that of the stakeholders about the social responsibilities of a company. More specifically, managers tend to have a cautious view, such as "do no harm" rather than the more proactive "do good" approach (European Commission 2011: 12). Managers perceive this responsibility as an obligation to follow the legal framework, while stakeholders (especially the external ones) take a more comprehensive approach that integrates the interests of large social groups and of the society as a whole (European Commission 2011).

How are these responsibilities shaped? Starting from the premise that today's students can become the managers of tomorrow, and consequently the attitudes about CSR depend on individual perceptions and knowledge, Singhapakdi et al. (1996) and Kolodinsky et al. (2010) found that idealistic students are more inclined to engage in morally and socially grounded actions, while their colleagues who are more inclined toward relativistic and materialistic views were negatively related to their CSR attitudes. Their conclusions are complemented by similar studies over practitioners in order to reach more useful and generalizable conclusions about managers' perceptions and attitudes about CSR in a given cultural context. Welford et al. (2008) in a large study in Hong Kong on managers and stakeholders perceptions on CSR found that the environment, health and safety, human resource management, and good governance are the most important factors in evaluating a socially responsible behavior. It is noteworthy to point out that philanthropy has a weaker importance as specific areas of CSR. Other studies, carried out in other developed and developing countries, on managers and stakeholders, have found that the most important aspects that CSR needs to tackle with include environmental degradation and improvement in working conditions (Cacioppe et al. 2008), community problems, followed by improving the demands of suppliers and customers (Azmat and Samaratunge 2009; Azmat and Zutshi 2012), the development of industry-specific and sector-wise regulation, such as pollution control, working conditions, and consumer protection, and adopting environmental management systems as a requirement for doing business (Rahim 2013). Often, the specific national context, cultural, social, religious, and moral values of entrepreneurs and managers influence the inclination toward certain types of CSR projects. Thus, researches have shown an inclination toward charity in Australia (Quazi and O'Brien 2000) or Bangladesh (Moyeen and West 2014), India (Chahoud et al. 2007), while in China, CSR geared toward consumer and employees development is more prevalent (Hofman et al. 2015). Moreover, Rahim (2013) cites a series of research in this area and argues that CSR understanding is different from one socioeconomic system to another and from one generation to another (Rahim 2013: 15) "for instance, its meaning in the Continental European welfare society is different to its meaning in the USA or in developing or transitional societies" (Daugherty cited in Rahim: 15). The managers of American companies "consider philanthropy as a dominant factor of CSR; in the Northern economies companies bear their social responsibilities by paying taxes" (Kakabadse cited in Rahim: 15).

Confirming some of these differences, Moyeen and Wash (2014) in their study over the business climate in Bangladesh found that "in spite of the prevalence of more positive attitudes to CSR, the perception that CSR is mostly concerned with philanthropic based initiatives" (Moyeen and West 2014: 110). In other words, a decrease in the importance of charity between the main areas of CSR (as was predicted by Carroll (1991) over two decades ago) is far from being achieved in most developing countries, which are still experiencing major social and economic problems. A second (partial) conclusion that can be observed is that the perception of the sense, importance, and role of CSR are highly influenced by location of specific factors (Dahlsrud 2006; Moyeen and West 2014), by the moral profile of managers and by their goals.

A reason that can explain the great variety in the understanding and application of CSR ideas is given by the cultural expectations in a given country (Waldman, et al. 2006). Even the sources of legitimacy are culturally dependent (Barkemeyer 2007). Companies' need for legitimacy and how it shapes the visibility of corporate social behavior also varies between different business areas (Chiu and Sharfman 2011). Thus, the fields that are highly visible to the public tend to have a need for greater legitimacy from stakeholders and if the number of stakeholders is greater, then they will be more directly involved in CSR projects.

In addition to this cultural dimension at the national level, a number of studies point to the role that managers have in their decision to become socially active (Hemingway and Maclagan 2004; Du, et al. 2013). This effect can be mediated through organizational culture (Ubius and Alas 2009; Baumgartner 2009). The different motivations for engaging in CSR are situated at different social levels, including the need of governments to stimulate such activities. Aguilera et al. usefully summarized these motivations (2007) in instrumental, relational, and moral. This study synthesizes the motivations and interests for engagement in CSR at the level of employees, managers, clients, both nationally and transnationally, pointing out the pressures at each level (clients, employees, etc.) that have an influence on CSR and its success. The authors do not address the differences between attitudes and behaviors of employees or clients—they keep a certain equivalence between the two although a pro-CSR attitude on the part of clients is not necessarily an indication of a behavior that sanctions the socially irresponsible firms, or a choice for socially responsible companies.

Maignan (2001) in an empirical study concerning the different attitudes of French consumers compared to American consumers over CSR underlines that business engagement in CSR is complemented by community pressure on those who have had success so that these can become socially engaged in communities. The differences between companies in their social performance in the same field of activity in different countries show the great impact of the sociocultural context on CSR (Ubius and Alas 2009; Williams and Aguilera 2008).

Organizational culture is also considered to be important in explaining how companies relate to CSR projects. The importance that a company may give to CSR is an indication of the type of organizational culture present in that company. As Baumgartner (2009) shows, the companies that have an integrated vision on sustainable development, present in the ethos of that company, are likely to be more successful in the implementation of CSR projects.

As far as the role of management styles on CSR implementation is concerned, it has been shown that the relation is not linear. Certain management styles are connected to certain CSR approaches. Du et al. (2013) demonstrate, in a major empirical study on managers in the USA, that transformation management style determines a certain strategy toward CSR. The management style has a different impact on the organizational results of the organizational CSR: the transactional one is more geared toward results. The transformational leader is the one who articulates a vision, which can be shared on followers, who stimulates people intellectually, and who pays close attention to employees' individual differences. The transactional leadership moderates the results of CSR projects.

Research has also shown that managers' personal values have a key influence on companies' engagement in CSR activities (Hemingway and Maclagan 2004). The freedom of action, especially in the area of entrepreneurship, influences the impact that these values have on engagement in CSR. The same argument is further supported empirically by the idea that values and social actions need to accompany an economic motivation (Joyner and Payne 2002). The interviewed managers noted better results in their CSR when these activities were complementary to economic activities.

Nonetheless, we need to remark that often these categories are interdependent. Values are part of the culture of a society as well as of an organization. Even the management styles are influenced by the values of managers: a utilitarian orientation is linked with a transactional management style, whereas a moral orientation or Kantian orientation is correlated with a transformational management style (Groves and La Rocca 2011). What is more, these authors also note the linkages between managers' orientation toward CSR and a transformational management style.

2.4 Methodological Framework

This study is based on data collected through a questionnaire elaborated and validated previously in a pilot study. There are 18 closed questions (regarding the profile of the firms, the CSR activities, fields of involvement, level of formalization of CSR-related aspects, and organizational CSR) along with 4 open questions regarding the definitions of and motivations for CSR, details regarding the CSR activities, and the legal framework.

This questionnaire was distributed to small and medium enterprises with the help of master's students from the Faculty of Economics, University of Oradea, Romania. The questionnaire was distributed both online and paper based. In this way, we have collected 109 valid questionnaires filled in March–April 2017 by managers/administrators of SME working mostly in Bihor County (75%) and especially in the county seat Oradea (52%). The sample is described in Table 2.1:

Table 2.1 Description of the sample

	Turnover in euro	Year of establishment	Current number of employees
Minimum	2,2	1991	1
Maximum	28764179,5	2017	188
Mean	1528457,35	2006	19,70
Median	114785,90	2007	8,00
Std. Deviation	4532801,21	7,853	32,614
Valid cases	104	108	105

Note The data was analyzed by the authors of the current paper using SPSS statistical package

2.5 Analysis and Discussion

2.5.1 What Companies Do Regarding Social Responsibility Actions

Based on this rather optimistic view, we will present in further paragraphs what definite measures they undertake regarding CSR, based on what has been reported. We must note that it is possible that some findings are over-reported, as we did not verify in any manner if what and how often the reported actions took place. Also, we have no control whether in some cases respondents correctly classified their actions.

Regarding the domains of involvement, there are 18 firms (representing 17.8%) that declare no activity in any of the declared areas. The most attractive areas are charity and environmental protection, as shown in Fig. 2.1.

Regarding the concrete actions in which the SMEs in our sample got involved, as shown in Fig. 2.2, they most frequently donate money or organize complementary services for their employees (training, transport facilities and other).

Fig. 2.1 Domains of social responsibility actions of companies in the sample, no. of cases

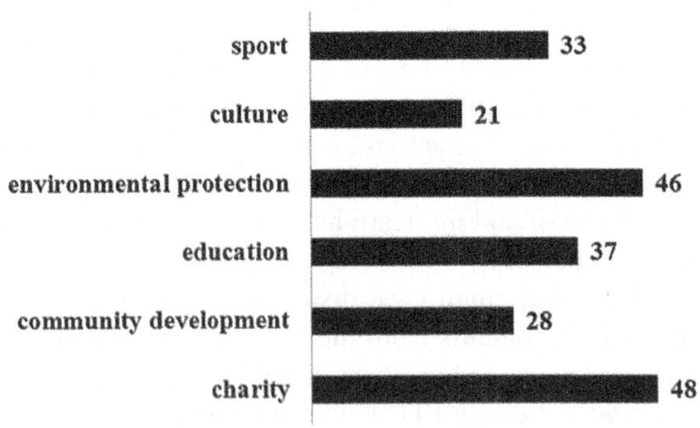

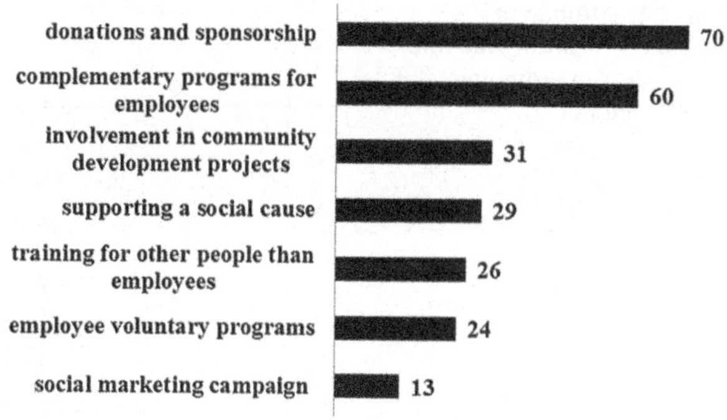

Fig. 2.2 Social responsibility actions organized by companies in the sample, no. of cases

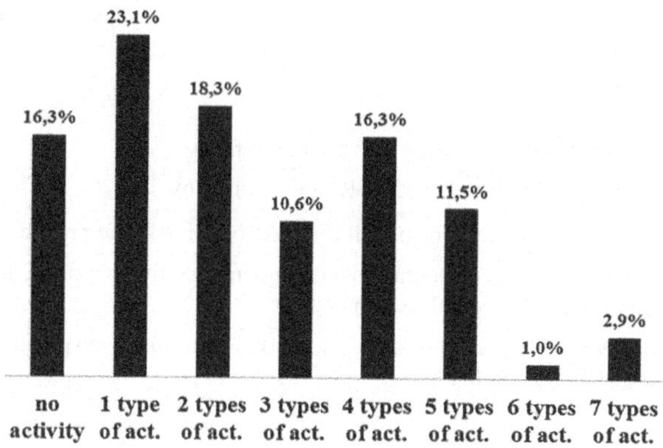

Fig. 2.3 The social responsibility type of actions scale, percentages

Based on the type of social activities undertaken by the firms, we computed a summative scale of social responsibility actions, considering that a company involved in more than one type of action is more involved in the community, and in other words has a larger propensity of social responsibility. On this scale (mean 2,4, median 2, std. dev. 1,85), we note that 17 firms have no action, 24 are involved in only 1, as presented in Fig. 2.3.

Nevertheless, the optimism derived from the previous observation regarding the level of social engagement is hindered by the size. In most cases, the sums of money spent on different types of actions are rather small—around 220 euros.

2.5.2 What Managers Say about the Role of Business in the Community

Regarding the role attributed to the business sector in providing social welfare, the opinions of managers of SMEs are rather optimistic. At the question "To what extent you consider the social welfare is the responsibility of the business sector?" (scale

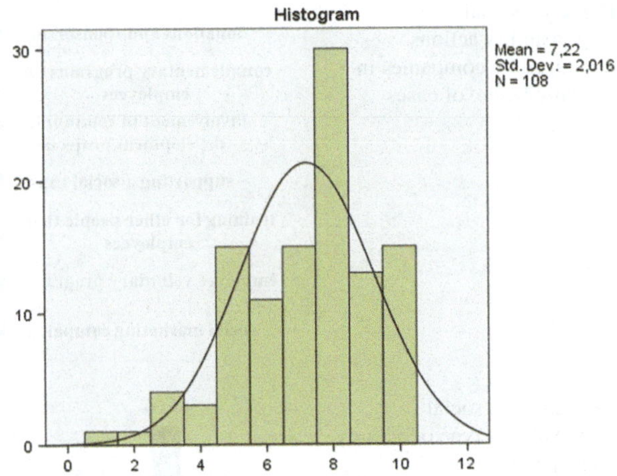

Fig. 2.4 Attitude of managers regarding the role of business in providing social welfare

Table 2.2 Formalization of CSR in the firms

Level of formalization of CSR in the company	Yes (%)
Are there any social responsibility components in the profile of your activity?	56.9
In your strategic or operational documents are there explicit any reference to values or principles of social responsibility?	47.7
Is there a department or a person employed to manage specifically aspects related to social responsibility?	22.9

with 10 points, where 1 meant that social welfare is solely the responsibility of governments and 10 that the welfare of the society should be a priority for the business sector), the majority assumed above average position. As one can see in Fig. 2.4, the average is of 7.22 and standard deviation is of 2.01 which indicates a bend to the left revealing the attribution of a stronger role of companies.

This is an optimistic outcome, suggesting that even small and medium enterprises consider they should engage in the community. This statement is supported also by the level companies declare that they incorporate CSR in their current activities. As shown in Table 2.2, most of the firms in our sample declare that they have CSR-related components in the profile of their activities. Even the percentage of firms who have a department or person dealing with CSR (23%) is higher than expected (previous research of the authors, on a smaller sample, indicated solely 4%). This higher reported engagement in CSR may derive from: (1) the self-selected sample—we expect that managers that are opened and interested in CSR would answer such a questionnaire, and (2) the constant promotion of CSR in the recent year would be reflected in a higher awareness of these issues among managers—the 3 years internal that passed from our previous research would account to some extent to improvements in this area (Table 2.2).

The important role of the managers is given also by the fact that they are the ones who decide, in most cases, in which activities to get involved (Table 2.3). To

Table 2.3 How companies choose their social responsibility actions

	Frequency	Valid percent
We base our choice on social or environmental diagnoses conducted by experts	3	3.1
We choose from the requests received from others	31	32.0
The company's manager chooses the domains of our involvement	63	64.9
Total	97	100.0

the question "Which of the following statements describe best how you choose CSR actions?", 65% of the answers referred to the fact that usually the manager chooses the domains of involvement. This percentage is even higher when we consider that 14 companies also added that the manager does the choice from the received requests.

2.5.3 *The Relation Between What Managers Say and What Companies Do*

We analyzed the link between the attitudes of managers regarding the role of companies in proving social welfare and their level of involvement in CSR activities: there is a strong positive correlation (Pearson = 0.308, sig. = 0.002) between these two indexes. The more the manager says a social welfare should be a priority for companies, the more the chance that his/her firm organizes several types of CSR activities.

There is a significant correlation (Pearson = 0.237, sig. = 0.014) between the existence of CSR-related components in the profile of firm's activities and the attitude of managers regarding the role of firms in providing welfare. In other words, the more the manager considers firms should hold social welfare as a priority, the more likely it is for their company to have concrete CSR-related components.

It is interesting to note that, contrary to other studies (Badulescu et al. 2016), there is no relation between the turnover or number of employees (as measures of the size of the firms) and the scale of the type of CSR activities. This is to say that the number of type of social activities undertaken by companies is not directly influenced by the size of the company. Also, the attitude of managers regarding the role of companies in proving welfare does not vary depending on the size of the company.

These results show that the most important factor explaining the level of engagement in social activities is related, according to our data, by the attitude of managers regarding the level at which a company should have as a priority social welfare. Given this role we consider it is important to investigate further the way managers shape the social activities the firms get involved in and how can we develop a more pro-social orientation from managers.

Based on these results, we consider that CSR can also be analyzed from the theories of active citizenship, which can be found in several domains: civil society, business, public sector, and politics (Holford and van der Veen 2003). Our data support the formulation of a future hypothesis: firms that are active in the social sphere or that of civil society are conducted by people that are socially active, interested, and involved in solving communities' problems.

2.6 Conclusions

The SMEs from our sample undertake several social responsibility actions, showing an interest in this area contrary to other views on Romanian CSR (Ciuperca 2011). Solely, 13% of our sample did not engage in any type of social activity. Nevertheless, most companies choose to donate money, and even in other cases the impact of this involvement in the community can be questioned. We consider that the level of interest of Romanian firms in solving social problems exceeds their purely economic role and is an important aspect that needs to be considered both by practitioners in the civil society and public arena as well as by scholars. Directing the efforts of companies in creating "the greater good" should be under public discussion.

Our study revealed that there is a strong link between the understanding of managers regarding the role of business in society and their social responsibility actions. This is argued for by the fact that solely the attitude of managers correlates with the scale of social responsibility types of action, while measures of size of the enterprise do not.

In other words, those who consider that companies need to take a proactive attitude are those who in fact do act, which supports one of the arguments according to which Romanian entrepreneurs are not socially active because they think they should not have this role.

They thus consider that social welfare is the job of governments; CSR actions are rather implicit, as an effect of national public policies rather than a bottom-up answer to certain social problems (Matten and Moon 2008). Likewise, the results of our research support the argument that managers' social attitudes explain companies' social engagement in CSR, thus bringing explanations over CSR at the individual level, and thus coming close to the active citizenship theory from the economic field (Holford and van der Veen 2003).

The lack of enthusiasm, reservations, and ambivalent attitudes of managers toward CSR have prevented the use of the full potential of CSR. Managers must perceive social responsibility to be vital in order for them to display socially responsible behaviors (Hunt et al. 1990; Moyeen and West 2014).

It is important to follow what the motivations are and what criteria are used by managers in their decision concerning engagement in CSR—an aspect that has received considerable attention in the literature (e.g., (Aguilera et al. 2007; Hemingway and Maclagan 2004; Joyner and Payne 2002). Moreover, the important role of managers means that this area of research comes close to research on civil participation of individuals at the community level.

In this sense, conceptualizing active citizenship (active engagement in producing collective goods) is built on three domains of activity: civil society, political and state actors, and the economic sector (Holford and van der Veen 2003; Hatos 2009; Hatos 2003). Both personal motivations and opportunities to participate play an important role in stimulating individual participation (Hatos 2009; Hatos 2015), which we expected to find concerning managers' decision to get involved in CSR. These aspects will be further researched in future work.

The main limitations of our study derive from the size of our sample, which is rather small. More, within the scope of the current study, we could not investigate the impact of the social actions carried out by small and medium enterprises in Romania. Further data is necessary also in determining the concrete mechanisms that link the attitude of managers and the social responsibility of their companies, and revealing other factors that hinder or promote the position of firms in the social sphere.

References

Aguilera, R., Rupp, D., Williams, C., & Ganapathi, J. (2007). Putting the S back in corporate social responsibility: A multilevel theory of social change in organizations. *Academy of Management Review, 32,* 836–863.

Azmat, F., & Samaratunge, R. (2009). Responsible entrepreneurship in developing countries: Understanding the realities and complexities. *Journal of Business Ethics, 90*(3), 437–452.

Azmat, F., & Zutshi, A. (2012). Perceptions of corporate social responsibility amongst immigrant entrepreneurs. *Social Responsibility Journal, 8*(1), 63–76.

Badulescu, A., Badulescu, D., Saveanu, T., & Hatos, R. (2016). *SMEs and social responsibility: Does firm age matter?* Bucharest: STRATEGICA Conference "Opportunities & Risks in the Contemporary Business Environment", Bucharest, October 2016.

Badulescu, D., & Petria, N. (2013). Social responsibility of Romanian companies: Contribution to a "Good Society" or expected business strategy? the annals of the university of oradea. *Economic Sciences, XXII, 1,* 590–600.

Barkemeyer, R. (2007). *Legitimacy as a key driver and determinant of csr in developing countries,* Amsterdam: Paper for the 2007 Marie curie summer school on earth system governance, 28 May–06 June 2007.

Baumgartner, R. (2009). Organizational culture and leadership: Preconditions for the development of a sustainable corporation. *Sustainable Development, 17,* 102–113.

Beck, U. (1997). *Reinvention of politics: Rethinking modernity in the global social order*. Cambridge, Massachusetts: Polity Press.

Blowfield, M., & Frynas, J. (2005). Setting new agendas: Critical perspectives on corporate social responsibility in the developing world. *International Affairs, 81*(3), 499–513.

Cacioppe, R., Forster, N., & Fox, M. (2008). A survey of managers' perceptions of corporate ethics and social responsibility and actions that may affect companies' success. *Journal of Business Ethics, 82*(3), 681–700.

Carroll, A. (1991). The pyramid of corporate social responsibility: Toward the moral management of organizational stakeholders. *Business Horizons, 34*(4), 39–48.

Chahoud, T., Emmerling, J., Kolb, D., Kubina, I., Repinski, G., & Schlager, C. (2007). *Corporate social and environmental responsibility in India—assessing the un global compact's role.* Bonn: German Development Institute.

Chiu, S. C., & Sharfman, M. (2011). Legitimacy, visibility and the antecedentes of corporate social performance: An investigation of the instrumental perspective. *Journal of Management, 37*(6), 1558–1585.
Ciuperca, E. (2011). *An explanatory model of corporate social responsibility implementation in Romania. In* International conference on social science and humanity IPEDR, 5, pp. V2–11-15. Retrieved February 5, 2017, from http://www.ipedr.com/vol5/no2/4-H10068.pdf.
Dahlsrud, A. (2006). How corporate social responsibility is defined: An analysis of 37 definitions. *Corporate Social Responsibility and Environmental Management, 18*(1), 1–13.
Deakin, N., & Walsh, K. (1996). The enabling state: The role of markets and contracts. *Public Administration, 74*(1), 33–48.
Devinney, T. M. (2009). *Is the socially responsible corporation a myth? the good, bad and ugly of corporate social responsibility.* Retrieved February 9, 2017, from https://aom.org/uploadedFiles/Publications/AMP/May09CorpSocialRespbyDevinney.pdf.
Du, S., Swaen, V., Lindgreen, A., & Sen, S. (2013). The roles of leadership styles in corporate social responsibility. *Journal of Business Ethics, 114*(1), 155–169.
European Commission. (2002). *Communication from the Commission concerning Corporate Social Responsibility: A business contribution to Sustainable Development.* Retrieved March 17, 2017, from http://ec.europa.eu/europeaid/sites/devco/files/communication-corporate-social-responsibility-sustainable-development-com2002347-20020702_en.pdf.
Commission, European. (2011). *Towards a greater understanding of the changing role of business in society*. Brussels: European Commission, Directorate-General for Research & Innovation.
Friedman, M. (1970). The social responsibility of business is to increase its profits. *The New York Times Magazine,* September 13.
Gibson-Graham, J., Cameron, J., & Healy, S. (2013). *Take back the economy*. Minneapolis: University of Minnesota Press.
Groves, C., & La Rocca, M. (2011). An empirical study of leader ethical values, transformational and transactional leadership, and follower attitudes toward corporate social responsibility. *Journal of Business Ethics, 103,* 511–528.
Hastings, G. (2016). CSR: The parable of the bad samaritan. *Social Marketing Quarterly, 22*(4), 280–289. https://doi.org/10.1177/1524500416631942.
Hatos, A. (2003). *Participarea comunitară în România. Acțiune colectivă urbană în postsocialism.* Iași: Institutul European.
Hatos, A. (2009). *Participarea comunitară în România urbană. Lideri, participanţi şi spectatori ai acţiunilor colective din vecinătăţile din blocurile construite înainte de 1990*. Oradea: Editura Universităţii din Oradea.
Hatos, A., Hatos, R., Badulescu, A., & Badulescu, D. (2015). Are risk attitudes and individualism predictors of entrepreneurship in Romania? *Amfiteatru Economic, 17*(38), 148–161.
Hemingway, C., & Maclagan, P. (2004). Managers' personal values as drivers of corporate social responsibility. *Journal of Business Ethics, 50,* 33–44.
Hofman, P., Moon, J., & Wu, B. (2015). Corporate Social responsibility under authoritarian capitalism: Dynamics and prospects of state-led and society- driven CSR. *Business & Society,* 1–21. https://doi.org/10.1177/0007650315623014.
Holford, J., and van der Veen, R. (2003). *lifelong learning, governance and active citizenship in Europe*. Retrieved April 4, 2017, from https://ec.europa.eu/research/social-sciences/pdf/etgace_en.pdf.
Hunt, S., Kiecker, P., & Chonko, B. (1990). Social responsibility and personal success: A research note. *Journal of the Academy of Marketing, 18*(3), 239–244.
Joyner, B., & Payne, D. (2002). Evolution and implementation: A study of values, business ethics and corporate social responsibility. *Journal of Business Ethics, 41,* 297–311.
Kolodinsky, R., Madden, T., Zisk, D., & Henkel, E. (2010). Attitudes about corporate social responsibility: Business student predictors. *Journal of Business Ethics, 91*(2), 167–181.
Maignan, I. (2001). Consumers'perceptions of corporate social responsibilities: A cross-cultural comparison. *Journal of Business Ethics, 30*(1), 57–72.

Matten, D., & Moon, J. (2008). "Implicit" and "Explicit" CSR: A conceptual framework for a comparative understanding of corporate social responsibility. *Academy of Management Review, 33*(2), 404–424.

Moon, J., & Vogel, D. (2008). corporate social responsibility, government, and civil society. In A. Crane et al. (Eds.), *The oxford handbook of corporate social responsibility* (pp. 303–323). Oxford: Oxford University Press.

Moyeen, A., & West, B. (2014). Promoting CSR to foster sustainable development: Attitudes and perceptions of managers in a developing country. *Asia-Pacific Journal of Business Administration, 6*(2), 97–115. https://doi.org/10.1108/APJBA-05-2013-0036.

Organisation for Economic Co-operation and Development (OECD) 2016. *What is corporate responsibility?* Retrieved February 26, 2017, from http://www.oecd.org/corporate/mne/corporateresponsibilityfrequentlyaskedquestions.htm.

Quazi, A., & O'Brien, D. (2000). An empirical test of a cross-national model of corporate social responsibility. *Journal of Business Ethics, 25*(1), 33–51.

Rahim, M. (2013). *Legal regulation of corporate social responsibility. Chapter 2. Corporate social responsibility, corporate governance and corporate regulation.* Berlin Heidelberg: Springer-Verlag.

Reich, R. B. (2007). *Supercapitalism. The Transformation of Business, Democracy, and Everyday Life.* NY: Knopf Doubleday Publishing Group.

Sandoval, M. (2015). From CSR to RSC: A Contribution to the Critique of the Political Economy of Corporate Social Responsibility. *Review of Radical Political Economics, 47*(4), 608–624. https://doi.org/10.1177/0486613415574266.

Sastry, T. (2011). Exploring the role of business in society. *IIMB Management Review,* 23, 246–256.

Singhapakdi, A., Vitell, J., Rallapalli, K., & Kraft, L. (1996). The perceived role of ethics and social responsibility: A scale development. *Journal of Business Ethics, 15*(11), 1131–1140.

Ubius, U., & Alas, R. (2009). organizational culture types as predictors of corporate social responsibility. *Engineering Economics, 61*(1), 90–99.

Waldman, D., de Luque, M., Washburn, N., & House, R. (2006). Cultural and leadership predictors of corporate social responsibility values of top management: A GLOBE study of 15 countries. *Journal of International Business Studies, 36,* 823–837.

Welford, R., Chan, C., & Man, M. (2008). Priorities for corporate social responsibility: A survey of businesses and their stakeholders. *Corporate Social Responsibility and Environmental Management, 15*(1), 52–62.

Williams, C., & Aguilera, R. (2008). Corporate social responsibility in comparative perspective. In A. Crane et al. (Eds.), *Oxford handbook of corporate social responsibility* (pp. 452–472). Oxford: Oxford University Press.

Chapter 3
Comparative Study Regarding Organizational Culture: Nonprofit Organization and Profit-Oriented Organization

Oana-Bianca Bercea, Elena-Simina Lakatos and Laura Bacali

Abstract This article presents the results of a comparative case study that identifies and analyzes the organizational culture differences between a nonprofit organization and a profit-oriented organization. For the analysis of the organizational culture, we used the Organizational Culture Assessment Instrument (OCAI) that approaches: dominant characteristics, organizational leadership, human resource management, organizational glue, strategic objectives, and success criteria of an organization. The participants of the study are executive employees and management members of the targeted organizations which facilitate local socioeconomic development. This case study identifies (1) the type of dominant organizational culture, (2) differences between the existent organizational culture and preferred organizational culture, and (3) differences between characteristics of existent cultural organization and characteristics of organizational culture that facilitates innovation in the targeted nonprofit organization and profit-oriented organization.

Keywords Organizational culture · Nonprofit organization
Socioeconomic development · Innovation · Management

3.1 Introduction

In a society that needs to respond to more and more complex challenges, organizations within social economy seem very important for the success of Europe 2020 Strategy as it contributes to intelligent growth by responding to social needs that are not satisfied with social innovation. Also, they determine sustainable growth through

---

O.-B. Bercea (✉) · E.-S. Lakatos · L. Bacali
Technical University of Cluj-Napoca, Cluj-Napoca, Romania
e-mail: bianca_bercea@yahoo.com

E.-S. Lakatos
e-mail: simina.lakatos@mis.utcluj.ro

L. Bacali
e-mail: laurabacali@gmail.com

S. A. Văduva et al. (eds.), *Civil Society: The Engine for Economic and Social Well-Being*, Springer Proceedings in Business and Economics,
https://doi.org/10.1007/978-3-319-89872-8_3

their positive impact on the environment and through their long-term vision, and at the same time, they are in the middle of inclusive growth process due to the emphasis on people and social cohesion (Barna 2014; Lakatos 2014).

Social economy represents solutions identified to solve some social problems at European and global level, that defines a group of organizations such as cooperatives, mutualities, associations, and foundations characterized by social goals and participative governance (Euricse 2013). According to this directive, social economy is regarded as a possibility to modernize the social European model as it generates employment and it develops new premises of entrepreneurship that responds to various social needs.

At European level, social economy represents 10% of existent businesses (Barna 2014) and it provides employment for more than 14.5 millions people, almost 6.5% of European Union workforce (Euricse 2013). Among them, 70% are employees in nonprofit associations, 26% in co-operatives, and 3% in mutualities (Barna et al. 2016).

The most common legal forms of social enterprises in European Union are (1) associations, foundations, and other similar forms in proportion of 92%; (2) cooperatives and other similar accepted forms in proportion of 7%, and (3) mutualities and other similar accepted forms about 1% (Euricse 2013). Most organizations pertaining to social organization are found in Great Britain with 875 555 organization in 2010, followed by Germany with 513 727 organizations and Spain with 200 769 organizations (CIRIEC 2012). Studies show an ascendent path for social economy structure in Romania with a 52.83% growth in 2012, when 39 347 organizations were reported, compared to 2010 with 25 744 organization.

The present study will analyze differences between a social economy organization and a profit-oriented entity from the organizational culture perspective. The following chapter will provide you some theoretical background regarding organizational culture while the next chapter is dedicated to an empirical study. Conclusions are presented in the last chapter.

3.2 A Theoretical Background for Organizational Culture

Research literature provides us with a variety of definitions for organizational culture. For example, Schein (1985) gives us a more formal definition for organizational culture: “A pattern of basic assumptions—invented, discovered or developed by a given group as it learns to cope with the problems of external adaptation and internal integration—that has worked well enough to be considered valid and, therefore, to be taught to new members as the correct way to perceive, think and feel in relation to these problems.”

Other authors answered the question regarding the definition of organizational culture in a manner that allows the average population to understand the concept by providing a more informal definition. Organizational culture describes “the way we do things around here” (Deal and Kennedy 1982). Organizational culture determines and guides the group behavior. It is a mental phenomenon that determines how individuals from a certain group think and assess reality in a similar way and how this thinking and assessment is different than other occupational groups (Alvesson and Sveningsson 2015; Oney-Yazıcı et al. 2007).

Therefore, organizational culture is a part of informal side of an organization that contains values, beliefs, and behavior models that are formed over time and that are passed to the new members. Organizational culture is created by the people in the organizations representing members' routine, their way of making the things to work.

There are several factors involved in the apparition of organizational culture such as (Hintea 2007): the culture of the society, traditions and success behaviors, the nature of organizational activities and close environment, founding members and crisis. Regarding the transmission of organizational culture, there are several ways such as the stories, organizational rituals, symbols, language, myths, heroes, norms to be followed or declaration of principles (Hintea 2007; Ojo 2009).

Cameron and Quinn (2005) have identified four types of organizational culture: clan culture, adhocracy culture, hierarchy culture, and market culture (Tables 3.1 and 3.2).

The research presented in this paper is based on the model developed by Cameron and Quinn (2005) and it is presented in the following section.

3.3 Comparative Study Regarding Organizational Culture: Nonprofit Organization and Profit-Oriented Organization

A comparative study regarding organizational culture in profit and nonprofit organization was conducted using the methodology developed by Cameron and Quinn (2005). The study has the following objectives:

1. To identify the type of dominant organizational culture in the targeted organizations;
2. To identify differences between the existent organizational culture and preferred organizational culture in the analyzed organizations;
3. To identify differences between characteristics of existent cultural organization and characteristics of organizational culture that facilitates innovation in the targeted nonprofit organization and profit-oriented organization.

3.3.1 Research Methodology

The research method used for this case study is the survey with a standardized questionnaire developed by Cameron and Quinn (2005) that is called Organizational

Table 3.1 Types of organizational culture (Cameron and Quinn 2006)

The clan culture	The adhocracy culture
A very friendly place to work where people share a lot of themselves. It is like an extended family. The leaders, or head of the organization, are considered to be mentors and, maybe even, parent figures. The organization is held together by loyalty or tradition. Commitment is high. The organization emphasizes the long-term benefit of human resource development and attaches great importance to cohesion and morale. Success is defined in terms of sensitivity to customers and concern for people. The organization places a premium on teamwork, participation, and consensus	A dynamic, entrepreneurial, and creative place to work. People stick their necks out and take risks. The leaders are considered to be innovators and risk takers. The glue that holds the organization together is a commitment to experimentation and innovation. The emphasis is on being on the leading edge. The organization's long-term emphasis is on growth and acquiring new resources. Success means gaining unique and new products or services. Being a product or service leader is important. The organization encourages individual initiative and freedom
The hierarchy culture	**The market culture**
A very formalized and structured place to work. Procedures govern what people do. The leaders pride themselves on being good coordinators and organizers, who are efficiency minded. Maintaining a smooth running organization is most critical. Formal rules and policies hold the organization together. The long-term concern is on stability and performance with efficient, smooth operations. Success is defined in terms of dependable delivery, smooth scheduling, and low cost. The management of employees is concerned with secure employment and predictability	A results-oriented organization. The major concern is getting the job done. People are competitive and goal oriented. The leaders are hard drivers, producers, and competitors. They are tough and demanding. The glue that holds the organization together is an emphasis on winning. Reputation and success are common concerns. The long-term focus is on competitive actions and achievement of measurable goals and targets. Success is defined in terms of market share and penetration. Competitive pricing and market leadership are important. The organizational style is hard-driving competitiveness

Source Cameron and Quinn (2005)

Table 3.2 Dominant organizational culture scores in profit-oriented organization

	Organizational culture—NOW	Organizational culture—PREFERRED
A (CLAN)	31.50	35.50
B (ADHOCRACY)	21.92	22.25
C (MARKET)	26.25	18.75
D (HIERARCHY)	20.33	23.50
Total	100.00	100.00

Culture Assessment Instrument (OCAI) adapted to approach the previously presented objectives. The instrument employs the Competing Values Framework that has been rated as one of the fifty most important models in the history of business study (Igo and Skitmore 2006).

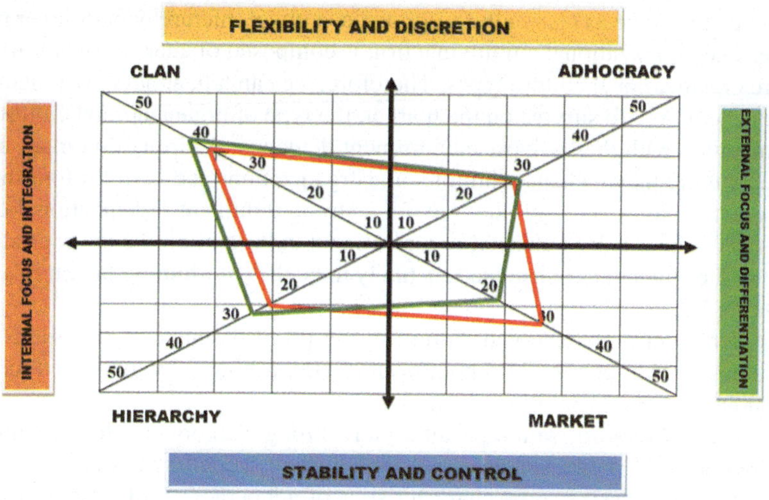

Graphic 3.1 Organizational culture in profit-oriented organization

The questionnaire was applied on the management and execution level of two organizations within the same field of activity—project management, but with different objectives: a profit-oriented organization—S.C. Pro Xpert Consulting S.R.L.—and a nonprofit organization—Civitas Foundation for Civil Society.

The OCAI questionnaire covers six key dimensions of organizational culture: (1) dominant characteristics, (2) organizational leadership, (3) management of employees, (4) organizational glue, (5) strategic emphasis, and (6) criteria of success. The OCAI consisted of six questions and each question had four alternatives. Respondents were asked to divide 100 points among those four alternatives. Based on management and executive employee's responses, we were able to depict the organizational culture profile for each participating organization. We had a response rate of 71.43% for the profit-oriented organization and a response rate of 53.85% for the nonprofit organization.

3.3.2 Organizational Culture: Actual Versus Preferred

(a) The case of profit-oriented organization

The general image of organizational culture in the profit-oriented organization is depicted in Graphic 3.1. Responses provided by the management team and executive teams were centralized and the mean was computed for each type of organizational culture.

The existent organizational culture is represented through the red quadrangle and the preferred organizational culture through the greed one. There is no pure organizational culture such as clan culture, adhocracy culture, hierarchy culture, or market culture. The organizational culture in a firm is composed of characteristics affiliated to more organizational culture types. Therefore, we can talk about a dominant organizational culture. To survive on the market, the type of organizational culture must be compatible with the business environment demands. A strong dominant organizational culture may be beneficial for some organizations and harmful for others. In some organizations, survival may rely on a strong dominant organizational culture while for others a more balanced organizational culture might be appropriate. The nature of the challenges a firm faces is likely to be the determining factor. (Cameron and Quinn 2005).

The dominant organizational culture in the profit-oriented organizations is the clan culture with a score of 31.5 points out of 100, followed by market culture with 26.25 points.

Personnel of the firm would prefer a more strong clan organizational culture, as the difference of 4 points suggests. At subculture or secondary cultures level, there is a desire to emphasize some characteristics of adhocracy and hierarchy cultures, and to give up to some characteristics of market culture. There is no major gap between actual organizational culture and preferred organizational culture. The balance between the dominant organizational culture and subcultures suggests an effort to adapt both to the internal and external environment as the field of activity requires flexibility and discretionary capacity in some situations, and stability and control in other cases.

The analysis on dimensions of organizational culture in the profit-oriented organizations shows differences higher than 10 points regarding the general characteristics of the organizational culture. According to the results, there is a need for a more structured and controlled organization. What it must be understood is that the dominance type of the hierarchy culture will be established at the organizational level according to characteristics of the developed activity. Once the need for change is identified, each member of the organization must define what a more dominating hierarchy culture means for them. Therefore, a change strategy will be established.

(b) The case of nonprofit organization

The general image of organizational culture in the nonprofit organization is summarized in Graphic 3.2. Responses provided by management and executive teams were centralized and the mean was computed for each type of organizational culture. As we can observe in the graphic above, the dominant organizational culture in the analyzed nonprofit organization is the clan culture emphasized with a red line in the upper left quadrant. The score of the clan culture is 30 points out of 100.

Interesting is that there are insignificant differences between the actual organizational culture and the preferred one. Based on general results, there is no need to change organizational culture. In Table 3.3 are presented the scores for each type of organizational culture.

According to our results, the actual and the preferred organizational culture type is the clan culture, with a difference in strength of 0.56 points. At the subculture level, personnel would like to strengthen some characteristics regarding hierarchy

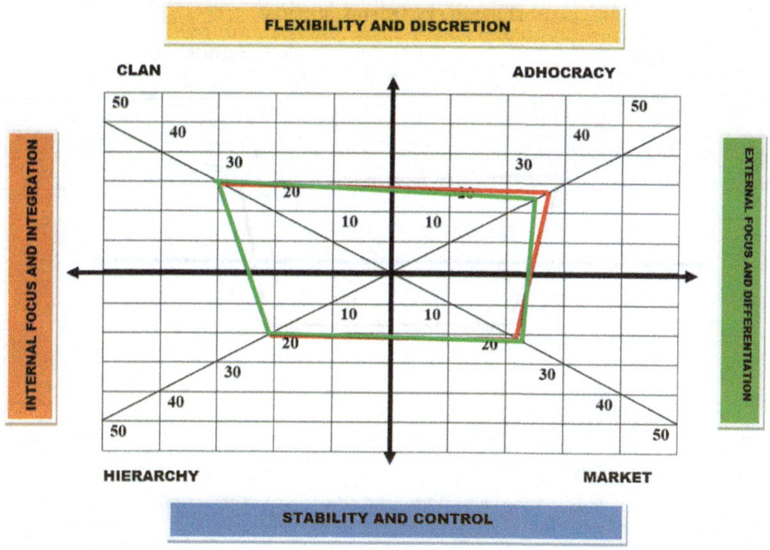

Graphic 3.2 Organizational culture in the nonprofit organization

Table 3.3 Dominant organizational culture scores in nonprofit organization

	Organizational culture—NOW	Organizational culture—PREFERRED
A (CLAN)	30.00	30.56
B (ADHOCRACY)	28.47	26.39
C (MARKET)	21.25	20.69
D (HIERARCHY)	20.28	22.36
Total	100.00	100.00

culture and give up to some characteristics of market culture and adhocracy. There are no major differences between actual and preferred organizational culture. Similar to profit-oriented organization, there is a balance between the types of organizational cultures. We can notice a difference of 9.72 points between the maximum score and the minimum score for the actual organizational culture and a difference of 9.87 for the preferred organizational culture.

Although the general actual organizational culture model and the preferred one are almost identical, a more detailed analysis identifies minor preferred changes regarding the last three dimensions: organizational glue, strategic emphasis, and criteria of success. We identified a desire to diminish the characteristics of organizational culture such as: (1) organizational glue maintained by commitment to innovation and development, (2) achievement of new resources and challenges, and (3) defining success through newest or most unique products and services. On the other hand, members of the organization would chose to accentuate some characteristics of the

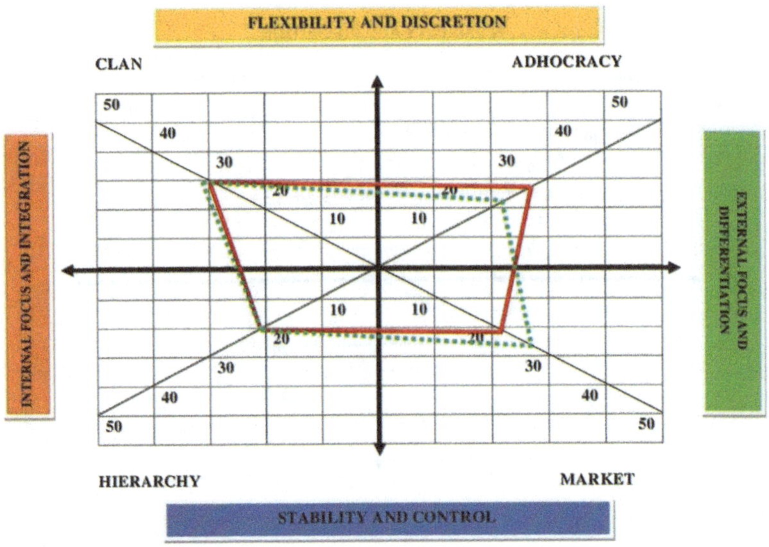

Graphic 3.3 Differences of actual organizational culture

clan culture such as: (1) organizational glue ensured by loyalty and mutual trust, (2) human development, high trust, and participation, and (3) success defined on the basis of the development of human resources, teamwork, employee commitment, and concern for people.

Differences lower than 10 points between actual and preferred organizational culture does not result in a need for change in the nonprofit organization.

3.3.3 Organizational Culture and Innovation

In Graphic 3.3 are represented the actual organizational culture and the preferred organizational culture in the nonprofit organization as compared to the profit-oriented organization. The organizational culture in the nonprofit organization is represented through a red quadrangle while the organizational culture in the profit-oriented organization is represented through a green dotted quadrangle.

Both organizations have a clan culture as a dominant organizational culture. The major difference between the two organizations can be observed in the upper right quadrant of the graphic. According to our analysis, the adhocracy culture, known also as a culture that fosters innovation, is stronger in the nonprofit organization compared to the profit-oriented one where a market culture is more important. The explanation is that in the case of a profit-oriented organization, market orientation has a certain importance. On the other side, for an organization with social objectives

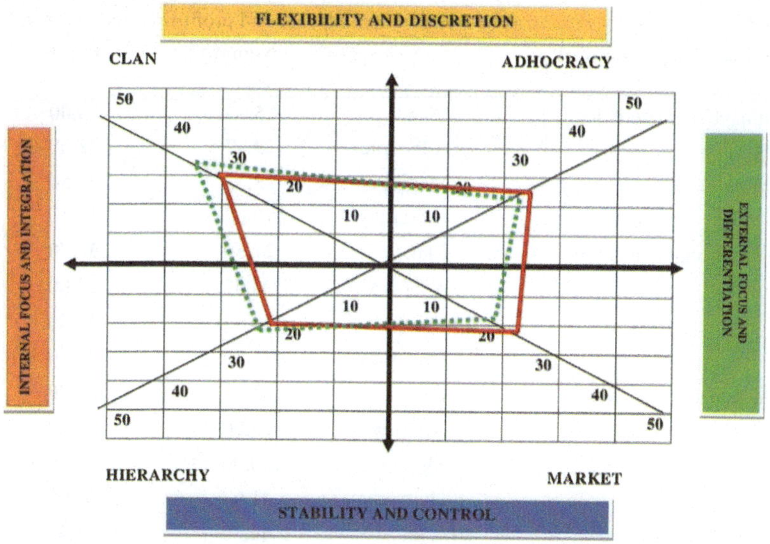

Graphic 3.4 Differences of preferred organizational culture

whose purpose is to address social issues and innovation, social innovation is critical (Graphic 3.4).

Regarding the model of preferred organizational culture in the two organizations, we can notice a greater emphasis on innovation in the nonprofit organization compared to the profit-oriented organization. The profit-oriented organization would prefer to approach to a greater extent some elements specific to hierarchy culture or clan culture. There are no major differences between the two organizations, but they portray two different actors of the local economy that contribute to socioeconomic development of the community.

In Table 3.4 are the scores of the two organizations for each component of the organizational culture. This way, we can analyze major differences in organizational culture of the profit-oriented and nonprofit organizations.

The dimension of dominant characteristics of the nonprofit organization is associated to the adhocracy culture—29.17 points out of 100, while in the profit-oriented organization, the dominant characteristics are related to the clan type of culture—38 points out of 100. The scores of dominant characteristics that are associated to the market culture are similar in both organizations. Both organizations are result oriented, with highly competitive employees, only that in the nonprofit organization, there is more emphasis on risk-taking while the profit-oriented organization dominates a family atmosphere.

The dimension of organizational leadership is specific to the clan culture in both organizations with a difference of only 3 points for the profit-oriented organization (30.50 points out of 100) in comparison with the nonprofit organization (27.50 points

Table 3.4 Dimensions of organizational culture in nonprofit and profit-oriented organization

Dimensions of organizational culture		Nonprofit	Profit
1. Dominant characteristics	Clan	25.83	**38.00**
	Adhocracy	**29.17**	22.00
	Market	28.33	28.50
	Hierarchy	16.67	11.50
2. Organizational leadership	Clan	**27.50**	**30.50**
	Adhocracy	26.67	24.00
	Market	20.83	25.50
	Hierarchy	25.00	20.00
3. Management of employees	Clan	**33.33**	**33.00**
	Adhocracy	25.00	20.50
	Market	20.00	18.50
	Hierarchy	21.67	28.00
4. Organizational glue	Clan	**42.50**	**31.50**
	Adhocracy	29.17	28.50
	Market	10.83	24.00
	Hierarchy	17.50	16.00
5. Strategic emphasis	Clan	*28.33*	**29.50**
	Adhocracy	**29.17**	19.00
	Market	22.50	*28.50*
	Hierarchy	20.00	23.00
6. Criteria of success	Clan	22.50	26.50
	Adhocracy	**31.67**	17.50
	Market	25.00	**32.50**
	Hierarchy	20.83	23.50

out of 100). Therefore, the leadership of both organizations is considered to exemplify mentorship and human development.

The management of employees dimension pertains to the clan culture in both organizations, with similar scores: 33.33 points for the nonprofit organizations and 33.00 points for the profit-oriented organization. Therefore, the management style in the two organizations is characterized through teamwork, consensus, and participation. Within the nonprofit organization, a more particular attention is dedicated to individual risk-taking, innovation, freedom, and unicity specific to adhocracy culture (25.00 points out of 100) while within the profit-oriented organization, job safety, commitment, predictability, and stability of human relationship specific to hierarchy culture are more important (28.00 points out of 100).

The dimension of organizational glue is kept in both organizations mostly through loyalty and mutual trust. If the scores regarding adhocracy culture and hierarchy culture are distributed in similar ways, it is not the case of characteristics regarding the dimension of organizational glue specific to market culture. In contrast to the nonprofit organization (10.38 points out of 100), for the profit-oriented organization (24.00 points out of 100), achieving of objectives is more important to maintain the organizational glue.

The strategic emphasis in the profit-oriented organization is represented by personal development that is specific to clan culture (29.50 points out of 100). It is important to maintain a high level of trust, openness, and participation. Also, personal development of employees represents a strategic objective for the nonprofit organization (28.33 points out of 100), but more important are acquiring new resources and creating new challenges specific to adhocracy culture (29.17 points out of 100). A strategic objective for the profit-oriented organization is success on the market (28.50). We can conclude that strategic objectives of profit-oriented organization are related to clan and market culture while those of nonprofit organization are associated to adhocracy and clan culture.

Criteria for success dimension of the nonprofit organizations are specific to an adhocracy type of culture while those of the profit-oriented organization are associated to a market culture. Therefore, the nonprofit organization defines its success by gaining unique services and products while the profit-oriented organizations define its success in terms of market share and penetration.

3.4 Conclusions

In conclusion, the main difference between the organizational cultures in the two organizations is defined by the importance given to innovation in comparison to market orientation. In the case of the profit-oriented organization, the purpose of gaining profit is more evident and it is highlighted by a market organizational culture. Albeit, the management of employees and the organizational glue of both organizations belong to a clan culture where mentorship is exemplified, professional development opportunities are created, teamwork, participation and commitment are encouraged while loyalty and mutual consensus held the organization together.

References

Alvesson, M., & Sveningsson, S. (2015). *Changing organizational culture: Cultural change work in progress*. Routledge.

Barna, C. (2014). *Social economy atlas Romania 2014*.

Barna, C., Irina, O., & Ancuța, V. (2016). Atlas of social economy 2014 edition-statistical overview of the reality of the social economy in romania. *Revista de Economie Socială, 6*(1), 19–34.

Ciriec. (2012). The social economy in the european union. http://www.eesc.europa.eu/resources/docs/qe-31-12-784-en-c.pdf.

Cameron, K. S., & Quinn, R. E. (2005). *Diagnosing and changing organizational culture: Based on the competing values framework*. Wiley.
Cameron, K. S., & Quinn, R. E. (2006). *Diagnosing and changing organizational culture: Based on the competing values framework.* John Wiley & Sons.
Deal, T. E., & Kennedy, A. A. (1982). *Corporate cultures*. Reading, Mass.: Addison-Wesley.
Euricse. (2013). *Social economy and social entrepreneurship: A social europe guide* (Vol. 4). European Commission.
Hintea, C. (2007). *Management public*. Accent.
Igo, T., & Skitmore, M. (2006). Diagnosing the organizational culture of an Australian engineering consultancy using the competing values framework. *Construction Innovation, 6*(2), 121–139.
Ojo, O. (2009). Impact assessment of corporate culture on employee job performance. *Business Intelligence Journal, 2*(2), 388–397.
Oney-Yazıcı, E., Giritli, H., Topcu-Oraz, G., & Acar, E. (2007). Organizational culture: The case of Turkish construction industry. *Engineering, Construction and Architectural Management, 14*(6), 519–531.
Lakatos, E. S. (2014). Abordarea responsabilităţii sociale corporative prin parteneriate între mediul de afaceri şi ong-uri pentru sustenabilitatea întreprinderii. In I. Pop (Ed.). MEGA. ISBN: 978-606-543-508-7. Edition: 2014.
Schein, E. H. (1985). Defining organizational culture. *Classics of Organization Theory, 3*, 490–502.
https://ocai.wordpress.com/2010/05/21/organizational-culture-assessment-instrument-ocai-explained/.

Chapter 4
Investigating the Different Roles of the Factors Affecting Ethically Questionable Consumer Behaviour

Ciprian-Marcel Pop, Andreea-Ioana Romonţi-Maniu and Monica-Maria Zaharie

Abstract Based on an empirical study in the context of Romania, this paper examines the different levels of importance regarding the determinants within the ethically questionable consumer behaviour. The quantitative study is based on the model of the theory of planned behaviour incorporating the factor of perceived unfairness. Confirmatory factor analysis was used to assess measurement structures and the proposed model was estimated using structural equation modelling. Significantly, perceived behavioural control is shown to have an obvious positive impact on the intention to behave unethically in terms of digital piracy context, but this is not significant in case of shoplifting. Instead, the influence of the perceived unfairness is shown to be considerable when it comes to the consumer action of stealing goods from a shop. As such, the influencing factors of ethically questionable behaviour change their importance depending on the type of the behaviour. In other words, companies need to understand the consumer perceptions toward the difficulty of engaging in ethically questionable behaviour and to consider their responsibilities in relation to their consumers. Limitations of the study and future directions for research are considered as well.

Keywords Ethically questionable behaviour · Digital piracy · Shoplifting
Theory of planned behaviour · Structural equation modelling

C.-M. Pop (✉) · A.-I. Romonţi-Maniu · M.-M. Zaharie
Faculty of Economics and Business Administration, Babeş-Bolyai University,
Cluj-Napoca, Romania
e-mail: marcel.pop@econ.ubbcluj.ro

A.-I. Romonţi-Maniu
e-mail: andreea.maniu@econ.ubbcluj.ro

M.-M. Zaharie
e-mail: maria.zaharie@econ.ubbcluj.ro

S. A. Văduva et al. (eds.), *Civil Society: The Engine for Economic and Social Well-Being*, Springer Proceedings in Business and Economics,
https://doi.org/10.1007/978-3-319-89872-8_4

4.1 Introduction

It is increasingly evident that ethics in business and consumer behaviour is more than a fancy word. Thus, the perception of ethics could differ in terms of specific cultural context, in order to explain how ethical concerns can have crucial implications for how companies consider their responsabilities related to consumers. Based on an empirical study in the context of Romania, this paper examines the importance of the factors affecting ethically questionable consumer behaviour. The findings of this research show how these factors could change their relevance depending on context and opportunities that arise.

The significance of ethically questionable behaviour has been recognized for some time, with retail fraud and digital piracy as probably its most prominent manifestations (Fukukawa and Ennew 2010). In this regard, researchers have studied ethically questionable behaviour in the context of software piracy (e.g. Aleassa et al. 2011; Cronan and Al-Rafee 2008; Hinduja 2007; Phau and Ng 2010), music piracy (e.g. Higgins et al. 2008), consumer insurance fraud (e.g. Miyazaki 2009; Tseng and Kuo 2014) or shoplifting (e.g. Egan and Taylor 2010; Smith and Clarke 2015). Such behaviours have proven their critical consequences on the marketplace. For example, the BSA Global Software Survey 2016 (BSA The Software Alliance 2016) explained how cybersecurity has become a great concern for companies around the world. The study shows that 39% of the global software installed on personal computers in 2015 were not properly licensed and the commercial value of the unlicensed installations stood at $52.2 billion (http://globalstudy.bsa). Regarding the context of Romania, the BSA report highlighted that the rate of software piracy in 2015 was 60%. Concerning shoplifting, the 2014–2015 Global Retail Theft Barometer reports that this behaviour was the main cause of total losses in Europe, representing 42% ($17.17 billion) (http://www.globalretailtheftbarometer.com). With these financial implications, companies undoubtedly find it difficult to cope with a range of strategic decisions to reduce the negative impact of such behaviours and understanding of how and why consumers engage in ethically questionable behaviour (Fukukawa and Ennew 2010).

The paper investigates the different roles of the factors affecting ethically questionable behaviour in the context of Romanian consumers. A key finding of the study is that context could change the importance of the influencing factors of ethically questionable behaviour. This finding raises implications for companies that need to understand the consumer perceptions toward the difficulty of engaging in ethically questionable behaviour and to consider their responsibilities in relation to their consumers.

This paper begins by reviewing the conceptual background of this study, including the theory of planned behaviour (Ajzen 1991) in ethically questionable behaviour literature. The research model and hypotheses will be explained in the second section followed by research methodology. The results of this empirical study will be discussed in the fourth section. The paper concludes with an analysis of the findings related to Romanian context which has several implications for consumer ethics research and business strategies.

4.2 Literature Review

4.2.1 Consumer Ethically Questionable Behaviour

Consumer ethics has greatly advanced in recent years (Vitell 2015) therefore there is a need for an understanding of why and in which context some consumers engage in ethically questionable behaviour. All aspects of consumer behaviour (the acquisition, use or disposition of products) could have an ethical component (Vitell 2003) and consumers may become opportunistic depending on the situation or their relationship with businesses. Although many companies make efforts to permanently apply ethical principles (Dabija et al. 2016), consumers might fail to act always in accordance with their moral norms in their consumption choices (Hassan et al. 2013). Research in relation to ethically questionable behaviour by consumers examines a variety of ethical dilemmas. In terms of measuring, Muncy and Vitell (1992) created and later updated (Vitell and Muncy 2005) the Consumer Ethics Scale, a reliable instrument that has been adapted by the present study as well. This scale offers a useful typology of ethically questionable behaviour, from which this study decided to focus on the most prevalent behaviours—digital privacy and shoplifting. Within the consumer ethics research, Sudbury-Riley and Kohlbacher (2016) have recently developed a new research instrument called the Ethically Minded Consumer Behaviour (EMCB) scale that offers researchers a valid instrument for measuring a variety of consumption choices pertaining environmental issues and corporate social responsibility.

The current study could be considered a complex investigation because it combines an attempt to identify the determinants of ethically questionable behaviour with the different roles of these factors within the consumer decision-making process.

4.2.2 Theory Development and Hypotheses

The present study builds on the theory of planned behaviour (TPB, Ajzen 1991), but also incorporates the possible impact of perceived unfairness in relation to ethically questionable behaviour to examine the extent to which consumers are motivated 'to redress an unfair imbalance between consumers and suppliers' (Fukukawa and Ennew 2010: 52). TPB, consisting of attitude, subjective norms and perceived behavioural control, remains one of the most significant attitude-behaviour theories due to its improved levels of prediction (Fukukawa 2002).

The influence of attitude on ethically questionable behaviour proved to be extremely varied in previous studies. When exploring software piracy, for example, Phau and Ng (2010) found that favourable attitude is likely to result in stronger intention to behave unethically. Accordingly, attitudes were the main influence on shoplifting intentions (Tonglet 2001). Instead, when investigating a range of ethically questionable behaviours, Fukukawa and Ennew (2010) emphasized that attitudes are less significant in predicting intention to adopt such behaviours than other situational factors. Based on these arguments, the present study suggests that attitude will be more favourable when consumers perceive significant benefits from the behaviour and less serious consequences. Thus,

H1 *Attitude toward performing an ethically questionable behaviour will be positively related to the consumer's behavioural intention.*

Social influence is an important determinant to consider in consumer ethics studies, because pressure from referent groups could challenge consumers to make certain choices in terms of a negative behaviour. For example, an individual may be using pirated software, but his/her friends or family may be using the licensed version, which they perceive to be ethical and legal as well (Phau and Ng 2010). To comply with the social norms, the individual could be tempted to conform to others behaviour. Therefore, when investigating piracy, Aleassa et al. (2011) found that the impact of perceived subjective norms on intention to pirate software was twice as great as that of attitude toward such a behaviour. In addition to previous findings about the crucial impact of others on consumer behaviour, Cherrier and Murray (2007: 22) emphasized 'the impermanence of such influence'. Thus, the current study expects that:

H2 *Social norm associated with performing an ethically questionable behaviour is positively related to consumers' behavioural intention.*

Perceived Behavioural Control (PBC) refers to the perception of the ease or difficulty of adopting a specific behaviour (Fukukawa and Ennew 2010), either in terms of the consumer's skills or the necessary resources to practice the behaviour. Yoon (2011) found PBC to be an influential factor in pirating digital materials. In the context of shoplifting, Tonglet (2001: 351) highlighted the importance of the consumer's 'perceptions of opportunity, low apprehension risks and ineffective security' when it comes to a wrong behaviour. In this case, when consumers consider that a specific behaviour is easy to be performed because they can control it, they are more likely to engage in that behaviour. Therefore, the following hypothesis is proposed:

H3 *Perceived behavioural control is positively related to consumers' intention concerning ethically questionable behaviour in consumption.*

However, in many cases, there are other situational factors that influence the consumer's intention to adopt a questionable behaviour. Fukukawa and Ennew (2010) research shows how attitudes and situational factors such as perceived unfairness influence intention to engage in the ethically questionable behaviour. The perception of unfairness is very useful to the current study, helping to identify the relationship quality between consumers and companies. For example, the perceptions of price unfairness (Bechwati et al. 2009) could influence shopping intentions. Moreover, when consumers feel they are treated unfairly in an exchange relationship, they are willing to respond in kind, with various negative actions (Fukukawa et al. 2007). Therefore, this research proposes that:

H4 *The perception of unfairness in relation to business is positively related to consumers' intention concerning ethically questionable behaviour in consumption.*

4.2.3 Research Methodology

4.2.3.1 Data Collection and Sample

A non-probability sampling technique was used for this research. The method was quota sampling based on two relevant characteristics: age and gender. The questionnaire was delivered to residents in Cluj-Napoca, the second largest city in Romania after its capital. The research used a self-administered questionnaire and respondents had no obligation to mention their identity, a fact that assured anonymity of the responses. A total of 413 (62.19%) valid and complete responses out of 675 were obtained over a period of 4 weeks. The SEM (Structural Equation Modelling) approach (with AMOS 20.0) was used to test the proposed hypotheses.

4.2.3.2 Measurements

The measurements for attitude, social norm, perceived behavioural control, perceived unfairness and intention concerning ethically questionable behaviour were adapted from the study of Fukukawa and Ennew (2010). The study used a seven-point scale to indicate the respondents' agreement or disagreement with the research items.

4.2.3.3 Findings

In accordance with Global Software Survey (2016), the high rate of software piracy for Romania (60%) justifies the analysis of this behaviour in comparison with another prevalent type such as shoplifting (Global Retail Theft Barometer 2014–2015).

Concerning Romanian consumers ethically questionable behaviour, attitude was found to be the strongest antecedent of intention, no matter what type of behaviour has been considered. This result supported H1, in accordance with previous studies (Phau and Ng 2010). At the same time, social norm seems to be an insignificant factor in this research in terms of the influence upon ethically questionable behaviour, therefore H2 was not supported, being similar with the results of Cronan and Al-Rafee's (2008). Taking separately, *perceived behavioural control* and *perceived unfairness* are related differently to consumers' intention concerning ethically questionable behaviour in consumption. Digital piracy is perceived as being acceptable by many Romanian consumers, which adopt it without any reservation, omitting some ethical issues that may arise. Thus, in accordance with the study of Aleassa et al. (2011), this research indicates that *perceived behavioural control* was found to have a great impact on intention to pirate, suggesting that the less difficult consumers believe an action to be, the more they will try to adopt that behaviour (see Table 4.1). In this case, H3 is supported, consumers feeling motivated to adopt such behaviour because they are able to control it and the risk is perceived to be minimum. In this way, consumers get over ethical considerations, moral standards or laws against piracy and find nothing

Table 4.1 Digital piracy

Causal relations				
Dependent variable		Independent variable	Standardized regression coefficients	P
INTENTION	<—	ATTITUDE	0.528	***
	<—	CONTROL	0.351	***
	<—	UNFAIRNESS	0.004	0.961

$p<0.05$*; $p<0.01$**; $p<0.001$***
Source (created by the authors)

Table 4.2 Shoplifting

Causal relations				
Dependent variable		Independent variable	Standardized regression coefficients	P
INTENTION	<—	ATTITUDE	0.400	***
	<—	CONTROL	−0.149	0.053
	<—	UNFAIRNESS	0.317	***

$p<0.05$*; $p<0.01$**; $p<0.001$***
Source (created by the authors)

wrong in downloading movies or music from Internet, even more considering it an unethical behaviour (Cockrill and Goode 2012; Robertson et al. 2012).

Instead, shoplifting is perceived as less acceptable, where the consumer actively benefits from an illegal activity. Interestingly, *perceived behavioural control* does not influence consumer shoplifting intention (H3 was not supported), but *perceived unfairness* has a strong impact on the intention to engage in a fraudulent behaviour, a result that supported H4. This finding is in line with previous research (Fukukawa et al. 2007: 193) where 'consumers are willing or prepared to engage in norm-breaking behaviour as consequences of a perceived unfair relationship with firms' (Table 4.2).

4.3 Conclusions

Although consumers may be tempted to be ethical and have strong moral principles, sometimes contextual factors could influence their behaviour. Therefore, the role of the context is decisive for understanding ethically questionable behaviour. The findings of this research show that *perceived behavioural control* and *perceived unfairness* vary significantly from one type of behaviour to another. These factors help us to understand how consumers make compromises depending on the type of the behaviour, their perception and their ability to perform a negative behaviour. In case of digital piracy, *attitude* has the strongest impact on intention (0.528, $p<0.001$***), which means that consumers perceive this behaviour as a common one, that brings them significant benefits and less serious consequences. This result is similar to Phau and Ng (2010) who show the great relevance of the attitude toward software piracy. *Perceived behavioural control* is also a strong and positive predictor of intention to pirate. Therefore, Romanian consumers consider that digital piracy can be easily performed, opportunity being a condition for engagement in criminal acts (Aleassa et al. 2011). In the same context, a relevant finding about *perceived unfairness* is that, compared with the shoplifting, this factor becomes insignificant. The result is perfectly justified because consumers have no serious reason to blame online companies. On the contrary, these companies seem to be too permissive and allow or even 'invite' people to piracy. In accordance with this 'invitation', consumers prepare a way to justify their unethical behaviour based on the consumer environment in Romania.

Concerning shoplifting, *attitude* is still a strong determinant of intention, but *perceived behavioural control* becomes an insignificant factor. A possible explanation is the relationship with the retail that becomes more important than consumers' ability to perform shoplifting behaviour. Exploring the role of *perceived unfairness* is of particular significance in the context of shoplifting, representing a key explanation of consumer theft or fraud (0.317, $p<0.001$***). This factor appears to indicate 'how strongly consumers are motivated to redress a perceived unfair imbalance with suppliers' (Fukukawa and Ennew 2010: 57).

4.3.1 Implications for Researchers and Business

The practice of digital piracy has been a real challenge for the development of the software and digital media industry (Yoon 2011). At the same time, shoplifting prevention is dependent on understanding why consumers decided to steal (Tonglet 2001). Therefore, this study provided support for companies, which are trying to understand their consumers and their motivation to adopt a wrong behaviour. For instance, in some cases, if an opportunity to perform a negative behaviour is presented, then consumers may try to take advantage of this opportunity, no matter what was their inner or first motivation. Therefore, companies should consider and permanently improve the quality relationship with consumers. More, these implications emphasize the variation in intention depending on the different types of behaviours and the significance of the influencing factors.

4.3.2 Limitations and Future Research

The findings provided meaningful implications for researchers and practitioners, but the current study has also some limitations. First, this research approached the intention instead of actual ethically questionable behaviour. Therefore, future research should consider actual behaviour in order to explore how this behaviour could be changed by certain situational factors. Another limitation refers to the sample of this study. This research was developed in the context of Romanian consumers, but it may be interesting to investigate how the factors affecting ethically questionable consumer behaviour may have a different role in different cultures.

References

Ajzen, I. (1991). The theory of planned behavior. *Organizational Behavior and Human Decision Processes, 50*(2), 179–211.

Aleassa, H., Pearson, J. M., & McClurg, S. (2011). Investigating software piracy in Jordan: An extension of the theory of reasoned action. *Journal of Business Ethics, 98*(4), 663–676.

Bechwati, N. N., Sisodia, R. S., & Sheth, J. N. (2009). Developing a model of antecedents to consumers' perceptions and evaluations of price unfairness. *Journal of Business Research, 62*(8), 761–767.

BSA The Software Alliance—Seizing Opportunity Through License Compliance (2016). http://globalstudy.bsa.org/2016/downloads/studies/BSA_GSS_US.pdf. Accessed 10 Apr 2017.

Cherrier, H., & Murray, J. B. (2007). Reflexive dispossession and the self: constructing a processual theory of identity. *Consumption Markets & Culture, 10*(1), 1–29.

Cockrill, A., & Goode, M. M. (2012). DVD pirating intentions: Angels, devils, chancers and receivers. *Journal of Consumer Behaviour, 11*(1), 1–10.

Cronan, T. P., & Al-Rafee, S. (2008). Factors that influence the intention to pirate software and media. *Journal of Business Ethics, 78*(4), 527–545.

Dabija, D. C., Postelnicu, C., & Pop, N. Al. (2016). Ethics of the garment retail within the context of globalization and sustainable development. *Industria Textila, 67*(4), 270–284.

Egan, V., & Taylor, D. (2010). Shoplifting, unethical consumer behaviour, and personality. *Personality and Individual Differences, 48*(8), 878–883.

Fukukawa, K. (2002). Developing a framework for ethically questionable behavior in consumption. *Journal of Business Ethics, 41*(1), 99–119.

Fukukawa, K., & Ennew, C. (2010). What we believe is not always what we do: An empirical investigation into ethically questionable behavior in consumption. *Journal of Business Ethics, 91*, 49–60.

Fukukawa, K., Ennew, C., & Diacon, S. (2007). An eye for an eye: Investigating the impact of consumer perception of corporate unfairness on aberrant consumer behavior. In *Insurance ethics for a more ethical world* (pp. 187–221). Emerald Group Publishing Limited.

Global Retail Theft Barometer (2014–2015). http://www.globalretailtheftbarometer.com/. Accessed 24 Mar 2017.

Hassan, L., Shaw, D., Shiu, E., Walsh, G., & Parry, S. (2013). Uncertainty in ethical consumer choice: A conceptual model. *Journal of Consumer Behaviour, 12*(3), 182–193.

Higgins, G. E., Wolfe, S. E., & Marcum, C. D. (2008). Music piracy and neutralization: A preliminary trajectory analysis from short-term longitudinal data. *International Journal of Cyber Criminology, 2*(2), 324–336.

Hinduja, S. (2007). Neutralization theory and online software piracy: An empirical analysis. *Ethics and Information Technology, 9*(3), 187–204.

Miyazaki, A. D. (2009). Perceived ethicality of insurance claim fraud: do higher deductibles lead to lower ethical standards? *Journal of Business Ethics, 87*(4), 589–598.

Muncy, J. A., & Vitell, S. J. (1992). Consumer ethics: An investigation of the ethical beliefs of the final consumer. *Journal of Business Research, 24*(4), 297–311.

Phau, I., & Ng, J. (2010). Predictors of usage intentions of pirated software. *Journal of Business Ethics, 94*(1), 23–37.

Robertson, K., McNeill, L., Green, J., & Roberts, C. (2012). Illegal downloading, ethical concern, and illegal behavior. *Journal of Business Ethics, 108*(2), 215–227.

Smith, B. T., & Clarke, R. V. (2015). Shoplifting of everyday products that serve illicit drug uses. *Journal of Research in Crime and Delinquency, 52*(2), 245–269.

Sudbury-Riley, L., & Kohlbacher, F. (2016). Ethically minded consumer behavior: Scale review, development, and validation. *Journal of Business Research, 69*(8), 2697–2710.

Tonglet, M. (2001). Consumer misbehaviour: An exploratory study of shoplifting. *Journal of Consumer Behaviour, 1*(4), 336–354.

Tseng, L. M., & Kuo, C. L. (2014). Customers' attitudes toward insurance frauds: An application of Adams' equity theory. *International Journal of Social Economics, 41*(11), 1038–1054.

Vitell, S. J. (2003). Consumer ethics research: Review, synthesis and suggestions for the future. *Journal of Business Ethics, 43*(1–2), 33–47.

Vitell, S. J. (2015). A case for consumer social responsibility (CnSR): Including a selected review of consumer ethics/social responsibility research. *Journal of Business Ethics, 130*(4), 767–774.

Vitell, S. J., Muncy, J. (2005). The Muncy–Vitell consumer ethics scale: A modification and application. *Journal of Business Ethics, 62*(3), 267–275.

Yoon, C. (2011). Theory of planned behavior and ethics theory in digital piracy: An integrated model. *Journal of Business Ethics, 100*(3), 405–417.

Chapter 5
Politicized Economy and Its Effects on Business Sustainability: A Case Study on Romania

Mihai Florin Talos, Pop Ioan and Oncica-Sanislav Dan

Abstract Globalization produces contradictory results and creates important loopholes in the socioeconomic dynamics of the world. In light of world politics and recent developments, (such as the proliferation of nationalist and populist parties and of the isolationist ideas culminating in the Brexit), the globalization idealists begin to understand that globalization is not an easy process to govern, given the fact that it implies the cohabitation of non-heterogeneous, multicultural populations. Besides the challenge brought by the stirred global context, Romania faces another complex challenge, consisting in the unprecedented interfering of the political sector in the very pillars of the society: democracy, the state law, and the market economy. The present paper intends to investigate the extent to which the politicization of the economy could have a major impact on the stability of the Romanian economy as a whole and on the sustainability of local businesses, in particular.

Keywords Business sustainability · Politicized economy · Globalization
Policymakers

M. F. Talos (✉) · P. Ioan
Universitatea Emanuel Din Oradea, Oradea, Romania
e-mail: mtalpos@yahoo.com
URL: https://www.emanuel.ro

P. Ioan
e-mail: ioan.pop@emanuel.ro
URL: https://www.emanuel.ro

O.-S. Dan
Universitatea Tehnica Din Cluj-Napoca, Cluj-Napoca, Romania
e-mail: oncicasanphd@gmail.com
URL: https://www.utcluj.ro

S. A. Văduva et al. (eds.), *Civil Society: The Engine for Economic and Social Well-Being*, Springer Proceedings in Business and Economics,
https://doi.org/10.1007/978-3-319-89872-8_5

5.1 Business Sustainability and Socio-Political Environment

Sustainable development was defined by the Brundtland Report as being the "development that meets the needs of the present without compromising the ability of future generations to meet their own needs", a development described as a "process of change in which the exploitation of resources, the direction of investments, the orientation of technological development, and institutional change are all in harmony and enhance both current and future potential to meet human needs and aspirations" (Brundtland 1987:43). The concept of sustainable development upholds the compatibility and complementarities of its three dimensions: economic, social, and environmental. It is a global, macroeconomic concept particularly through its social and environmental facets (Oncică-Sanislav and Cândea 2016).

We can interpret the concept of sustainable development as the ideal of a human society thriving indefinitely. Pop (2015) asserts that development is sustainable if it leads to an increased number of human options, both locally and globally, to meet the needs of the present and future generations and defines resilience (R), viability (V), and subsistence (disaster) (S) as three levels of eco-economic reality, three different stages in the functioning of eco-economic systems in the context of sustainable development. These levels are measurable by identifying energy interdependencies with the three pillars of sustainable development in a trans-disciplinary context: the environmental (environmental) sector, the socio-community sector (human habitats), and the economic sector (market).

At macroeconomic level, the development process interconnects the global with the local levels, through what is defined as the concept of "glocalization".[1] Possible human choices are determined by the available resources and personal creativity. There is a resource limit at the matergical level, but fortunately, there is no limit to creativity at the informational level. The least used potential is the human one, the knowledge in its complexity, which integrates the two seemingly difficult issues to manage together (Pop 2015).

At microeconomic level, the sustainable development concept relates to "sustainable business" concept, a concept (business sustainability) that can be regarded as the correspondent of sustainable development for the business sector (Oncică-Sanislav and Cândea 2016). By analogy with the three pillars of the sustainable development concept: economic development, social development, and environmental protection, the generally held view is that companies should strike in all their actions a balance between their economic, social, and environmental performance (Cândea 2010). Addressing the higher level context of corporate sustainability, Werbach (2009) extends the number of sustainable development dimensions to include the cultural aspect, in other words the local level, and holds that a corporation will not be sustainable unless its strategy for sustainability addresses all these four dimensions simultaneously.

---

[1]Glocalization: the idea that in globalization, local conditions must be considered—Cambridge Dictionary 2017.

Fig. 5.1 Business sustainability depends on and, simultaneously, affects the social and natural environments. *Source* (Morris 2000)

In this context, we can define business sustainability as the capacity of a business to prosper in the long term, with no foreseeable time limit. As the engine of economic development, for-profit business is a very important actor and stakeholder of sustainable development.

On one hand, its activity and its sustainability (or lack of) have a significant impact on its social and natural environments. The well-being of society depends upon profitable and responsible/sustainable business enterprises. On the other hand, business sustainability (its long-term prosperity) is conditional on the sustainability of the social system and both depend on the sustainability of the natural system (Morris 2000) (Fig. 5.1).

This hierarchy implies that the organizational performance on which business sustainability hinges is determined by higher rank conditions that shape the activity of the organization. Namely, certain performance criteria of a company that strives to be sustainable can be limited by the way the broader, social, and natural system works.

The natural system includes interrelated factors like physical resources, wildlife, and climate. The social system (or societal environment) includes general forces that can be divided in at least four interrelated subsystems (Wheelen and Hunger 2006): the economic subsystem (forces that regulate the exchange of materials, money, energy, and information), the technological subsystem (forces that generate problem-solving inventions), the political–legal subsystem (forces that allocate power and provide constraining and protecting laws and regulations), and the sociocultural subsystem (forces that regulate the values and customs of society).

The lists of factors comprising each subsystem are relatively long and as more and more markets become global, the number of factors becomes huge and much more complex. All these factors could prove important for business sustainability: the long-term survival of the firm. In order to achieve the purpose of this paper, we will further focus on the factors comprising two interrelated subsystems that are, usually, providing a major individualization at the national level: the sociocultural and political-legal subsystems.

The sociocultural subsystem is shaped by factors, such as national identity, values, religion, social organization and language, demographic trends, legal/justice system, the level of corruption, the level of government control, cultural understandings, and the list could continue. These factors are critically influencing the way the organizations are managed (Hofstede et al. 2010), the prevalence of long-term view as opposed to short-term view in managing organizations, the interpretations given to and actions related to Corporate Social Responsibility (Tilt 2016), and the importance granted to environmental sustainability (Băcanu 2006: 66).

As an example, the level of corruption is a factor that can be an important source of environmental and social degradation, with negative impacts on sustainable development, thus hindering company's prospects for sustainability. For a company, the level of corruption in the society it operates can directly affect all the three dimensions, previously discussed, of business sustainability: economic, social, and environmental. Corruption and bribery escalates costs, undermines fair competition, and poses serious legal and reputational risks (UN Global Compact 2017). It also can be an important source of environmental degradation, especially in developing countries—it may reduce the stringency of environmental and labor regulation or the effectiveness with which these regulations are enforced (Welsch 2003).

The political factors comprising the political-legal subsystem can impact business organizations in many ways. Their evolution can add substantial risk to business operations and profitability, thus affecting directly business prospects for sustainability. A list of political factors affecting business (and business sustainability) can be considered to be (without claiming to be exhaustive): protectionism as opposed to free trade, level of bureaucracy, freedom of the press, education and education law, environmental law and laws that regulate environment pollution, tax policy (including here tax rates, incentives and tax administration), government stability and its involvement in trade unions and agreements, employment, immigration law, health and safety law, and so on (Wheelen and Hunger 2006). Also, a country's political stability, government efficiency, and central bank independence are to be considered as important factors with impact on state sustainability (RobecoSAM 2016) and, as a direct consequence, on business sustainability operating locally.

At the global level, the recent evolutions of the political landscape are rising doubts regarding the evolution of the globalization process, populist, and nationalist movements, based on anti-elitist, anti-immigration, and protectionist platforms gaining more and more traction and popularity.

At the Western society's level, the political environment is rocked by the populist successes at the polls in Western Europe and the United States, the proliferation and flourishing of nationalist and populist parties in EU, and by the democratic deterioration and authoritarian consolidation in the postcommunist countries of Eastern Europe.

Examples of these political evolutions are the United Kingdom's popular vote to withdraw from the EU and the election of Donald Trump as president of the United States, victories achieved through political campaigns based on anti-elitist, anti-immigrationist, and on economic protectionist platforms.

France is the latest country to deal with a blow to politics as usual, its voters rejecting the political parties that have governed in the last decades, in favor of Emmanuel Macron (a pro-European liberal) and the far-right challenger, Marie Le-Pen, who has vowed to take on globalization and France's relationship with the EU (BBC 2017).

This political evolutions, which are rejecting diversity of identity and of opinion within society and are discarding basic principles of modern constitutional thinking that democracy requires constraints on the will of the majority and checks on the decisions of the executive (BBC 2017), are also manifesting in the political-geographic area of Romania.

Thus, the political situation in the postcommunist countries (now members of UE) seems to indicate, after years of populism and corruption have eroded once-promising democratic institutions, a constant drift toward authoritarian types of regimes—Two outstanding examples being the recent political evolutions in two of the recent champions of transition from communism to democracy: Hungary and Poland (Balogh 2017). The EU and Britain are now focused on the Brexit phenomenon and governments in the region are also unsure of the positions of the Trump administration. As a result, the EU's capacity to encourage and support the commitment to democratization and a stable, rules-based order, seems to be weakened.

In Romania, the current political power seems to interfere with all the major pillars of the democratic society, an interference that could lead, in our opinion, to the elimination of the existing checks on its power, restrictions on democracy, and corruption strengthening. In the following, we will review some of the signs of the politicization of the Romania society and the potential impact on the local and corporate businesses sustainability.

5.2 Detectable Signs Toward a Politicized Romanian Society and Their Impact on Business Sustainability

5.2.1 The Main Modalities of Political Influence on Justice and the Negative Effects of Such an Influence

After the Revolution from 1989, under the influence of former communist leaders and nomenclature's members that still enjoyed political influence, the Romanian justice program has been politicized and delegitimized (Simic and Volcic 2013). As such, Romania unfortunately enrolled in the group of similar postcommunist countries and emerging democracies, in which independent courts are rarely found (Papova 2014).

Under the influence of a deficient legislative framework and with the intelligence services permission (still populated with former Securitate agents), the politicized leadership of the Supreme Court and Constitutional Court has contributed to the perpetuation of a partially independent justice, which in fact continued to be (in many regards) a politically driven tool (Stan 2013).

The European Commission (EC) report published on January 25, 2017, in regards to Romania shows that important improvements are still necessary in the justice field, especially in regards to aspects like the mutual respect between the state's institutions, and the independency of the legal system from the parliament (Cristea 2017). Unfortunately, after the publication of the EC report, the new Grindeanu government adopted a controversial emergency ordinance amending the Criminal Procedure Code and the Criminal Code, in spite of the opposition of civil society, manifested in massive street protests. The emergency ordinance stated the decriminalization of the abuse of office, if the damage caused falls below 200,000 lei. Such a stipulation was about to cancel years of effort made by DNA (National Anti-corruption Division) to identify and punish policymakers who are guilty of abuse of office. Such a legislative measure could also affect many companies that have contracts with the local authorities and who noted the tendency of some representatives of local government to impose (abusively) certain views regarding the commercial relations existing between the two parties.

Fortunately, after weeks of unprecedented massive street protests, the Grindeanu government repealed the abovementioned emergency ordinance and accepted the resignation of the Justice Minister, who initiated the controversial ordinance. Moreover, the Grindeanu government asked the Justice Ministry to initiate—in the coming period—public debates with the civil society and political parties on all the important topics from the repealed ordinance.

Political and social developments like the ones described above can have a direct impact on the sustainability of Romanian businesses from several perspectives.

On one hand, the political-legal regulations are usually considered foreseeable by the business environment, contributing to the stability of the business environment by allowing timely adaption of the organizations. "Overnight" changes to regulations can greatly damage the interests and chances of long-time prosperity of firms, leading to an unstable and unpredictable business environment. They also affect the long-term confidence the investors have in the stability of the political and legislative environment of the country and in the capacity of the political class to govern.

Also, a weak social climate can easily result in violent turmoil, disrupting important economic activity and/or paralyze policymaking (RobecoSAM 2016).

On the other hand, regulations like the above mentioned, proposed by the Grindeanu government, may lead to the rise of corruption level, and greatly expand the extent to which public power is exercised to protect the interests of a small group at the expense of the economy and society at large. As mentioned before, this can have a direct negative impact on business sustainability.

It is true that the social events that followed the Grindeanu government's decision also bring good news from the perspective of business sustainability as they are demonstrating the development in Romania of a strong social cohesion around the anti-corruption fight. This strong social cohesion can support orderly conflict resolution and can facilitate the implementation of the necessary reforms, thus contributing toward sustainable economic development (RobecoSAM 2016) and business sustainability.

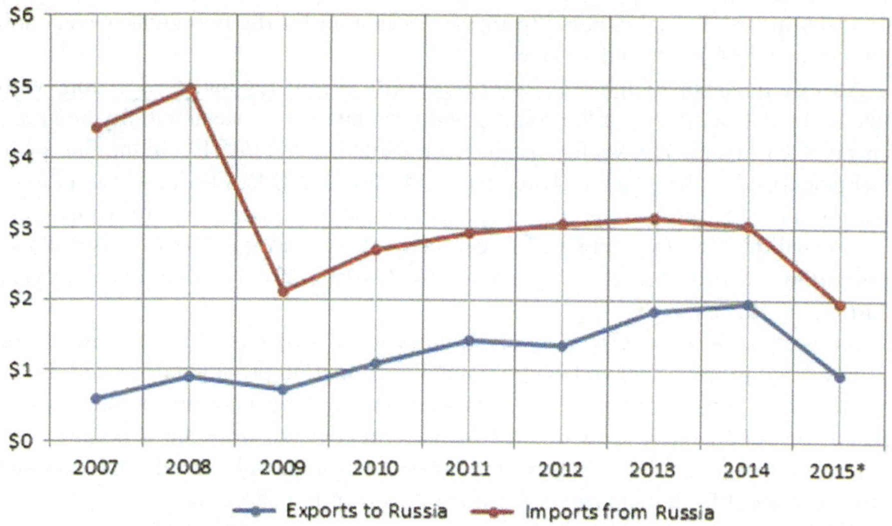

Fig. 5.2 The evolution of the Romanian-Russian bilateral trade. *Source* http://www.rusexporter.com/research/country/detail/3901/

5.2.2 *The Main Modalities of Political Influence on the Economy and the Negative Effects of Such an Influence*

In relation to the state's economy, the political factor can manifest its influence on two major ways: (a) from outside to inside (e.g., interstate embargoes imposed on divergent foreign policy considerations); and (b) from inside to inside (e.g., misleading actions on different critical points and institutions of the society, such as the education system, the religious institutions, the national bank, the national media, the tax administration system, etc).

(a) Outside to inside influence
As a member of the European Union, Romania must obey the union's external political decisions, assuming all the effects, negative or positive.

A good example of European external political decisions with negative effect is the embargo imposed by the United States and the European Union against Russia in 2014, as a response to the Russian military intervention in Ukraine. This embargo had tremendous effects on the Romanian exports and imports (as seen in Fig. 5.2), given the fact that Russia is one of the traditional Romanian commercial partners. In only 20 months (in 2015), the Romanian-Russian bilateral trade volume decreased by 33% and reached 2.8 billion USD compared to 4.3 billion USD in 2014.[2]

In this context, the compensatory measures that the European Union and/ or the United States of America have worked in the commercial relations with Romania

[2]www.rusexporter.com/research/country/detail/3901/.

are insignificant, Romania being (primarily) a market for the two great powers and not a provider of goods and services.

An example, but of internal European political and regulatory decision, with potential positive effects on the country and local businesses sustainability and their sustainable practices can be, for instance, the Directive 2014/95/EU of the European Parliament and of the Council (Directive 2014/95/EU, 2014). The laws, regulations, and administrative provisions necessary to comply with this Directive are brought into force at national level starting with December 6, 2016, and apply to all undertakings within the scope of Article 1 (Directive 2013/34/EU, 2013) for the financial year starting on January 1, 2017.

Its purpose is to raise to a similarly high level across all Member States the transparency of the social and environmental information provided by undertakings in all sectors. Thus, starting in 2017, it is necessary for large enterprises and business groups of public interest, as defined in the Directive, to draw up a nonfinancial statement containing information on at least environmental, social, and personal aspects, respect for human rights, Combating corruption and bribery.

This, in turn, could improve the business practices regarding CSR and environmental practices and reporting of companies which operate in Romania, thus improving their prospects for sustainability.

(b) Inside to inside influence
This kind of political influence manifests on different critical segments and institutions of the society, such as:

b1. Education
The most important personnel recruitment and selection agent that a nation has, in order to ensure the covering of certain roles or economic positions in the societal structure, is—for sure—the educational system (Cicea and Dobrin 2015). As such, the political factor is constantly interested in controlling the educational system, detrimental to the private sector, which is engaged in an unfair competition of attracting valuable young persons from the educational system.

In Romania, probably the most used way to politically control the educational system is to appeal to the school principals, who are appointed on political criteria and not on performance criteria, by contest (Tanase 2016). According to the information included in an official interpellation addressed to the Ministry of Education in the autumn of the year 2016 by Valerian Vreme (a deputy from Bacau district), in the already mentioned district (Bacau), there has never been organized a contest for the selection of a school principal for more than 8 years (idem). However, in the same period of time, important changes have been made in regards to the management of the schools in Bacau district, appointments being done on the basis of direct decisions made by a general inspector, surely supported by a political party. In such a manner, in the Bacau district alone, 45 school principals were changed in 2011, 88 school principals and 30 deputy directors were changed in 2012 and 50 school principals in 2014 (ibidem), decreasing once again the credibility of the Romanian educational system.

It is obvious that a powerful and developed contemporary nation depends both on economic strength, and on the vigor of the educational system (Phillips 2010). That is why the independence and performance of the educational system are crucial for the normal development of the society in general and of the economic environment in particular.

b2. Media

Information has always been an essential resource for the life of humans. By using information, humans were able to improve the society, take important decisions, economically develop, or elect better politicians (Levitin 2015: 55–56). In the Internet era, given the overload of information, the public has real difficulties in distinguishing the true information from the false ones. In other words, people do not know whom to believe anymore and they do not have time to investigate the information on their own. As such, the public's decisions are made based on the information and opinions emulating from so-called "trustworthy entities" such as newspapers, TV stations, Radio stations, or even books (idem). Sometimes such entities deserve our trust, sometimes they don't.

After the Romanian Revolution from 1989, the majority of the post-communist journalists involved in the daily media are in fact leftovers from the communist regime (Stan and Vancea 2015). Besides that, the main media corporations are owned and financed by the state (e.g., TVR, The National Romanian Television; Radio Romania Actualitati) or by legal entities/individuals who were not strangers to the communist regime (e.g., Dan Voiculescu, the owner of Intact Media Group, a press trust that includes: TV Stations such as Antena 1, Antena 2, Antena 3, Antena Stars, Euforia Lifestyle TV, Antena International, Happy TV; written press such as Jurnalul National or Gazeta Sporturilor; and Radio stations such as: Romantic FM and Radio ZU[3]). Dan Voiculescu is an important representative of the communist regime, former General Manager of the Romanian Foreign Trade Department and a proven Securitate informer (Romania Curata 2012).

Under the circumstances, the standards of accuracy, fairness, or social responsibility manifested by several of the Romanian media major corporations remain questionable and help perpetuate the phenomenon of politically influencing the media message.

b3. Religion

Important societal values such as the relationship with the natural environment, treatment of others, fairness, justice, and work ethic seem to be intrinsically linked to the extent to which religion has an important place in the life of a nation, because religious people usually have better values (Sandor and Popescu 2008).

Romania is considered to be the sixth most religious country in the world and the Church is constantly present in all the sociological studies and polls as the most trusted institution of the nation (Dale-Harris 2012). The Church claims to have 18 million followers in Romania, which is over 80% of the total population (The Economist

[3]www.intactmediagroup.ro/.

2012). As such, the Romanian Church is an inalienable authority and a terrible factor for influencing the public opinion.

Under the circumstances, the policymakers are constantly interested in keeping a "good relation" with such an important institution. Although Romania doesn't have an official state religion, the Orthodox Church is the biggest religious institution in Romania, and it is getting public funding from the government (idem).

It was noticed by the press the fact that certain politicians received (over the years) help from different clerics, who are not making a secret of their political activities (ibidem). This explains why, in the election years, churchgoers find campaign leaflets in the churches and probably why the government has donated 11 hectares of land for the project of The National Cathedral of Redemption, a gigantic and luxurious church, which is currently being built in Bucharest. This casts a dense shadow on the Romanian State–Church relationship.

A modern relationship between the State and the Church should concentrate on the purpose of improving publicly shared values such as moral values, work ethic, and tolerance. Any other kind of entanglement between those two brings unfortunate results in the long term.

b4. National Bank

The National Bank of Romania (NBR) is the central bank of Romania, an independent public institution that supports the general economic policy of the Government.[4] The National Bank of Romania is run by the Governor of the bank together with a Board of Directors. The members of the Board of Directors are usually renowned specialists that enter their mandates only after receiving the consent of the Parliament. Unfortunately, the Parliament may refuse to grant the consent for a certain proposed specialist in favor of a person politically sustained. An episode of this kind took place in October 2009, when Mr. Lucian Croitoru (a renowned economist and banker) was passed over by the Romanian Parliament in favor of Bogdan Olteanu (a lawyer by profession but a leading member of the National Liberal Party), for the position of National Bank vice-governor. This provoked harsh accusations from the press and the economic establishment that the Parliament was politicizing the NBR. In the year 2014, in the context of political elections, new accusations were made in regards to elude the independence of this fundamental institution of the state: The National Bank. According to the financial analyst Florin Cîțu, the Parliament "*legalized the subjugation of the monetary policy to political interests*" and "*the NBR has never been politically independent, but that was harder to prove*" (Rechea 2014). Recent evolutions (August 2016), in regards to the resignation of Bogdan Olteanu from the position of deputy governor of Romania's National Bank, in the context of a big corruption scandal (Popescu 2016), brought the institution—once again—in a shadow side.

There are voices that claim that Bogdan Olteanu's removal is only a political approach (Euractiv 2016), which aims to prepare the ground for the nomination of a new deputy governor, politically sustained by the actual governing party, which

[4] http://www.bnr.ro/National-Bank-of-Romania-1144.aspx.

Table 5.1 List of the Romanian districts that received bigger amounts of money than the ones they paid toward the state budget

District	Contributions to the state budget (euro)	Reimbursements received from the state budget (euro)
Vaslui	66.166.667	104.952.381
Botoşani	67.595.238	100.904.762
Teleorman	52.666.667	75.500.000
Călăraşi	49.095.238	66.095.238
Vrancea	63.261.905	81.642.857
Caraş-Severin	64.952.381	77.142.857
Suceava	143.976.190	165.833.333
Neamţ	101.261.905	116.571.429
Mehedinţi	57.238.095	65.595.238
Dâmboviţa	98.166.667	106.785.714
Ialomiţa	55.857.143	60.523.810
Tulcea	57.523.810	61.238.095
Gorj	78.428.571	83.023.810
Maramureş	112.119.048	116.833.333
Olt	95.666.667	96.809.524

Source Pele (2012)

no longer is the National Liberal Party, the party that promoted Olteanu in the first instance.

The National bank has an important role in the financial stability of the country's economy. As such, the destabilization of Romania's economy will probably continue under the surveillance of a National Bank which seems unable to get rid of the curse of political influence, directly affecting the economic subsystem and, as a direct consequence, the sustainability (long-term viability) of the businesses operating in it.

b5. Tax administration

A balanced tax administration system for the state centralized budget involves a direct correlation between the collected fees from the different districts of the country and the amounts redistributed into the districts, after the collection. Yet, many people feel that the Romanian tax administration system does not reflect such a value and that the budgeting process is politically influenced, meaning that the reimbursements toward the districts are made according to the number of voters that the ruling party has, in each district (Pele, 2014).

According to public data offered by the Ministry of Public Finance, at national level, from every 100 Euros collected for the centralized state budget, only 25 Euros are being reimbursòed to the districts. However, 15 districts of Romania (out of 41) received bigger amounts of money than the ones they paid toward the state as taxes and fees (see Table 5.1).

Table 5.2 Top 20 of the districts with the biggest rates in terms of PSD voters (the ruling party), during the latest elections (December 2016)

District	PSD voters' rates for the senate[a](%)	District	PSD voters' rates for the chamber of deputies (%)
Galati	51.46	Neamţ	52.64
Teleorman	51.95	Călăraşi	52.87
Buzau	52.85	Bacău	52.91
Bacău	53.04	Galaţi	53.09
Gorj	53.14	Hunedoara	53.18
Mehedinţi	53.64	Vrancea	54.05
Vâlcea	54.83	Gorj	54.06
Timiş	55.23	Vâlcea	54.84
Tulcea	57.13	Vaslui	56.84
Brăila	58.70	Brăila	57.97
Argeş	58.88	Argeş	58.96
Harghita	59.56	Ialomiţa	59.73
Dâmboviţa	60.34	Dolj	61.10
Ilfov	61.58	Botoşani	61.31
Botoşani	61.59	Teleorman	61.57
Sibiu	62.09	Mehedinţi	62.26
Covasna	62.47	Dâmboviţa	62.90
Bucureşti	64.71	Buzău	64.94
Mureş	67.15	Olt	67.14
Dolj	68.85	Giurgiu	68.73

Source Cozmei and Popica (2016)
[a]Percent out of the total numbers of voters in that district

If we analyze the same districts in terms of the number of voters for the ruling party (PSD), we will see that many of the favored districts are among the one to provide the biggest numbers of voters (see Table 5.2). 40% of the favored districts are included in the top 20 of the districts with the biggest rates in terms of PSD voters for the Senate (see Table 5.2 and the gray boxes in Table 5.2), and 80% of the favored districts are included in the same top with the biggest rates in terms of PSD voters for The Chambers of Deputies (see Table 5.2 and the boxes marked with a diagonal line, in Table 5.1).

In the other extreme, of the districts that benefit from reimbursements much lower than their contributions to the state budget, we mention: Ilfov district (with the capital—Bucharest included), Cluj district, or Timisoara district.

From every 100 Euros collected for the centralized state budget from Bucharest, only 11 Euros are being reimbursed to that district. From every 100 Euros collected for the centralized state budget from Cluj district, only 44 Euros are being reimbursed to that district. From every 100 Euros collected for the centralized state budget from

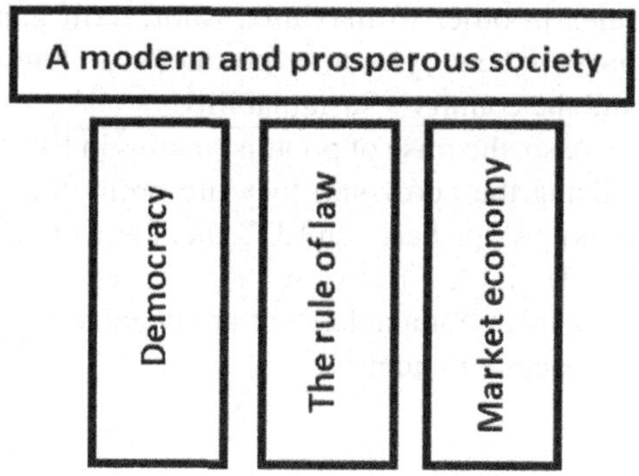

Fig. 5.3 The three pillars of a modern and prosperous society

Timisoara district, only 44, 6 Euros are being reimbursed to that district (Pele 2012). All those districts are usually among the ones with the lowest rates in terms of PSD voters (the ruling party).

5.3 Conclusions

Business sustainability depends on internal and external factors. In order to be sustainable, companies should strike in all their actions a balance between their economic, social and environmental performance. But business does not operate in a vacuum—it is part, and depends on the social and natural system in which it operates. As such, business sustainability contributes but also depends on the sustainability of its economical and social environment.

A modern and prosperous society is based on three major pillars (as shown in Fig. 5.3): democracy (political factor), the rule of law (justice), and market economy (economy). The independent effort of each of these three pillars contributes to the sustenance of the society; as such, those pillars should not interfere with each other (Minea 2015).

Democracy should provide businesses a safer long-term investment climate, by offering a level playing field and universal rules for competitors (Buchanan 2016). In a democracy, these rules should be devised and implemented by neutral state apparatus and enforced by a politically neutral judicial system. The politicization process of all the key financial, educational, and legal factors of the Romanian society, an unpredictable legal and economical environment, and an increased level of corruption seems to point toward a business environment which can prove very detrimental to business sustainability: a false democracy and rule of law, in which power arbitrarily exercised to protect the interests of a small group at the expense of the economy and society at large with policymakers that are more concerned about their own welfare than they are about the smooth running of the economy. This could lead the way to unfair competition and, determined by an unstable and unpredictable business environment, temptation for businesses in cutting corners and playing loose with rules in order to maximize short-term gains. Continuation of this process would prove to be very counter-productive to long-term viability of firms, business sectors, and the country's sustainability.

Also, the raise of populist parties in EU, and the protectionism policies (including leaving the eurozone) they are promoting could put at risk the existing free trade relationships between EU's member countries, and even threaten the very existence of EU and the Eurozone, putting under risk the future and sustainability of many Romanian companies that are depending on the commercial relationships with the EU member countries.

References

Balogh, L. (2017). Hungary and Poland: Drifting towards downgraded democracy. Internet article. Retrieved April 27, 2017, from http://www.voxeurop.eu/en/2017/central-europe-s-hybrid-regimes-5120961.

Băcanu, B. (2006). *Practici de management strategic: Metode si studii de caz*. Iasi: Polirom.

BBC. (2017). French election 2017: Why is it important? 5 May, 2017. Retrieved May 5, 2017, from http://www.bbc.com/news/world-europe-39130072.

Brundtland, G. H. (1987). *Report of the World Commission on environment and development: our common future*. Oxford, Oxford University Press.

Buchanan, P. (2016). Political risk and sustainable enterprise. Retrieved April 10, 2017, from http://36th-parallel.com/2016/03/31/political-risk-and-sustainable-enterprise/.

Cambridge Dictionary. (2017). Retrieved March 15, 2017, from http://dictionary.cambridge.org.

Cândea, D. (2010). Sustenabilitatea în afaceri—procesul, finalitatea, organizaţia. In D. Cândea (Ed.), *Dezvoltare durabilă şi responsabilitate social corporativă* (pp. i–iv). Cluj-Napoca, Romania: U.T.Press.

Cicea, C., & Dobrin, C. (2005). Contribuţia educaţiei la dezvoltarea economică. Economia, seria Management, anul VIII, nr 1. Retrieved January 15, 2017, from http://www.mer.ase.ro/files/2005-1/6.pdf.

Cozmei, V. & Popica, O. (2016). Rezultatele alegerilor parlamentare: Cum arata harta Romaniei politice—Rezultate zdrobitoare pentru PSD in judetele tarii/Unde a castigat PNL, UDMR sau USR, Internet article. Retrieved March 24, 2017, from http://www.hotnews.ro/stiri-alegeri_parlamentare_2016-21465073-harta-interactiva-rezultatele-alegerilor-parlamentare-cum-arata-harta-romaniei-politice-rezultate-zdrobitoare-pentru-psd-judetele-tarii-vezi-unde-castigat-pnl-udmr-sau-usr.htm.

Cristea, C. (2017). Justice in Romania under the spotlight. Retrieved February 27, 2017, from http://www.rri.ro/en_gb/justice_in_romania_under_the_spotlight-2559480.

Dale-Harris, L. (2012). Romania: Church and state. Retrieved March 19, 2017, from https://www.opendemocracy.net/luke-dale-harris/romania-church-and-state.

Directive 2014/95/EU of the European Parliament and of the Council. Retrieved February 27, 2017, from http://eur-lex.europa.eu/legal-content/EN/TXT/?uri=uriserv:OJ.L_.2014.330.01.0001.01.ENG.

Directive 2013/34/EU of the European Parliament and of the Council. Retrieved February 27, 2017, from http://eur-lex.europa.eu/legal-content/EN/TXT/?uri=celex:32013L0034.

Euractiv. (2016). Internet article. Retrieved March 20, 2017, from http://www.euractiv.ro/justitie/viceguvernatorul-bnr-bogdan-olteanu-retinut-in-urma-denuntului-lui-sov-5062.

Hofstede, G., Hofstede, G. J., & Minkov, M. (2010). Cultures and organizations software of the mind intercultural cooperation and its importance for survival.

Levitin, D. J. (2015). *Mintea organizata* (pp. 55–56). Bucuresti: Editura Publica.

Minea, C. (2015). Pilonii unei societăţi prospere. Internet article. Retrieved April 10, 2017, from http://imperiulmizil.blogspot.ro/2015/07/pilonii-unei-societati-prospere.html.
Morris, J. (2000). Defining the precautionary principle. In J. Morris (Ed.), *Rethinking risk and the precautionary principle* (pp. 1–14). Oxford: Butterworth–Heinemann.
Oncică-Sanislav, D. & Cândea, D. (2016). *Business sustainability: Is the learning organization one step ahead?* Cluj-Napoca: Ed. U.T. PRES. ISBN: 978-606-737-163-5. Retrieved March 15, 2017, from https://sites.google.com/site/bussustlo/.
Phillips, J. (2010). *The educational system in Romania: An overview of how communism has influenced current aspects and programs.* Liberty University. Retrieved March 19, 2017, from http://digitalcommons.liberty.edu/cgi/viewcontent.cgi?article=1195&context=honors.
Pele, A. (2012). Harta banilor din Romania. Cât dă şi cât primeşte înapoi de la bugetul de stat judeţul tău. Internet article. Retrieved March 24, 2017, from http://www.gandul.info/financiar/harta-banilor-din-romania-cat-da-si-cat-primeste-inapoi-de-la-bugetul-de-stat-judetul-tau-9444892.
Pop, I. (2015). Economie ecologică, Paperback. Universitatea Divitia Gratiae Chişinău.
Popescu, I. (2016). Romanian central bank deputy governor resigns amid corruption scandal. Internet article. Retrieved March 20, 2017, http://www.romania-insider.com/romanian-central-bank-deputy-governor-resigns-amid-corruption-scandal/.
Popova, M. (2014). *Politicized justice in emerging democracies: A study of courts in Russia and Ukraine.* Cambridge University Press.
Rechea, C. (2014). The national interest is being undermined by the shameless politicization of the national bank of Romania. Internet article. Retrieved March 20, 2017,http://www.bursa.ro/the-national-interest-is-being-undermined-by-the-shameless-politicization-of-the-national-bank-of…&s=print&sr=articol&id_articol=240076.html.
RobecoSAM. (2016). Retrieved March 12, 2017, http://www.robecosam.com/en/sustainability-insights/about-sustainability/country-sustainability-ranking/index.jsp.
Romania Curata, (2012). Candidatii cu functii in administratia regimului communist. Citeste cum s-au descurcat in cariera antedecembrista cei care azi vor votul tau. Internet article. Retrieved March 12, 2017, http://www.romaniacurata.ro/candidatii-cu-functii-in-administratia-regimului-comunist-citeste-cum-s-au-descurcat-in-cariera-antedecembrista-cei-care-azi-vor-votul-tau/.
Simic, O., & Volcic, Z. (2013). *Transitional justice and civil society in the balkans.* Springer. Retrieved February 27, 2017, https://books.google.ro/books?id=oAACPNWX41gC&printsec=frontcover&hl=ro#v=onepage&q&f=false.
Stan, L. (2013). *Transitional Justice in Post-Communist Romania: The Politics of Memory.* Cambridge University Press. Retrieved February 27, 2017,https://books.google.ro/books?id=vtEhAwAAQBAJ&pg=PA21&lpg=PA21&dq=justice+in+Romania+politicized&source=bl&ots=uPmqJ_sdK&sig=Sd6lAzXIA1C44nC2IWQkzXfIOaA&hl=ro&sa=X&ved=0ahUKEwii2d62m7DSAhXC1ywKHb8RB344ChDoAQgbMAE#v=onepage&q=justice%20in%20Romania%20politicized&f=false.
Stan, L., & Vancea, D. (2015). Post-communist Romania at twenty-five: Linking past, present, and future, Lexington Books. Retrieved March 13, 2017, https://books.google.ro/books?id=I2zHCQAAQBAJ&printsec=frontcover&hl=ro#v=onepage&q&f=false.
Sandor, S. D., & Popescu, M. (2008). Religiosity and values in Romania. *Transylvanian Review of Administrative Sciences, 22E*(2008), 171–180.
Tanase, F. (2016). Despre schimbarea directorilor de scoli. Internet article. Retrieved March 13, 2017, https://presaonestilor.wordpress.com/tag/schimbari-pe-criterii-politice/.
Tilt, C. A. (2016). Corporate social responsibility research: The importance of context. *International Journal of Corporate Social Responsibility, 1*(2), Springer. Retrieved February 04, 2017, https://jcsr.springeropen.com/articles/10.1186/s40991-016-0003-7.
The Economist. (2012). Religion and politics in Romania: The mystery of God's way in Romanian politics. Internet article. Retrieved March 19, 2017, http://www.economist.com/node/21556646.
UN Global Compact. (2017). Principle ten: Anti-Corruption. Retrieved March 19, 2017, from https://www.unglobalcompact.org/AboutTheGC/TheTenPrinciples/anti-corruption.html.

Werbach, A. (2009). *Strategy for sustainability: A business manifesto*. Boston, MA: Harvard Business School Publishing.
Welsch, H. (2003). Coruption, wealth and environment—A cross—country analysis, Discussion Paper, German Institute for Economic Research.
Wheelen, T. L., & Hunger, J. D. (2006). *Strategic management and business policy*. Upper Sadle River, NJ: Pearson Prentice-Hall.

Chapter 6
Developing a Culture of Service Utilizing the Civil Society in Romania: Needs Assessment and Training Preparation for the Hospitality Industry

Joseph Takacs III, Sebastian A. Văduva and Robert Miklo

Abstract The theme we intend to research in this paper is the creation of a culture of services in Romania, understanding the hospitality management sector. The focus will be on the analysis of training initiatives within the hospitality industry in comparison with the hospitality industry in the western, more developed nations that benefit from significant data and studies already undertaken. There is a necessity to analyze the individuals who comprise this service sector, who they are, how do they behave, what motivates them, what results do they currently generate, and how can corporate training better equip and train them to achieve a higher, more western level of quality of service. Further, we plan to analyze and understand the current industry perspective along with its values, norms, and practices that can be improved through education. This would, in turn, improve the overall customer satisfaction, increase sales, and enhance the profitability and long-term sustainability of those companies that would excel in providing such superior service.

Keywords Hospitality management · Service sector · Training · Tourism

6.1 Introduction

Business has long recognized the need to be hospitable, to be of service and to win customers. Morrison and O'Gorman (2008) summarized general principles of hospitality, including matters of business principles, guest principles, hospitality

J. Takacs III
University of Florida, Florida, USA
e-mail: joetakacs@themvpservices.com

S. A. Văduva (✉)
Emanuel University of Oradea, Oradea, Romania
e-mail: sebastianvaduva@emanule.ro

R. Miklo
The Academy of Economic Studies in Bucharest, Bucharest, Romania
e-mail: robert.miklo@gmail.com

S. A. Văduva et al. (eds.), *Civil Society: The Engine for Economic and Social Well-Being*, Springer Proceedings in Business and Economics,
https://doi.org/10.1007/978-3-319-89872-8_6

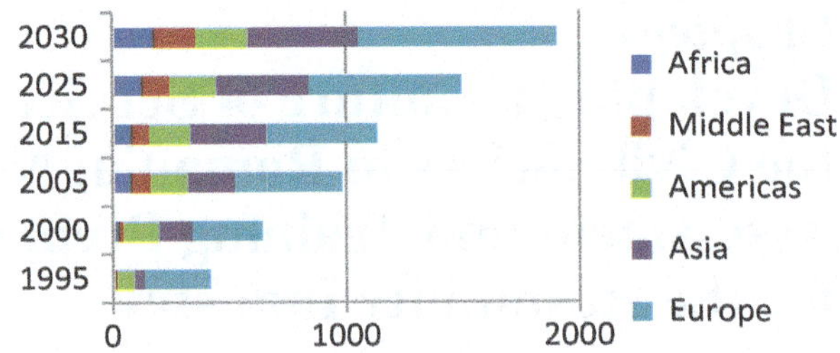

Fig. 6.1 Projected international tourism arrivals. *Source* (Statista 2016)

provision principles, staffing principles, and management principles, further suggesting a direct correlation between training methods adopting advance hospitality curriculums in efforts to support local businesses. The learning and training experience that incorporates a liberal and vocational approach is more likely to prepare professionals for tomorrow's industry leadership. Payment for services rendered has been at the heart of the business transaction since internal tribal trading for resource allocation (Adams 1974).

Simon Cooper of Ritz Carlton talks about customer service and hospitality this way; "*If you equate customer satisfaction with meeting guests' expectations, we equate customer loyalty to that element that surpasses expectations. We try to layer experiences and an outstanding memory on top of a perfect stay*" (Gensler 2006). Mr. Simon Cooper goes on to discuss the original slogan for Holiday Inn "no surprises." He feels that today hoteliers like Ritz are in a different business where consistency exists in the hotels that expect loyalty and repeat business believe that creating experiences and memories is critical to the customer of today.

In business tourism and those services that are expected and desired go hand in hand. Tourism and hospitality services affect almost every country in the world. Services are increasing at a quicker rate than agriculture and manufacturing combined. Tourism-related business is the leading producer of jobs all around the world. Tourism has developed into a truly international business that knows no political, ideological, geographic, or cultural constraints. Tourism can survive a recession because it is often viewed as a necessity and performs very well during expansions seen as a luxury good; travel and tourism's future economic forecasts look bright. Growth prognoses indicate that tourism will support nearly 350 million jobs worldwide by 2025. That's an increase of over 78 million jobs when compared to 2015 (Cook et al. 2018) (Fig. 6.1).

Tourism and hospitality have become more than just the leading industry; it is now a vital component of the economic makeup of most communities, regions, and countries. Activities have historically followed an upward trend in numbers of participants as well as revenues. The tourism industry responds well to economic ups and downs, and then at the same time is able to quickly come back from negative economic factors impacts. Even during the dramatic 2008 mess, the influence on international travel and tourism was not as significant as the downturn experienced in foreign trade and industrial production. Over the past 60 years, tourism has experienced continued expansion and became one of the largest and fastest growing economic segments around the globe.

6.2 Hospitality as a Relationship

Hospitality is a relationship between individuals who adopt roles of host, or roles of the guest. The host provides for the well-being, comfort, and entertainment of the guest. Typically, hospitable behavior includes offering food, drink, sleeping accommodation, and entertainment. Alternatively, hospitality can mean providing comfort and a location away from the guest's home, which is secondary, or irrelevant to the act of hospitality itself. Essentially, hospitality represents the cordial reception, welcoming and entertainment of individuals from diverse social backgrounds and cultures into one's home to dine, or to lodge, temporarily. Depending on circumstance and context, the degree to which the hospitality offering is conditional, or unconditional, may vary.

Additionally, this relationship between host and guest may be commercial or private (e.g., social). In a commercial relationship, the guest's only obligation is to pay and to behave reasonably. The guest holds power to go elsewhere for service if the hospitality provided is not satisfactory. Private, or social hospitality, assumes an equality of power and the guest has a social obligation to contribute to the relationship by being good company, as well as to reciprocate to the host in some way.

Further, keys to successful hospitality, in both commercial and private spheres, include knowing how to please the guest and how to deliver services flawlessly and generously. Moreover, hospitality is a process that begins with the guest's arrival and upon arrival, being hospitable involves the host greeting and making the guest feel welcome, providing comfort and fulfilling the guest's wishes. The process concludes upon departure, at which time, the host thanks the guest and extends an invitation to return. At each step of the process, these courtesies, or social rituals, define the status of the guest and the nature of the guest–host relationship.

Regardless of the length of time, it takes for a service provider to deliver a particular service, a relationship develops between the guest and host. Skilled hosts have a mannerism and method about them which allow them to establish that relationship. While that skill is on an understanding of a biblical mandate, the golden rule or some other foundation important to the host, the ability to build report or relationship it is critical and foundational to establishing the relationship between host and guest.

6.3 Failures of Hospitality Services

Blum (1996) summed up service failures in the hospitality industry as follows: "*How management defines quality service is insignificant; how the customer defines it is paramount*" (p. 25). When individuals faced with violations of justice, or in the case of hospitality, receive service that has not met their expectations, they may adjust their beliefs, so that they value their outcomes as equal to those of the other group. In other words, they may rationalize differences by belittling the service provider (Stone-Romero and Stone, as cited in Beldona and Karthik 2006). Receiving poor service may cause customer reactions that include decreased satisfaction and loyalty, as well as a higher propensity to switch service providers. Such attitudes can lead to behavioral reactions, such as negative word-of-mouth and a customer who simply will not come back (Beldona and Karthik 2006).

Based on that, arguably, one of the best times to measure and examine customer reactions and how they feel about an organization is when service has gone bad. Interactions between customers and service providers include a mix of social, work, and consumer behaviors. As such, it is reasonable to expect that customers' cultural orientations will influence how customers experience and evaluate service failure and recovery and make judgments concerning fair treatment (Mattila and Patterson 2004). Again, the ultimate judgment about the fairness of treatment rests solely with the customer.

Scholars have argued that influential forces such as colonialism and its legacy, foreign education, media, economic modernism, travel and indigenous culture, moderate people's birth cultural values and affect consumer behavior (Schutte and Ciarlante 1998). Behavioral dispositions allow an individual to protect a social self and function integrally in society. Research supports the importance of interactional justice as a potential threat to many of our core values. Mattila and Patterson (2004) observed that people from Eastern cultures tend to have an interdependent view of self. Consequently, interactions with others are a salient measure of one's self-worth. The implication for hospitality service providers is to manage service interactions efficaciously and assiduously to meet customers' needs and expectations.

A firm's service management approach targets how customers from similar or different cultural source markets make sense of and assign meaning to service interactions. A key measure of service satisfaction score follows failure and subsequent recovery, or lack thereof. However, most insights about service failure and recovery issues are derived almost exclusively from Western societies. It is not clear to what extent such insights are generalizable across cultures. For example, Clark (1990) suggests that principles of customer satisfaction derived from studies of Western consumers are less appropriate for universal application; and Schutte and Ciarlante (1998) are known for their attempts to apply consumer behavioral theories across cultures, but these attempts have been proven ineffective, unless those theories are modified to account for cultural differences.

Studies have shown that customers of different cultures evaluate service quality differently and exhibit different complaint behavior in hospitality settings (Cheung et al. 1999; Liu et al. 2001). There is also evidence of cultural differences in the perception of service failure and service recovery provision (Magnini and Ford 2004), as well as perceptions of justice in complaint handling (Mattila and Patterson 2004). Therefore, the customers recognize both good and bad experiences, which lead to brand loyalty to the specific providers of hospitality services.

The globalization impact is key to this examination of the customer experience. Globalization has produced a consumer base high in cultural diversity and makes culture a critical consideration when managing customer relationships (Becker 2000). The success of any strategy to recover a failed customer relationship will depend on some interrelated factors, one of which is the individual expectations of the customer and social and cultural norms that define appropriate behaviors from that customer's perspective. Expectations are not homogeneous across all customer segments, and important differences must be recognized if a recovery effort is to succeed. Failure to recognize these meaningful differences may amount to a recovery mistake that is worse than no attempt at recovery at all.

In the twenty-first century, the term service recovery is used to describe any actions designed and implemented to alter negative perceptions of dissatisfied customers (Schweikhart et al. 1993). The service recovery strategy, including the management of service failure events of an organization, must be culturally relevant, suggesting that it must have accurate insights into customers' culture because these values often determine preferences for problem management (Becker 2000). Evidence suggests that service recovery efforts have more influence on a customer's overall satisfaction and future intentions to repurchase than a well-executed initial service encounter (Spreng et al. 1995).

6.4 The Hospitality Industry in Romania

According to the National Institute of Statistics, Romania was host to over 1.5 million foreign tourists through October of 2013, a 3.5% increase over 2012. Previously, Romania has experienced a decrease from the years 2008–2010, after reaching a maximum value of 1.55 million arrivals in 2007, as reflected in Table 6.1.

Due in large part to the economic crisis in 2008 and 2009, Romania lacked the appeal of foreign visitors. In 2011, only 22% of all visitors were generated by foreign countries. This value is tremendously low as compared to Bulgaria for example; which was nearly 68% (Bulgarian Institute of Statistics, 2012). This lack of foreign visitors, as a competitive measure, is reflected in the classification elaborated by the World Economic Forum, as part of the Travel and Tourism Competitiveness Report World. Romania ranks 63rd in this classification and is lagging behind even smaller but growing economies in the EU like Czech Republic 31st, 33rd ranked Slovenia, 34th ranked Croatia, 38th ranked Hungary, 48th ranked Bulgaria, 49th ranked Poland, and 54th ranked Slovakia. There are simply far too few private tourism entities that are organizing and providing or permitting, public visits with the main cause of this being weak support of public authorities.

There remain close links between tourism-related needs and other growth priorities, and the strong support for tourism development is noticeable. Moreover, tourism needs and plans would more than likely contribute to the creation of a competitive regional profile for potential visitors to experience, in which tourism would be correlated with other economic and social activities, to increase regional employment and

Table 6.1 Comparison of Romanian Tourists 2013 versus 2012

Year 2013 compared to year 2012						
	Arrivals[a]			Overnight Stays[a]		
	Year 2012 thousands	Year 2013 thousands	Year 2013 compared to year 2012 (%)	Year 2012 thousands	Year 2013 thousands	Year 2013 compared to year 2012 (%)
Total	7653.4	7918.5	103.5	19091.4	19301.8	101.1
Romanian tourists	6000.0	6204.0	103.4	15799.9	15830.6	100.2
Foreign tourists[b] out of which:	1653.4	1714.5	103.7	3291.5	3471.2	105.5
• Europe	1344.2	1381.0	102.7	2662.2	2793.3	104.9
• The European Union	1158.3	1184.1	102.2	2272.0	2364.3	104.1
• Asia	148.3	168.4	113.7	313.3	360.0	114.9
• North America	103.7	105.6	101.3	190.6	194.9	102.3
• South America	12.7	12.0	94.5	27.6	25.9	93.8
• Africa	14.1	13.8	97.9	42.7	32.5	76.1

Source The National Institute of Statistics Tourism—December 2013
[a]Registered in the establishments of tourists' reception
[b]By the country of residence

income. Along with challenges specific to infrastructure, security, marketing, and delivery, talent (people) to implement all the preceding is required in every phase, product and delivery; therefore, that talent becomes the centerpiece in any growth planning that envisions tourism as a significant factor.

In 2013, the National Tourism Authority, the National Tourism Research, and Development Institute and the Romanian Ecotourism Association, created a set of criteria consistent with and based on priorities defined by the National Strategy for the Development of Ecotourism in Romania 2009. One of these criteria refers to the establishment of a minimum level of tourism services (e.g., accommodation and catering facilities, tourist rescue services) and public services, such as ATMs, medical and educational facilities, waste collection system. Specific issues related to the measurement of satisfaction lead to corrective management actions, ensuring the provision of quality services (Association of Ecotourism in Romania, 2015).

During that economic downturn and from 2010 through 2015, Romania began to reverse the downward trend and found the formula for growth. In fact, since 2015 and again in 2016, Romanian tourism revenues not only maintained but outpaced similar period over period results in all of Europe. Additionally, Romania lagged behind the EU average in service sector employment statistics. From 2000 to 2012, the EU reported an increase in service sector employment, from 62% to 70%, respectively.

However, in Romania, a mere 43% employment in the service sector was reported. This trend reversed in 2013 as Romanian GDP began an upward trajectory, subsequently outpacing all other EU economies. It seems evident that Romania is on the uptrend and rising in Tourism revenues. Additionally, there exists a tremendous upside. Statistics released January 2017 show Romania as enjoying less than 1% of the total room nights occupied for Europe as a total (Baltescu and Borcor 2014).

Romania is no different from the rest of the world and has enjoyed even more significant growth. According to the National Institute of Statistics, Romania was the choice for 1.5 million visitors through October of 2013, more than a 3% increase on the year before (Xia 2015). Since 2015, the Romanian economy has outpaced the other European Union economies. The tourism was supported by two distinct components: landscape and historical, which have helped to provide economic growth.

Today, the definition of tourism and hospitality includes a wide array of people, activities, and facilities, and most would agree that it is comprised of a unique group of industries. Services are tied together by a common denominator. No matter the industry, if the service provider caters to a traveling public, hospitality will be central to generating new guests and especially to the notion of creating a repeat client. Much debate exists as to be the exact definition of tourism. Critics have even suggested using a different more far-reaching term such as *visitor-service industry* to describe the traveling public and the services of demand. No matter the definition that one chooses for tourism, it doesn't take significant imagination to see a common thread of hospitableness throughout. Hospitality is a business and one that is significant, generates revenue, and creates jobs.

Consistent with this industry growth and world view, tourism and tourism development in Europe and especially the EU is strong, albeit, not uniform. The development of the tourism industry relies not only on policies and strategies elaborated and adopted at the EU level but also on the policies of each country within the EU as their participation is critical. According to the Eurostat Statistical Yearbook from 2012, the main EU tourist's regions are concentrated in only six countries; those being Spain, France, Italy, United Kingdom, Austria, and Germany. These are recognized countries and destinations that enjoy a long tradition in tourism. However, other countries with less developed do not enjoy the same revenues from tourism; countries like Latvia, Lithuania, Estonia, Slovakia, Bulgaria, and Romania are among regions with the least tourist's arrivals (Blanke and Chiesa 2011). In fact, the SW area of Romania called Oltenia remains the region with the least tourists from outside Romania; only 3.1% of the total number being foreign (National Institute of Statistics 2012).

Romania's joining the European Union has favored the growing involvement of decision factors at the national level for the valorization of cultural heritage as part of the European cultural heritage. In this respect, Romania introduced a National Cultural Heritage for the period 2008–2013, which generated increased performance in the operational framework of cultural heritage management and the quality increase of the heritage field by sustainable investments in preservation, training, and management of sites.[1]

6.5 Conclusions

International tourism and hospitality have emerged and developed as the world's largest most robust sector, a rapidly growing industry, which impacts not only the global economy, but also the local economy, Romania being an illustrative example of this reality. To become and maintain a successful local and international tourism service provider, industry professionals need to understand the cultural differences among consumers, as well as between tourists and the society within which they live and thereby serve those guests and tourists (Meng Fang 2010). Identifying the kind of relationships that are acceptable and desirable is important because cultural influences are involved. Understanding what it takes to survive and thrive in today's international hospitality economy is beneficial for any company and can help position that company for expansion and profitability. Those companies whose leaders can listen, learn, adapt, and change to meet customer needs are better equipped to survive and thrive. Those companies whose leaders refuse to do so will likely fail.

The findings that Romanian managers feel that older employees are better qualified to meet customer expectations could lead to hiring practices that deliver an older workforce. The associated risk could eventually lead to a failure in meeting a younger clientele need state, as millennial customers might interact more positively with younger hospitality staff. Additionally, maintaining an older workforce could also minimize talent development for future and expected employee turnover among the older staff.

Younger employee development is not new, but is further supported in this study. Training material in the areas of problem-solving and interpersonal skills were present in younger applicants, Romanian managers might feel more secure in hiring younger staff. A younger staff ensures that hospitality companies can meet the needs of younger patrons, while also ensuring a longer period of employment among qualified staff.

Companies in Romania are established and exist to generate bottom line profits, and therefore any increase in the satisfaction of consumers that translated into an increase in higher patronage and subsequent higher profits is good. This western standard of hospitality then, being already established and measured, at least in other countries and cultures, provides a target or groundwork for Romania and its schools and institutions. If hospitality industry leaders were to seek employees who provided a higher level of service to customers, specific training in the identified areas of this study makes the most sense.

---

[1]Baltescu, A. & Borcor, D. (2013). Bulletin of the Transilvania University of Braşov Vol. 6 (55), No. 2-2013 Series V: Economic Sciences An Analysis of the Cultural Tourism Development in Romania.

Finally, graduates of hospitality programs in which training methods were tailored to meet the needs of the marketplace would be better prepared to move into companies and have a prompt and positive effect on the bottom line of their employers. Thus, also providing a lift to the overall hospitality industry output in Romania and subsequently adding value to the economy.

References

Adams, R. (1974). Anthropological perspectives on ancient trade. *Current Anthropology, 15*.

Baltescu, C. A., & Boscor, D. (2014). The assessment of hotel services in Poiana Brasov Resort. *Bulletin of the Transilvania University of Brasov Economic Sciences Series V, 7*(2), 65.

Becker, C. (2000). Service recovery strategies: The impact of cultural differences. *Journal of Hospitality and Tourism Research, 24,* 526–538.

Beldona, S., & Karthik, N. (2006). Gender and demand-based pricing: Differences in perceived (un) fairness and repatronage intentions. *Journal of Hospitality and Leisure Marketing, 14*(4), 89–107.

Blanke, J. E. N. N. I. F. E. R., & Chiesa, T. H. E. A. (2011). The travel & tourism competitiveness index 2011: Assessing industry drivers in the wake of the crisis. *The Travel and Tourism Competitiveness Report 2011: Beyond the Downturn* (2011), 3–33.

Blum, S. C. (1996). Organizational trend analysis of the hospitality industry: Preparing for change. *International Journal of Contemporary Hospitality Management, 8*(7), 20–32.

Cheung, G. W., Murrmann, K. F., Murrmann, S. K., & Becker, C. (2004). Noninvariant measurement versus traditional approaches for studying cultural differences: A case of service expectations. *Journal of Hospitality and Tourism Research, 28,* 375–390.

Clark, T. (1990). International marketing and national character: A review and proposal for an integrative theory. *Journal of Marketing, 54*(4), 66–79.

Cook, R., Hsu, C., & Taylor, L. (2018). *The business of Tourism* (6th ed.). Pearson Publishing.

Gensler (2006). The business of hospitality. Dialogues with Gensler #12. www.dialogue.gensler.com.

Liu, T. C., Warden, C. A., Lee, C. H., & Huang, C. T. (2001). Fatal service failures across cultures. *Journal of Hospitality and Leisure Marketing, 8*(1/2), 93–110.

Magnini, V. P., & Ford, J. B. (2004). Service recovery in China. *International Journal of Contemporary Hospitality Management, 16*(5), 279–286.

Mattila, A. S., & Patterson, P. G. (2004). Service recovery and fairness perceptions in collectivist and individualist contexts. *Journal of Service Research,* 6(4), 336–346.

Meng, F., Li, X., & Uysal, M. (2010) Tourism Development and Regional Quality of Life: The Case of China: *Journal of China Tourism Research,* 6(2), 164–182.

Morrison, A., & O'Gorman, K. D. (2008). Hospitality studies and hospitality management: A symbiotic relationship. *International Journal of Hospitality Management, 27*(2), 214–221.

Schutte, H., & Ciarlante, D. (1998). *Consumer behavior in Asia*. Basingstoke, UK: Macmillan.

Schweikhart, S., Strasser, S., & Kennedy, M. (1993). Service recovery in health services organizations. *Hospital and Health Services Administration, 38*(1), 3–12.

Spreng, R., Harrell, G., & Mackoy, R. (1995). Service recovery: Impact on satisfaction and intentions. *Journal of Services Marketing, 9*(1), 15–23.

Xia, C. F. (2015). Romania tourism industry strategic thinking. *Internal Auditing and Risk Management 10*(1).

Chapter 7
Semiotics and the Entrepreneurial Creation's Myths

Mihai Florin Talos and Sebastian A. Văduva

Abstract In the context of the mutations occurring due to the development of a new transdisciplinary knowledge paradigm, sciences are increasingly concerned by the integration of rational approaches (knowing things) with the relational ones (knowing and understanding the world). In other words, sciences understood that the two perspectives are essentially complementary and not at all opposed.Such a dialog, between the entrepreneurial science and the creation's myths, based on the rational–relational perspective of transdisciplinary knowledge, may constitute an important challenge for the academia, business in general and entrepreneurs in particular. For entrepreneurs, the exercise of escaping from the routine of the actions performed in a monodisciplinary framework, in order to reorient toward a pluri-disciplinary and multidisciplinary framework, jettisoned by the limitations of excessive specialization, can represent the chance of developing a new entrepreneurship style, marked both by rational and relational thought.The main purpose of the present paper is to argue based on the thesis that the condition of animation of the entrepreneurial creation (defined as the human need to transpose a business vision into a new built reality), obeys the universal laws of the creation of cosmos, under certain methodological dimensions, that gravitate around the notion of "entrepreneurial knowledge".

Keywords Entrepreneurship · Creation · Transdisciplinary knowledge
Paradigms · Semiotics

7.1 What is Creation?

According to the majority of archaic beliefs, creation represents the process through which a transcendent, omnipotent and omnipresent universal reason generates and

M. F. Talos (✉) · S. A. Văduva
Emanuel University of Oradea, Oradea, Romania
e-mail: mtalpos@yahoo.com
URL: https://www.emanuel.ro

S. A. Văduva et al. (eds.), *Civil Society: The Engine for Economic and Social Well-Being*, Springer Proceedings in Business and Economics,
https://doi.org/10.1007/978-3-319-89872-8_7

orders all "things" of the seen and unseen world. Such a definition of creation also assumes the presence of a preexistent script, which is due to an all-creating force that generates causal-natural determinations (laws of universe).

Cosmogenetics, situated at the intersection between theology, science and philosophy, presents creation as the moment of selection, from the phenomenological field, of a shape which through transformation is going to signify something else than its own substance (Diaconu 2011).

Thus it is sketched a semiotics complementary to the divine one, in which can manifest possible coauthors of the primary universal creation, entities presenting a capacity of choosing totally or partially independent from the all-signifying conscience of the all-creating force. Included in the category of "artificial" (human) semiotics, creation manifested at this level, allowed through the privileges given by the all-signifying conscience fit in a series of boundaries created by the same laws of the universe, which the "artificial" (human) constructions cannot overcome. In other words, the order of ideas (pure meaning that is not manifested) is transposed in the order of things (concrete forms of existence): "Whatever is, is either in itself or in another" (Spinoza) (Nadler 2016).

Understanding the fact that creativity is manifested at all cosmic levels (Diaconu 2011), Mircea Eliade sensed the fact that the measure of understanding "the show of creation", of reflection of the "divine semiotics" into the "artificial semiotics" (human), is the one which will give the measure of the creation genius of Homo sapiens (Stănciulescu 1995).

Creation, as a typically human process, is an attribute, a capacity or a function of some special aptitudes that the human can hold, in general, and of his imagination in particular (Diaconu 2011). Creation in humans represents for A. K. Koestler the result of a process both intellectual and emotional, but also a field of manifestation of performances that vary according to the individual endowment of the creator.

7.2 On the Matter of Creation and the Requirements for "Animating" the Entrepreneurial Creation

The primary particles used by the Creator in building Cosmos can be grouped in three large categories: neutral (the majority—90%), passive (a minority—9%) and active (very few—1%) (see Fig. 7.1).

In a similar manner, in the entrepreneurial world there are (become active) barely 1% of people (Robinson 2015), the rest of them preferring other forms of earning a living. Same as particles, some people have more will and less intelligence, others have more intelligence and less will (Zirbo 2012).

Once arrived in the Divine Sphere (Creation Lab), the particles enter an existing circuit between the two important parts of the Creation Lab: the thinking center (placed in the central area of the sphere) and the creative center (placed in the peripheral area of the sphere). The thinking center issues periodically microscopic luminous

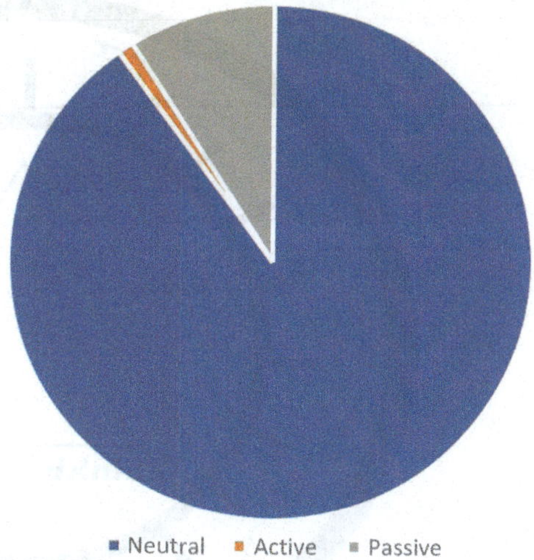

Fig. 7.1 Distribution of primary particles of creation, categorized

parts, called divine sparkles/ideas, which can be associated to business ideas, in the endeavor of comparing the two forms of creation: divine and entrepreneurial. There is a permanent movement (vibration) in the creative center, which stimulates the evolution of idea-particles up to the point in which these become fully formed, being capable of the act of knowledge, meaning to judge, reason and choose, forming a conclusion from two or more existent hypothesizes (Zirbo 2012) (Fig. 7.2).

The requisite of animation of the entrepreneurial creation in people, in other words the need of transposing a business vision in a newly constructed reality is subject to universal laws of creation, with extremely interesting methodological dimensions that gravitate around the notion of *entrepreneurial knowledge*.

The essential characteristic of the before-mentioned entrepreneurial knowledge is that it represents a synergic process, developed between three steps of knowledge:

a. The *subconscious* knowledge, manifested in entrepreneurs, many times, in a psychogenetic manner, proving true the folk wisdom saying, "*not everyone can become an entrepreneur, the entrepreneurial spirit is something one is born with*" (Schiopu 2015). On this step of subconscious knowledge is born the entrepreneurial revelation, of the genesis of the future business vision.
b. The trans-conscious knowledge, which is linked to cognitive landmarks of emotions, manifested in becoming entrepreneurs through anxiety feelings and fear without object, which affects people that are waiting for the moment of their entrepreneurial launch. It is, therefore, a matter of subjective feelings, which can be controlled voluntarily by developing the so-called *entrepreneurial conscience*. Entrepreneurial conscience is the one that allows entrepreneurs to become aware of the way in which they perceive the business world and is, most times, the mere reflection of their own mental projections, which resulted from the set of beliefs, perceptions, values entrepreneurs have in their subconscious and being,

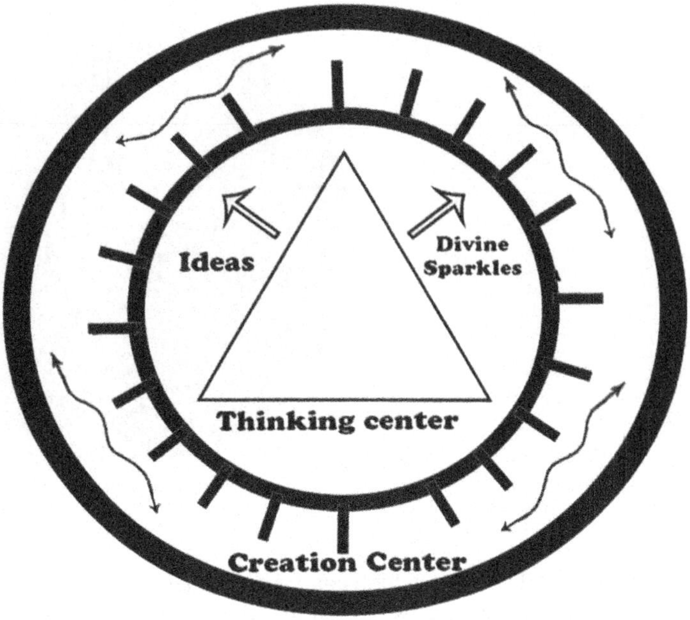

Fig. 7.2 Section in the Divine Sphere (Creation Lab)

manifested on the already-mentioned level of subconscious knowledge (Filip, n.a.).

c. Conscious knowledge, the one that allows entrepreneurs a realist-factual transfiguration of the business vision, including aspects related to the operational area (coherent and systemized) of the entrepreneurial endeavor (e.g., studying the feasibility of a business idea, planning the business, identifying and attracting the needed resources etc.)

7.3 Entrepreneurial Creation, Reflex of Divine Creation

In compliance with the archaic beliefs, human creation in general (therefore, the entrepreneurial makes no exception) is a reflex of the divine creation (Filip, n.a.). In consensus with Aranyaka Upanishad, "it can be stated that the universe of a business is comprised of three elements: name, shape and actions" (Morretta 1993). Explained in less formal terms, this triad denotes with much eloquence the ternary nature of any entrepreneurial endeavor (to be explained in Fig. 7.3) by responding to three questions: (1) Who creates?—**signified** (name/business name/brand); (2) How does he or she create?—**signifier** (form); 3) What does he or she create?—**signification** (the action of unifying name with form) (Stănciulescu 1995).

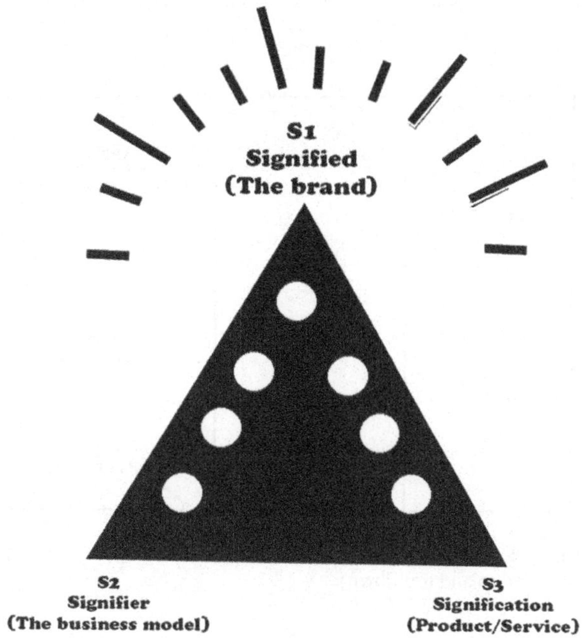

Fig. 7.3 The 3S entrepreneurial model

Undoubtedly, the name (brand) has an extensional effect for its designated, such that within the relationship with the ones he meets it gets to play a capital part, serving to the identification (by denotation) of a special significance (Pop and Vereș 2010). Reporting one's self to name (brand) and its meanings help customers/potential clients identify the product or the wanted service.

In the context of the entrepreneurial creation, seen as a reflex of divine creation, it is interesting to follow and analyze the way in which the two perspectives of gaining a name intersect (see Fig. 7.4):

a. The *bottom-up* perspective, in regard to acquiring—through a personal effort—one's own name/brand (curve no. 1 from Fig. 7.4)
b. The *top-down* perspective, in regard to acquiring—through inheritance/notoriety transfer—a name/brand (curve no. 2 from Fig. 7.4)

The first perspective, *bottom-up*, is naturally overlapped on the stages of a business' lifecycle (launch, development, maturity, decline), and the second perspective, *top-down*, overlap on the dramatic succession of the stages the man had in Eden, as the Bible presents: creation, fall, restoration and resurrection (Chen, n.a.; Pop and Vereș 2010).

Concrete examples in the sense of the two aforementioned perspectives are the cases of the following two businesses:

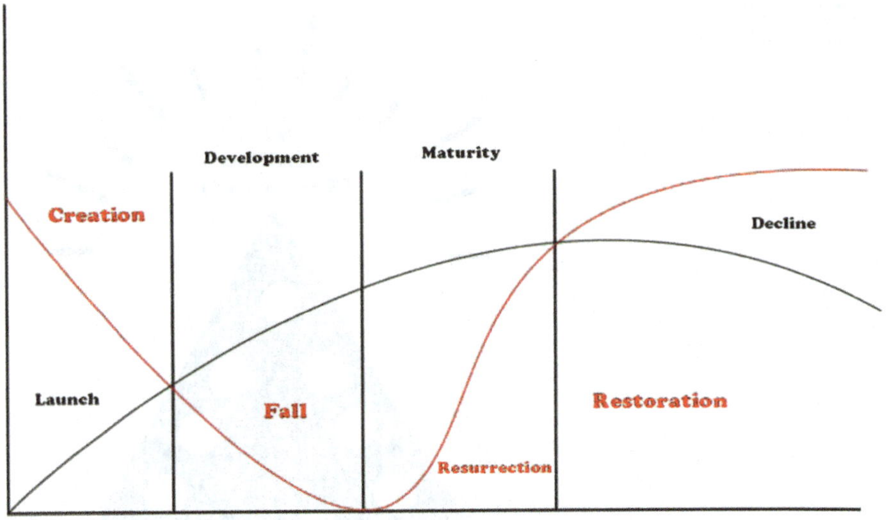

Fig. 7.4 Graphic of the intersection zone between the two perspectives of acquiring a new name (bottom-up and top-down)

a. BitDefender, business initiated by entrepreneur Florin Talpeş and which has gained, in time, worldwide notoriety by using a bottom-up approach in creating a name (brand) (*BitDefender—o afacere românească globală* 2011);
b. ProTV Chișinău, a private TV channel from the Republic of Moldova, which benefited from a remarkable transfer of notoriety from the most watched TV channel in Romania, thus using a top-down approach in creating a brand (*De 12 ani, Moldova gândește liber împreună cu PRO TV* 2011)

Such an analysis, on creating a name (brand) opens the gates of another area interesting to be investigated, meaning one of the types of entrepreneurial creation, from the perspective of the authenticity of the creation. From such a perspective, we can distinguish three main categories of entrepreneurial creation:

1. Authentic entrepreneurial creation, based on the purest form of creation (innovation/divine inspiration) and which requires creating a competitive advantage by taking on the foregoing character of the entrepreneurial endeavor. A good example in this respect is constituted by the Informal School of IT, which in the year of its launch (2013) stood for a pioneering initiative in respect to the informal education (on short term) in the IT and software industry (Pintea 2016). Another example from this category is Psychometric Systems, Corp (mindmisystem.com), producer and distributor of the first system of psychometric evaluation complementary to an individual's psychological profile (*Un român a inventat un aparat care îţi spune ce personalitate ai şi pentru ce job eşti cel mai potrivit*, n.a). The entire business endeavor is founded on an invention unique in the world and capable of completely changing the paradigm of psychological evaluations,

so useful in almost all activity areas that require the involvement of the human factor (Talpoş, Pop and Oncica-Sanislav 2015).

2. Mimetic-imitative entrepreneurial creation, generated by appealing to the memory of the collective unconscious or superconscious and which is activated in the factual-informational field of the initiator. This mimicry can sometimes get, in today's wild entrepreneurship, too far: companies that imitate (conscious or unconscious) from work methods to corporation image elements (logos), everything that looks like it can be successfully replicated in their environment. A good example in this respect is the case of Panemar Morărit și Panificație, LLC company, accused on multiple occasions to have been generated imitatively this business, inspired by the success story of the Spanish company Panamar (Fartusnic 2014). Another example, positive this time, of entrepreneurial creation is the one of the social enterprises Valea Barcăului, LLC, generated by a sum of traditions received genetically and by experience from parents, grandparents and even grand-grandparents and which came to condition, develop, motivate, and transform continuously the said business, ensuring the values to which it should relate (Alin Prunean, ardeleanul care a transformat mierea in produs de lux si i-a invatat si pe altii valoarea muncii cinstite 2014; (Nicolae 2014). Valea Barcăului, LLC social enterprise produces and packages honey specialties with edible boletus following traditional Romanian recipes, which have been proved to be extremely appreciated on Western markets such as the UK, Austria, France, etc.
3. Sympathetic entrepreneurial creation (by contamination), generated under the influence of entrepreneurial initiatives which become "centers of radiation" and which create true chain reactions within the group (community/society) in which they manifest (Stănciulescu 1995). These chain reactions stabilize and stop barely at the moment where it is reached a balance between the manufacturing capacity of the mentioned entrepreneurial group and the power of absorption of the market. Still, this balance is relative, because it manifests (many times) due to tensioned interactions between the entrepreneur's members of the same community. It is somehow paradoxical the fact that the mentioned tension participates as well at the becoming and formation of the sympathetic entrepreneurial community. Several concrete examples of such entrepreneurial communities generated by contamination are:

    (a) The community of small pottery and ceramics workshops from Horezu, renowned even on a global level. According to a study conducted in 2013 within a project co-financed by the European Social Fund through the PoS-DRU 2007–2013 program "Invest in people!", in the area of Horezu locality (6,300 inhabitants), Vâlcea County, there were identified no less than 97 craftsmen and producers, most of them in ceramics (*Lista mestesugari si producatori judetul Valcea* 2013).
    (b) The community of producers of musical instruments from Reghin, Mureș county, which has also gained notoriety at an international level. In this community, the role of a radiation center has been played by the musi-

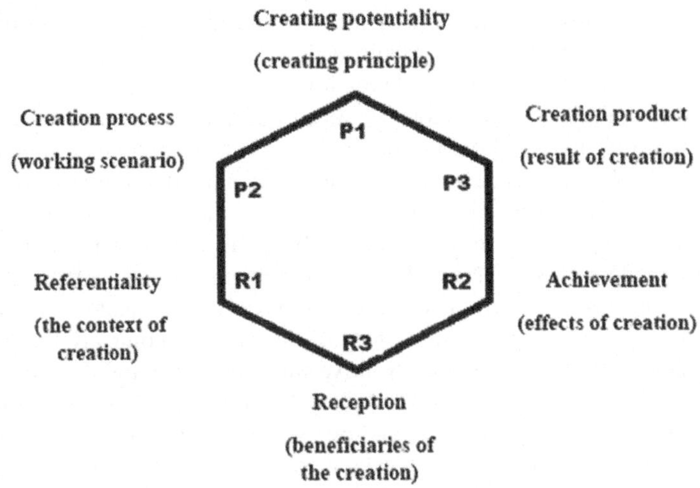

Fig. 7.5 Phenomenological–hexadic model of entrepreneurial creation (Stănciulescu 1995)

cal instruments factory Hora Corp., which started its activity since 1951, being the main supporter of the practical school of construction of musical instruments, where most of the luthiers learned that today build the musical instruments in Reghin have studied (Matei 2014).

(c) The community of small handcrafts merchants concentrated near the driveway, in the Izvoru Crișului locality, Cluj county (Neagoie 2006). In Cluj county, Izvoru Crișului municipality is constantly among the richest communes, this success being due to the fact that within the commune there are registered and function a high number of family associations and freelancers that have the main occupation producing and selling traditional crafts specific to the area.

The act of entrepreneurial creation can also be analyzed through the perspective of the parameters established by the phenomenological hexahedron of creativity (Stănciulescu 1995) (see Fig. 7.5).

From the perspective of the entrepreneurial creation, the three Ps (see Fig. 7.5) gain the following meanings (Stănciulescu 1995):

P1—entrepreneurial creating potentiality (*Who is creating?*)
P2—the creation process (*How is it being created?*)
P3—the product of the creation (*What is it being created?*)
R1—referentiality (*In which space–time context is the creation being created?*)
R2—achievement (*With what purpose is the creation being created?*)
R3—reception (*To whom is the creation being addressed?*) In relation to its effect, the entrepreneurial creation can be:

- Entrepreneurial creation with a private effect—it brings satisfactions (most times material ones) to one person or a small group of people;
- Entrepreneurial creation with public effect—brings satisfaction and benefits to both associates/shareholders behind the entrepreneurial endeavor and the entire community.

7.4 Conclusions

Synchronic entrepreneurial coordination, inspired from the coherence of the myths of cosmic creation can reduce disorientation of the entrepreneurs lost in the labyrinth of the superficial shapes (Stănciulescu 1995), helping them have a better vision regarding their own business (the micro-medium) but also regarding the economic macro-medium, two elements ontologically linked. From this connection can derive the so necessary structural and functional coherence of the entrepreneurial world.

From a functional point of view, entrepreneurial creation is subjected, such as the cosmic genesis, to some causal-natural determinations (laws of the universe), more exactly to the law of entropic cycle and the law of informational continuity (Stănciulescu 1995). In essence, this means that, once born, a business will inexorably have to subject to the process of growth, maturing, and decline. Even the passing of cosmos through death (return to chaos) can find its correspondent in the entrepreneurial or economic sphere, because the difficult times from an economic perspective only represent the preparing stage of a future rebirth in a transformed manner, benefitting from the "genetic code" inherited from a world that has just destroyed its structures. In such an agreement will be interesting to follow the evolution of the worldwide automobile sector that is, in professionals' point of view, borderline with the "return to chaos", the stage which, most probably, will lead to the reinventing of the sector in a completely new paradigm, one of the electrical or non-polluting automobiles, in general (Pam Matei 2016). As it has already been stated in this paper, human creation is limited both by the natural laws (of the universe) and by the variable performances, which are connected to the individual inheritance of the creator. As such, in entrepreneurship as well, there is unequivocally the chance of one being transformed into a victim of his own creation (Gerber 1995).

Finding again the fundamental unit of creation must, therefore, preoccupy not only theologians, scientists, or philosophers, but also entrepreneurs, who will gain new perspectives of understating their own businesses and the economic macro-medium. That will happen as soon as they realize that, in many ways, the entrepreneurial creation is nothing but a natural reflex of divine creation.

In other words, the naturalization of the entrepreneurial creation concept (replacing the natural causality with an "artificial" causality—a human one—overlapping with the "natural truths" of the universe) can generated the manifestation of a new form of entrepreneurship, based on a new values system, on new ways of action (signifier) and new products or services (signification).

Decoding the divine speech of creation, as a manifestation of the entrepreneurial curiosity can be simplifying and can bring a supplementary efficiency to entrepreneurs, allowing them to transform their own businesses in "syncretic constructions". Within these constructions, different elements of vivid micro-universes combine with elements of extremely complex macro-universes, in an ensemble of interpretative variants, which only the process of cosmic creation can suggest to business initiators.

References

BitDefender—o afacere românească globală (2011) *adevarul.ro*. Retrieved February 6, 2017, from http://adevarul.ro/international/europa/bitdefender—afacere-romaneasca-globala-1_50ad72c17c42d5a663955863/index.html.

De 12 ani, Moldova gândeşte liber împreună cu PRO TV. (2011). Retrieved February 7, 2017, from http://www.timpul.md/articol/de-12-ani-moldova-gandeste-liber-impreuna-cu-pro-tv–26770.html.

Diaconu, O. A. (2011). *Creaţie şi creativitate în viziunea lui Mircea Eliade*. Iaşi: Sedcom Libris.

Fartusnic, A. (2014). *Panemar, slogan şi logo furate de la spanioli* Available from: Alin Prunean, ardeleanul care a transformat mierea în produs de lux şi i-a învăţat şi pe alţii valoarea muncii cinstite (2014) *stirileprotv.ro*. Retrieved February 8, 2017, from http://stirileprotv.ro/stiri/social/alin-prunean-ardeleanul-care-a-transformat-mierea-in-produs-de-lux-si-i-a-invatat-si-pe-altii-valoarea-muncii-cinstite.html.

Filip, A. (n.a.). *Antreprenor spiritual versus spirit antreprenorial*, Internet Article.

Gerber, M. E. (1995). *The E-myth revisited, Why most small businesses don't work and what to do about it*. New York, NY: HarperCollins.

Matei, R. (2014). *Peste 4 milioane instrumente produse la Reghin*. Retrieved February 9, 2017, from http://online.reghinulnostru.ro/articole/reportaj/peste-4-milioane-de-instrumente-produse-la-reghin.html.

Morretta, A. (1993). *Spiritul Indiei*. Bucharest: Tehnica.

Nadler, S. (2016). Baruch Spinoza. Retrieved February 19, 2017, from https://plato.stanford.edu/entries/spinoza/.

Neagoie, L. (2006). *Romania la şosea: Imperiul artizanatului*. Retrieved February 9, 2017, from http://jurnalul.ro/campaniile-jurnalul/romania-la-sosea/romania-la-sosea-imperiul-artizanatului-16292.html.

Nicolae, R. (2014). Businessul dă dependenţe! I Romania Libera. RomaniaLibera.ro. Retrieved February 8, 2017, from http://www.romanialibera.ro/economie/business/businessul-da-dependente–349568.

Pam, Matei, C. (2016). *Schimbări dramatice în energia mondială—Vremea combustibililor fosili se apropie de sfârşit*. Retrieved February 19, 2017, from http://www.cotidianul.ro/vremea-combustibililor-fosili-se-apropie-de-sfarsit-282820/.

Pintea, V. (2016). *PROIECT PRIVAT DE SUCCES: Şcoala Informală de IT de la Cluj, număr dublu de cursanţi în 2016*. Retrieved February 8, 2017, from http://www.buzznews.ro/146604-proiect-privat-de-succes-scoala-informala-de-it-de-la-cluj-numar-dublu-de-cursanti-in-2016/.

Pop, I. G., & Vereş, O. L. (2010). *Elemente de semiofizică aplicată*. Cluj-Napoca: Risoprint.

Retrieved February 6, 2017, from http://andreafilip.com/antreprenor-spiritual-vs-spirit-antreprenorial/.

Retrieved February 9, 2017, from http://www.i-dealis.ro/wp-content/uploads/2013/02/Lista-mestesugari-si-producatori-Judetul-Valcea.pdf.

Retrieved February 1, 2017, from http://www.ziardecluj.ro/panemar-slogan-si-logo-furate-de-la-spanioli.

Robinson, M. (2015). *Only 1 out 100 people become Financially Free*, Internet Article. Retrieved February 8, 2017, fromhttps://www.linkedin.com/pulse/only-1-out-100-people-become-financially-free-marco-robinson.

Schiopu, D. (2015). *Antreprenoriatul e ceva cu care te naști sau care se învață?*, Internet Article. Retrieved February 8, 2017, fromhttps://dragosschiopu.ro/concurs-antreprenoriatul-ceva-care-nasti-care-invata/.

Sheen, C. (n.a.). *What Are The Stages of a Business Lifecycle and Its Challenges?* Retrieved February 7, 2017, from https://www.aabacosmallbusiness.com/advisor/stages-business-lifecycle-challenges-100036770.html.

Stănciulescu, T. D. (1995). *Miturile creatiei—lecture semiotice*. Iași: Performantica.

Talpoş. M. F., Pop. I., & Oncica-Sanislav, D. (2015). *Managerial creativity, between native enhancing factors and environmental influencers*, Proceedings of the International Conference: GSMAC 2015– Dezvoltarea, finanțarea și creșterea organizațiilor. Oradea, Romania.

Un român a inventat un aparat care îţi spune ce personalitate ai şi pentru ce job eşti cel mai potrivit, Available from: http://www.mediafax.ro/life-inedit/un-roman-a-inventat-un-aparat-care-iti-spune-ce-personalitate-ai-si-pentru-ce-job-esti-cel-mai-potrivit-15454861 (Accessed 8 February 2017).

Zirbo, G. (2011). *Despre lumile create*. Cluj-Napoca: Casa Cărții de Știință.

Chapter 8
The Role of the Civil Sector in Contribution to Social Well-Being and in Shaping Active Citizenship

Márta Nárai and Adrienn Reisinger

Abstract Nowadays social and economic issues can have unfavourable consequences; social problems both at the global and local level are outstanding and it is essential to find solutions because of the efficient functioning of the economy and the society. Also, state and for-profit actors can take part in solving these problems, but there are lots of services which can be provided only by civil organizations. The first part of the paper presents the concept of civil organizations and current issues of them in Hungary. After that, it describes the way of their contribution to the active citizenship and to social well-being based on theoretical and empirical background. We made a questionnaire research in 2013 among civil organizations at the regional level in Hungary; we would like to show the main results of it. This paper presents a review of the main participatory forms of the organizations through which they can contribute to the improvement of the services and to the expanding of the supply. An important message of the paper is that civil organizations cannot operate without active citizens, our study will also show the methods how civil organizations can contribute to the active citizenship and what kind of elements and barriers have this process. This paper can add to the literature of the civil organizations and can be useful both for policy makers, researchers and citizens.

Keywords Civil sector · Organizations · Society · Participation · Active citizens

8.1 Introduction

The current social, economic changes and processes have unfavourable consequences; social problems—both at global and local levels—become more conspicuous, and it is vital to handle and solve them for the acceptable operation of the society.

M. Nárai · A. Reisinger (✉)
Széchenyi István University, Győr, Hungary
e-mail: radrienn@sze.hu

M. Nárai
e-mail: naraim@sze.hu

S. A. Văduva et al. (eds.), *Civil Society: The Engine for Economic and Social Well-Being*, Springer Proceedings in Business and Economics,
https://doi.org/10.1007/978-3-319-89872-8_8

Public and private actors may also take part in the accomplishment, however, we, as self-conscious and liable civilians cannot leave these actors alone to manage social problems, to represent individual and community interests, as well as to shape and influence public affairs. The actors of civil society have also become determining players by now. Civil organizations have become important actors in creating and ensuring social welfare and well-being by producing public goods, providing services, creating jobs, influencing developments and participating in their realization. However, besides their role in these fields, their role in community development, social organization, value preservation, etc., are also not negligible, since community experience, togetherness, trust, solidarity are as determining factors of well-being as financial security or public order.

In our study, we present the social engagement of civil organizations based on theory and a territorial questionnaire survey conducted in Hungary. We introduce the engagement's most important forms with which civil organizations can contribute to social well-being. Civil organizations cannot operate without active citizens, thus we also discuss how organizations can contribute to active citizenship.

8.2 The Concept of Civil and Non-profit Organizations in Hungary

It is not easy to define civil and non-profit organizations exactly, because there are several approaches of these organizations, and there are several different names for them like the third sector, voluntary sector; depending on the attributes of the sector. Mária Anna Bartal (1999:14) defined the definition of civil organizations as follows: civil society includes those citizens' initiatives which are voluntary for the citizens, and are free from state interventions.

Nowadays this definition is often confused with the definition of the non-profit organizations, which can be an incorrect approach in Hungary. Non-profit organizations are only those ones, which have legal status in the civil society. It means that non-profit sector is a narrower category, but it is also a wider one in Hungary, because non-profit sector also includes organizations, which are established partly or completely by state actors (Kuti 1998: 15). These organizations are out of civil sector because of their establishment. In our study, we write about those non-profit organizations which are also civil as a whole (for example foundations and associations), and we call them civil organizations.

During the period spent since the transition of the regime, a diverse civil/non-profit sector with an extremely heterogeneous composition has emerged in Hungary as well; the number of the organizations exceeds 62 thousand (KSH 2016), and most of the organizations mean determinant social actors in view of their engagement and field of activity. Nevertheless, recent years have seen an unfavourable process; the 'deprivatisation' of civil society has begun. A greater acceptance and support of civil organizations close to the power can be observed as well as the attack and the hampering of those ones that are either far from power or real ones, furthermore, the emergence of so-called pseudo-civil organizations can be experienced, which adumbrates the evolution of the institution of state corporatism organized from the top (Ágh 2016).

8.3 The Role of Civil Sector in Shaping Active Citizens

Civil sector cannot exist without active citizens who not only care about their own life, but also about social issues. These active citizens can support the civil sector in many ways, by being members or leaders, donating, volunteering, etc. 'Citizenship defines rights and responsibilities, in turn creating a dynamic debate about the duties of citizens as members of the community. Traditionally, active citizenship has included participating in elections or referendums, standing for a political office, and actively or passively engaging as member of a political party or politically affiliated organization. However, this strict definition has expanded. A core element of active citizenship is now seen as engagement in civil society through membership in or support of organizations, involvement in political debates and public consultation processes, participation in demonstrations or protests, volunteering, and awareness of topical issues.' (Policy Paper on… 2013: 3). 'Active citizenship means primarily active involvement of citizens in the life of their communities and thus in democracy, in terms of activity and decision-making.' (Policy Paper on… 2013: 4).

The question arises who teach the citizens how to be active in these areas. The question is important because nobody was born with those skills, which make them active. People can learn the skills from the followings (e.g. Breen and Rees 2009; Delatny 2007; Gáti 2010):

- family
- formal learning (in school system)
- non-formal learning (organized learning but not in the formal system)
- informal learning (during everyday life and in the communities where people live)

We think the first two types do not need any explanations, the other two will be shown very briefly. 'Non-formal education involves learners voluntarily opting to engage in self—directed learning from an organized body of knowledge, directed by a designated teacher.

Informal education or training is more incidental and spontaneous.' (Breen and Rees 2009: 16–17) It means that people can learn in such a way that they are not aware of being thought actually. In the literature, there are no exact viewpoints about which form of learning is the best; we think that all of them can have an important role in a certain situation. The most important thing is that learning these skills can be a lifelong learning process and the emphasis is on the activity. Formal education can contribute to the learning of active citizenship but such activities which are not formal can be also effective.

There are many platforms for learning the skills of active citizenship in practice, and one of them is civil organizations. This means that these organizations can help people to be more active, and if people are more active, they can contribute to the social goals of the organizations at a higher level. 'One of the most important roles of civil organizations [...] lies in their ability that they can activate people, strengthen their community bonding, and have them connected to the circulation of the society thought informal networks between them and within the organizations.' (Nárai 2004: 627). The more active the citizens are, the better the society where they live will be, or in other words 'active citizenship is the glue that keeps society together...' (Active Citizenship For..., 2012: 6).

Civil organization can take part in the informal education of active citizenship with the following types of activities[1]:

- They make people have their voice heard.
- They can ensure opportunities to learn how to act with other people, how to behave in community.
- They can help in assertive communication.
- They can ensure opportunities for self-organization.
- They can ensure public relations—social integration.
- They can ensure an opinion-influencing and—shaping, value—and behaviour-forming socializing medium.
- They can help building social capital and trust.
- The can contribute to understanding democracy.
- They can provide such courses, which can be useful for people who would like to learn more about themselves, about effective communication, etc.
- Working for organizations can help people learn how to manage everyday life issues in an organization and how to manage formal issues (e.g. go to the post office, go to offices, etc.)
- They can help learn how to enforce public interests.
- They can help learn how to make decisions in everyday and professional life.

It is important to emphasize that civil organizations can be the teacher in the learning process but they are also the platforms where people can practice what they have learnt in the organization. That is to say, people can immediately try out in practice what they have learnt in the organizations.

As we can see, civil organizations can teach people lots of kind of skills of active citizenship, now we would like to show in detail the following ones: ensuring the opportunity of self-organization, ensuring socializing medium and practicing social participation as a learning scene of democracy.

An important social relevance of establishing civil organizations is that they ensure an appropriate frame and opportunity for *self-organization*. By establishing associations, clubs, coalitions, foundations, etc. people can express their demands and enforce their interests. They intensify the diversity of individual interests into group interests and are also adapted to link the formed and pronounced group interests to the greater community or public interests (Jenkins 1997; Lévai 1998; Putnam 1993; 1995). Public and private actors are not always able to find those problems with

[1]The list is based on the following literature: (Jochum 2005; Nárai and Reisinger 2016).

which people face day by day, and are not always able to meet the more and more special demands. By founding civil organizations and volunteering in these types of organizations people also have the opportunity for solving the occurred problems according to their own ideas, as active actors of the society, and for meeting the occurred demands.

By membership in civil organizations as well as activities carried out in such organizations people have the opportunity for expanding their personal relationships. These organizations strengthen individuals' community bonding and *integrate them into the society* through informal networks, public relations and social activities. Without the rich network of civil initiations society becomes atomized, however, we can infer diverse social relations from their huge number (Kuti 1998), by which relations the emotional and informational networks between people strengthen and trust and solidarity will have a greater degree (Putnam 2000).

Civil organizations also mean important *opinion-influencing and—shaping, value—and behaviour-forming socializing medium*, 'they inculcate receptivity for cooperation and participation in social life in their members' (Putnam 1993: 89–90). They provide opportunity, for e.g. participation in decision-making, the deployment of the initiative, or even the development of the ability to compromise. Participation in civil organizations is also the perfect field for practicing tolerance, empathy, solidarity and the 'evolution' of this kind of willingness (namely e.g. to be solid with others), or increasing sensitivity to social problems.

These abilities, skills, knowledge and activities are essential for democracy, thus if we talk about the role of civil organizations, the fact has to be emphasized that these organizations can be interpreted as the basic elements of civil society, an *essential keystone of democracies* (Jenkins 1997). Back in the 19th century Tocqueville (1835, 1993) saw voluntary, autodynamic organizations as the bailees of democracy. According to this role, besides interest representation, the linking of individual and community interests and aims, the establishment of horizontal networks and political socialization, they promote the participation of individuals in the operation of community level, and enable the involvement of individuals in community activity and democratic processes. For many people activity in associations, clubs and foundations is the only opportunity for *active social participation*. Thus, these organizations visualize the right of autonomous, free activity, so they are essential for the emergence of participatory democracy (Brachinger 2005).

8.4 The Engagement Forms of Civil Organizations Responsible for Society

Civil organizations are not only able to promote citizens' social activity, but they can also be active social players, which may have the following forms according to us (Nárai and Reisinger 2016):

(1) fundraising,
(2) support to private persons,
(3) support to institutions, organizations,
(4) providing special services,
(5) performing community/public tasks,
(6) maintaining the institutions,
(7) acting as employers—job creation,
(8) publishing publications,
(9) organizing and conducting events,
(10) participation in the decision-preparing work of the local government,
(11) active participation in the elaboration of development documents,
(12) participation in the implementation of investments, developments affecting the settlement,
(13) the implementation of social control, the 'monitoring' of the actors of power sphere, a so-called watchdog (Szabó 2004) or voice role (Ferge 1997, 1998), social organization, providing social integration,
(14) community-building and—shaping, community organization.

These diverse engagement forms suggest and show that civil organizations have several and often closely linked psychological, socio-psychological, socio-political, social and economic functions for individuals and smaller and larger communities and also for the society as a whole. Thus, civil organizations mean such organizational resources the social value of which highly exceeds their financial basics and economic performance, and this diverse social role confirms that they are the embodiers of social responsibility only with their bare existence.

Hereinafter a review of the most common forms of engagement takes place.

8.4.1 Fundraising and Largition, Support, Assistance

An important engagement form of civil organizations, mostly foundations[2] is the support of different institutions, organizations and private persons. Fundraising is not only important to have something to give from, but these organizations take charge of coordinating activity, e.g. by collecting different donations-in-kind and passing them to individuals and organizations in need of support. This is a significant thing because the majority of people are helpless to whom and how to pass, e.g. the assets redundant for them; and civil organizations undertaking these help them and thus activate the inhabitants to donate.

Besides foundations that are specifically organized to collect donations, numerous autodynamic organizations contribute to the operation of an institution (mainly nursery school, school, common lodging house, healthcare institution) or to the support

[2]In her previous pieces of research, Nárai (2008) found that private foundations are more open to individual needs and problems than the other elements of non-profit sector.

of private persons by their financial support or donation-in-kind. These organizations play an important redistributive role in society.

According to the data of Hungarian Central Statistical Office, one-fifth of civil organizations give donations, and in 2014 the amount of support distributed by them reached 140 billion HUF from which 125 billion HUF were financial donation (89%). On a national scale, most of the donations addressed to private persons derive from self-organizations that are active in the field of social care, while in case of donations addressed to organizations, institutions the redistributive role of foundations and associations operating in the fields of culture and education is prominent. Spatial concentration is very significant in the redistribution of supports, as the majority of financial supports given to both the inhabitants and the institutions (overall, nearly three quarters of the donations) get to Budapest, the capital.

8.4.2 Providing Services, the Production of Public Goods

There are some civil organizations which are involved in performing community/public tasks and population's needs by providing a kind of service, and they usually perform additional services and special activities (Horváth 2002). Several organizations provide *special services* for their members and most commonly for others (population, institutions and organizations) in their settlement, region. These organizations extend and improve the existing service supply as in most cases they gratify alternative demands which are different from the average, or they often perform activities which are required by the majority but not provided by other organizations (e.g., fire protection, damage control, safeguarding, elderly care, home care and legal protection).

One part of the organizations is involved in *performing public tasks and providing public services* correcting and balancing this way the negativities and lacks of the public welfare service system as well as offering alternatives and implementing the practice of a more flexible, a more direct and a more anthropocentric performance. In many cases they 'just' help in providing services, but there are also several examples when they completely take over the performing of tasks from the local government, or perhaps they maintain a self-dependent institution (e.g. temporary home for children and families, school, library, community house). It happens that by reacting to the occurring social demands, needs they introduce new services, perform tasks or try to reach the state or local governmental support of these tasks which were not present earlier in public services or still do not have a place in the current networks usually because these could be provided with higher costs within state, institutional frames (e.g. the care for and rehabilitation of addicts). A good example of the involvement in performing public tasks is the activity of Hungarian Maltese Charity Service who involve in, for e.g. the care for disabled people or homeless ones in numerous settlements.

Today it is typical that several local governments entrust performing one or more (public) tasks to civil organizations. More and more local governments realize that they can ensure their obligations of performing public tasks as well as their advantages, positivities not only by maintaining own institutions, but also by involving other social actors like civil/non-profit organizations in performing public services. In the middle of the 1990s, only one-tenth of local governments involved civil partners, while in the middle of the 2000s this rate increased to 22%, and nowadays it is 21%. However, due to the centralization, re-deprivatisation of public services the number of involved organizations has significantly decreased (to one-fourth) (Sebestyén 2015). Currently, in Hungary, the actors of civil society can be involved in the following public tasks:

- performing public educational tasks;
- performing public cultural tasks;
- maintaining and operating social institutions providing personal care;
- providing child protection services ensuring personal care;
- ensuring health care;
- performing communal tasks.

Local governments usually involve civilians in performing such tasks that significantly contribute to the wealth and the well-being of the settlement's inhabitants as well as the improvement of their way they feel. In Budapest and in the bigger cities, local governments count on civil actors in performing tasks in the fields of education, culture, social care and health care, while in villages rather in the establishment of development aims (Sebestyén 2015). Obviously, the delegation and the outsourcing of tasks can take place within appropriately controlled frames which provide guarantees for both parties as well as their accountability, thus usually in the form of contract (of public utility) or cooperation agreement, in order to supply the inhabitants continuously and appropriately. Civil organizations need suitable human and material background to be able to continuously ensure the performing of undertaken tasks at an appropriate level; thus this type of engagement presumes a more balanced and more professional operation from civil/non-profit organizations.

8.4.3 Employment, Job Creation

A part of civil organizations also *apply paid workforce* besides or in some cases instead of volunteers to continuously and reliably perform the undertaken tasks. Operation mainly or exclusively with volunteers does not necessarily mean amateurism since the work provided for free of charge by suitable professionals enables the organization to perform the undertaken tasks at an appropriate level and reach its aims. However, in most cases, especially in case of organizations involved in performing public services and tasks, the continuous provision of the service or the activity as well as the reliability of the organization's operation and task-performing activity require continuously employed and paid workforce. They usually apply professionals in accordance with the organization's field of activity, in addition, accountants, financial and accounting staff, and/or the administrative workforce. Several organizations apply paid professionals in the fields of leadership, management and legal consultation, representation to operate more professionally.

Civil organizations often transform such works and activities into services and 'occupation', which works were previously done by potential consumers or were performed with the help of relatives, friends and acquaintances (mainly different time-consuming and work-intensive activities, personal, social or communal services), or were used within the frames of informal economy. However, sometimes civil sphere creates jobs due to social sensitivity as a part of the organizations enables individuals who have unfavorable chances in labour market (e.g. people with changed working ability, disabled people) to get jobs by creating jobs outside the mainstream of labour market and implementing employment projects. In their case, it is an important aim to impede to get to the absolute periphery, to exclude from society and to help them got (re)integrated to the society (Frey 2001).

However, it is also important to emphasize that civil/non-profit sphere cannot provide a mass solution to the handling of employment problems. And although a more dynamic development can be seen in the employment by civil/non-profit organizations, nationally only 3% of all employees work for these organizations.

8.4.4 The Gratification of Cultural and Leisure Time Demands

By organizing different events, civil organizations significantly contribute to the gratification of cultural demands, the substantial spending of leisure time, the ensuring of recreational opportunities as well as to the extension of people's knowledge. From this viewpoint, civil/non-profit organizations have important roles especially in villages and smaller towns, where there are only a few organized or institutionalized opportunities for doing leisure time cultural activities and gratifying such demands. It is common that civil organizations take part in the organization and the provision of the programs of village days which are more widespread nowadays, but they also organize various competitions, cultural and other festivals, summer camps, different conferences, training, informative presentations and study trips.

8.4.5 Community-Building, Community-Shaping—Development

The bases of local societies are local communities in the organization, shaping of which and in their functioning as real communities, civil organizations are important. By joining people together and activating them they *create communities* and encourage them to do community activities. They enable them to bond, provide them the feeling of belonging to somewhere, and ensure them *communal and social embeddedness*. From this viewpoint, mainly the engagement of associations can be highlighted, as smaller-greater organized communities are formed with the establishment of associations. Of course, it is not necessary to be a member of a civil organization so that we could talk about communities (e.g. neighbourhood relations, different informal groups).

The engagement of civil organizations in community organization and community—building prevails broadly as well, not only with the organization of membership, since through their activity or different actions, appeals they contribute to the forming, catalyzation and the development of the broadly defined community life. It also includes that they try to involve people in social activities and they encourage them to participate in common activities by which individuals are not only passive viewers, the endurers of things surrounding them, but can become active players, generators of changes. From this viewpoint, the role of civil organizations is important from more aspects as on the one hand they convey the importance of the how, the when and the wherefore and the validation of public civil and civil roles, while on the other hand, a certain level of organization is necessary by all means to determine common aims, to recognize common interests, to effectively enforce interests, to influence power players. '… during communal activity civilians recognize their own opportunities, […] A civil community becoming an organization […] as a result of its activities, realizes its own power as well, which enhances its consciousness and makes it motivated to act further.' (Nagy et al. 2014: 51).

There are organizations which during their community organizing and community developing activity pronouncedly undertake the development of the ability of inhabitants who are unable to represent their own interests, do not have means and are on the periphery of the society to fight back disadvantages.

8.4.6 Active Engagement in Settlement—and Regional Development

We can interpret the contribution of civil/non-profit organizations in development tasks as the complexity of development functions, roles and activities.

There are civil organizations which help the good meeting and the edification of a given village, city or region by their activities affecting the built and natural environment, e.g. by making the environment more beautiful, arranged or planting flowers to the streets. In several cases, it was the result of the appearance of social self-organizations that buildings were renovated, monuments and statues were set up, but we can also find examples for participation in the followings: the road-reconstruction of the given settlement, the development of public lightning, the establishment of memorial park, the renovation of sport clubhouse, the establishment of playground or even building a gym (Nárai 2008). A part of civil initiations also try to get involved in planning and shaping development policy.

The planning of a settlement, region is basically a top-down process (in relation to local governments and settlements activities initiated by local governmental actors are seen as top-down ones), which becomes effective and meets the criteria of active democracy, according to us, if top-down initiations couple with bottom-up ones which are initiated by the society and the economic actors. Although the conception of community planning is now a part of the EU development policy too, it is not so common in Hungary. The community model of development builds upon local resources, local values, human capital and local initiatives. In this model, both the citizens and the civil/non-profit organizations are active participants. The implementation of plans ensures effective development in the long run as well, because development is not only directed from the top, but also reflects the ideas and interests of local actors. As a consequence of this, such developments take place which better meet the needs, and it increases cost-effectiveness (Erdősi and Knyihár 2015). During community planning, a major emphasis is put on the planning itself as well as on coordination; gathering information is based on primary data collection, the basics of future plans are mainly provided by the opinion and the ideas of those affected, therefore such plans can be created which are well founded and accepted by the majority, which is also the basis of sustainability.

8.4.7 Involvement in the Decision Preparation Work of the Local Government, Civil Control

Efforts to influence the decisions of power and public affairs are also decisive forms of participation for the enforcement of the voice role of civil organizations and the implementation of civil control; and these efforts are mainly fulfilled by involvement in the decision-making process of local governments, and especially in its preparatory phase.

Organizations participating in decision-making process usually try to help the work of local governments and implement civil control by estimating proposals of local governments (documents, plans and ideas) as well as by permanent committee membership, making different statements, and consultancy. The opportunities of civil society for managing and influencing public affairs highly depend on local governments' initiative and receptivity as determining the frames of cooperation mainly depends on them. According to Sebestyén (2015), it does not only depend on the commitment of local governments towards democratic operation, but financial interests may influence it too.

8.4.8 Own Research

We conducted a questionnaire research among civil organizations in 2013 (Nárai and Reisinger 2016). The goal of the organization survey was to get information from civil/non-profit organizations about their opinion and actions regarding social participation and the forms of their activity. The research area was the North-Transdanubian Region (5 counties), we sent the questionnaire to 3 800 organizations by e-mail, about 7.7% of them answered. Our sample does not represent the organizations in the region (but the ratio of the organizations by activity and form is quite the same as in the region), so we draw up the results only about those who participated.

During our research, it was proved that the establishment of civil organizations takes place along diverse dimensions; a part of the organizations focus on more aims and concentrate on more fields. Our results show that their activity is organized averagely around two aims and three fields. Based on previous research findings (Nárai 2008), it can be stated that multipurposeness is present at the moment of foundation in case of a significant part of the organizations, which also adumbrates their *multifunctionality* regarding their activities. Only one-fourth of the respondent organizations operate in only one area, while half of them operate in three or more fields. They mainly perform cultural (49.6% of them) and leisure time, hobby activities (43.1%), but education and training (37.7%), environmental protection (28.6%), sport (27.2%), social care (18.3%), settlement development (15.3%) and international relations (15.3%) are also decisive. Like national characteristics, in our sample, the lowest rate (under 6%) belong to those who undertake tasks related to policy, economy development and legal protection, from which the former two should not primarily belong to the tasks of civil actors.

Their activities, engagement are driven and motivated by diverse aims; a significant part of them (52%) are multilateral in this respect too, so they mentioned more aims when we wanted to know why they had been established. It seems that the organizational form has a significant effect on the diversity of objectives. Typically public foundations and foundations mentioned more than one objective; however, the majority of non-profit business organizations operate with only one objective. Our findings also show that among organizations operating in chief towns of a county, the rate of those mentioning one or two objectives was slightly higher (with 4–5%) than in smaller towns and in villages, and there were not any organizations operating along more than three objectives.

Figure 8.1 illustrates the objectives mentioned by the organizations.[3] Their establishment was mainly motivated by the cultivation of diverse traditions, preserving traditions, the achievement of a specific aim, the performing of specific tasks and assistance, but the collaboration of people, the promotion of the development of the settlement, information-giving, knowledge development and interest representation were also mentioned. The diversity and ambiguousness of objectives adumbrate the heterogeneity of the undertaken and performed tasks. However, it can also be stated

[3]The question related to objectives was an open one and we executed the categorization of the answers afterwards.

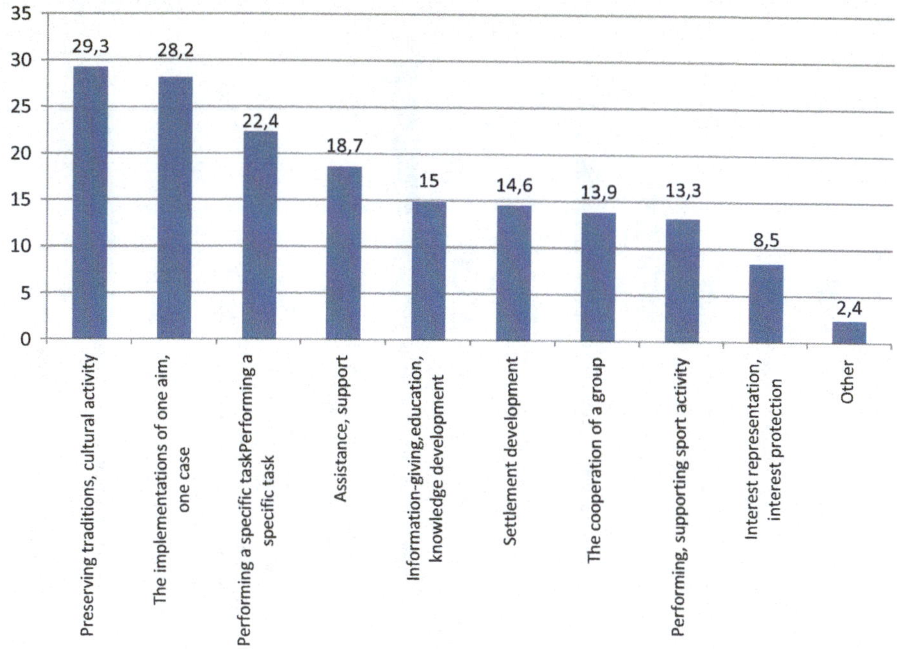

Fig. 8.1 The objectives of the respondent organizations, %, n=294 *Source* (Own questionnaire research among civil organizations 2013)

that although the majority of civil organizations (90.8%) concentrate on population, diversity characterizes target groups as there are other civil/non-profit organizations, local governments, but also state institutions and even the actors of market sector among the target groups of tasks undertaken by our respondents. However, the latter ones were mentioned at a lower rate (8.5 and 7.8%).

In order to reach their aims, a significant part of analyzed foundations, associations and other social organizations involve in and participate in more ways in the life of their home settlement. Organizations mentioned averagely three specific forms of engagement. Only less than one-fourth of them indicated only one form, almost a half of them mentioned 2–3, while one-fifth of them mentioned 5–6 or more forms with which they try to contribute to making the life of the population and the local community/society better, to handling social problems, and to achieving common good. Among communal organizations the rate of those who indicated only one form of engagement was significantly lower than among those operating in chief towns of a county and in other cities (10% versus 1% and 23.3%). On the other hand, it can be said that the rate of those who are engaged in only one form (25%) is typically higher among foundations compared to actors operating in other organizational forms; however, it can also be observed that public foundations and foundations are over-represented among those engaging in diverse activities (who mentioned at least

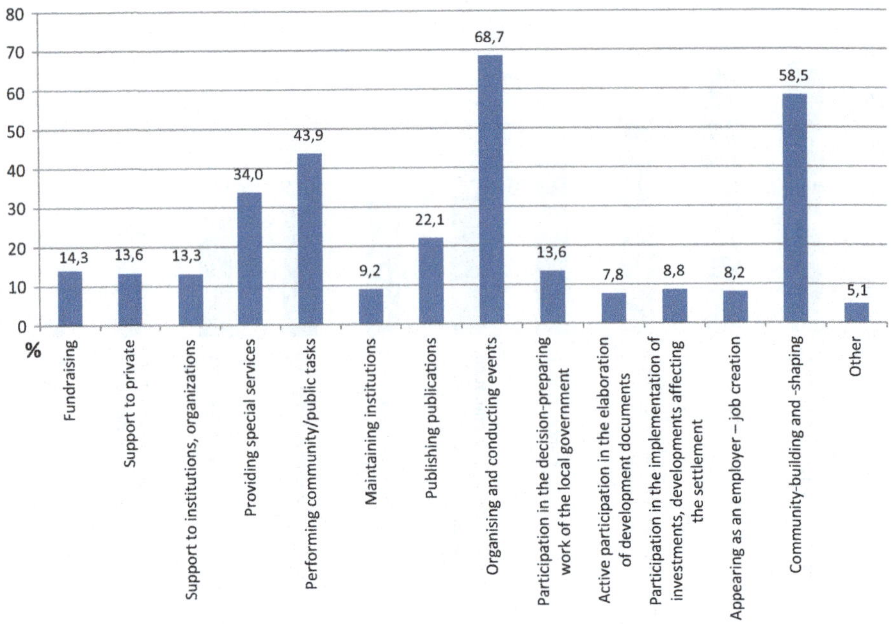

Fig. 8.2 The frequency of different forms of engagement among the respondent organizations, %, n=294 *Source (Own questionnaire research among civil/non-profit organizations 2013)*

five forms of engagement). However, in this respect, a significant relationship was only found in organizational form.

Most civil organizations mentioned the organizations of diverse events, thus this form of engagement characterizes two-thirds of them (see Fig. 8.2). They organize sports events, cultural and environmental protection events, actions, but also professional training and conferences. These events contribute to the formation of local communities if the events are open to the inhabitants of the settlement. The second most commonly mentioned form of engagement was community-building—organization as more than half of the respondents appear in this role (see Fig. 8.2) and try to catalyze community processes.

Besides these two dominant engagement forms, the role of civil actors in providing services is also stressed as more than two-fifth of them mentioned that they are engaged in performing different community/public tasks, while one-third of them provide a kind of special service, which shows that their role in gratifying community needs is significant. Of course, there are overlaps between these two fields. The performed community tasks are diverse, as they mentioned the provision of health care and social services, crime prevention, patrol service for enhancing the inhabitants' sense of security (e.g. militiamen), drug prevention at school or even activities regarding the protection of animals (e.g. teaming and caring for stray dogs).

A lower rate of the organizations (approximately one-tenth of them) performs the provided services within institutional frames. We can find civil organizations as employers mainly among those providing diverse services, and it is especially true for those ones that function as institutions, which does not require further explanation. Performing professional service-provider role cannot take place only based only on volunteers, as steadily ensuring services with appropriate standards requires the employment of paid workforce.

All in all, the rate of those organizations that work with employees as well (18%) is higher than that of those ones which (also) determine themselves as employers and job creators (8.2%). This latter rather characterizes those one which have more employees. Employing paid workforce has a significant relationship with the organization forms, and it mainly characterizes non-profit business organizations and public bodies, almost all of these organizations as well as almost one-fifth of foundations and public foundations have employees, while one-tenth of associations appear as employers.

Almost one-third of our respondents (28.5%) perform redistribution activity, and by raising and/or distributing donations they try to contribute to the improvement of the position of those in need and who need support. Of course, there are overlaps, but not necessarily the same actors appear as supporters as who indicated fundraising. Practically, the rate of those who provide support to private persons and those who provide support to organizations, institutions is the same, but only 5% is the rate of those organizations which support both the private persons and the institutions.

One of the most effective ways of shaping processes and public tasks of the given settlement is if civil/non-profit organizations try to influence the decisions regarding the fate of the settlement, region and to shape local public opinion. A form of this can be, for e.g. the participation in the decision-preparing work of the local government as well as striving for doing so, participation in the settlement development processes like in the form of the elaboration of planning documents or engagement in the implementation of investments, developments. According to our results, appearance in these forms of engagement is not general; what's more (!), only less than one-tenth of organizations play an active role in settlement development, and influencing the work of the local government characterizes only one-seventh of them (see Fig. 8.2). From this viewpoint, these results prove a significantly lower level of engagement than that we found as a result of our research in the middle of the 1990s, when two-fifth of the respondent organizations participated in the decision-preparatory work of local governments or at least tried to do so, and one-fifth of them (also) had an active role in settlement development (Nárai 2008). Maybe the reason for this decline is that the civils' strive for engaging in public tasks as well as their efforts to influence power decisions did not meet with a warm response or did not have big results, and in some cases these were not so effective, thus nowadays a part of civil/non-profit organizations does not even try to act in this field and they rather undertake the task of community-shaping, service-providing and responding to cultural–leisure time needs.

8.5 Conclusions

Although the majority of civil organizations do not serve directly the whole society, just only some narrower groups of it, and the value and effectiveness of their activity is hard to measure and estimate, we think that the importance and the social value of organizational net that organizes individuals into communities, provides opportunity for civil participation and control and helps the everyday life of people is indisputable. The forms of engagement introduced in our study illustrate well that the contribution of civil organizations to the life and the development of a settlement (region), the provision of social well-being, and the implementation of active citizenship is more complex than it is shown by statistical data and numbers. Several examples prove that these organizations more and more find those fields where they can successfully engage in the life of the local society, and they can show what they can do and who they are. There are some fields where they do this more spectacularly and louder, as it is visible, sensible for almost everybody or at least for the majority of the inhabitants, however, there are some fields where their activity and their results are only sensible for a narrower group. The results of a part of the undertaken roles are well-quantifiable (e.g. the amount of distributed supports, the number of employees, the event organized), however, the other part cannot be measured in an exact way, but these are the proofs of the work and activity of civilians and their contribution to the life of their narrower–broader environment. Without them, democracy is in danger as well as the opportunity for autonomous, free activity.

The future of the sector is the responsibility of the following: the whole society, the decision-makers, the supporters (state, companies, private persons, and non-profit organizations), those who are supported, and the organization providing support and services. Every member of the society is a part of one if not more groups. Therefore it is our joint responsibility that the organizations, which work to make our life and environment better, could achieve their aims, and the existence of their majority should be governed by the joy of assistance and not by uncertainty.

Aknowledgment Supported By The Únkp-16-4 New National Excellence Program Of The Ministry Of Human Capacities.

References

Active Citizenship For a better European Society. (2012). European Economic and Social Committee.

Ágh, A. (2016). A védekező társadalom, avagy a civilek hatalma: töprengések a magyar civil társadalom helyzetéről. (Defensive society, alias the power of civils: speculations about the status of Hungarian civil society.) *Civil Szemle*, *13*(1), 5–29.

Bartal, A. M. (1999). *Nonprofit ismeretek kézikönyve*. (Handbook on Nonprofit Knowledge.) Ligatúra Kiadó, Budapest.

Erdős, B. M., & Knyihár, É. (2015). Pécs partnerség: lépések a közösségi tervezés felé. (Pécs partnership: steps toward community planning.) *Civil Szemle, 12*(1), 25–47.

Brachinger, T. (2005). Civilek és a politikai hatalom. (Civils and the political power.) *Civil Szemle, 2*(1) 45–59.

Breen, M., & Rees, N. (2009). *learning how to be an active citizen in Dublin's docklands: The significance of informal processes*. Working Paper 09/08. Combat Poverty Agency.

Delanty, G. (2007). Citizenship as a Learning Process—Disciplinary citizenship versus cultural citizenship. Retrieved March 1, 2017, from www.eurozine.com.

Ferge, Z. (1997). Az állami szociálpolitika változásának trendjei a rendszerváltás óta; ezek illeszkedése nemzetközi (nemzetközileg változó) paradigmákhoz. (Changes in the trends of state social policy since transformation; their conformation to international (internationally changing) paradigms.) *Politikatudományi Füzetek*, XX. MTA Politikai Tudományok Intézete, Budapest.

Ferge, Zs. (1998). Egy mítosz társadalmi ára. Nemzetközi paradigmaváltás és a magyar szociálpolitika. (The social price of a myth. International paradigm shift and the Hungarian social policy.) *Társadalmi Szemle, 53*(8–9), 74–92.

Frey, M. (2001). *Nonprofit szervezetek a munkaerőpiacon*. (Non-profit organizations in labour market.) Országos Foglalkoztatási Közalapítvány Munkaügyi Kutatások Szakmai Műhelye, Budapest.

Gáti, A. (2010). *Aktív állampolgárság Magyarországon nemzetközi összehasonlításban*. (Active citizenship in Hungary in international comparison.) TÁRKI-TUDOK. Retrieved October 23, 2014, from http://ess.tk.mta.hu/wpcontent/uploads/2013/04/Gati_Annamaria_TARKI_TUDOK.pdf.

Horváth, M. T. (2002). Civil szerveződések szerepe a közszolgáltatásokban. (The role of civil organizations in public services.) *Helyi közszolgáltatások szervezése*. Dialog Campus Kiadó, Budapest–Pécs. pp. 157–175.

Jenkins, R. M. (1997). A nonprofit szféra és a politikai rendszer kapcsolata Magyarországon. (The relationship between non-profit sphere and political system in Hungary.) In Balogh, E., Bullain, N., & Simon, I. (eds), *Egymás jobb megértése felé. Tanulmányok az állam, az önkormányzatok és a nonprofit szervezetek viszonyáról Magyarországon,* A Civil Társadalom Fejlődéséért Alapítvány, Budapest. pp. 7–14.

Jochum, V., Pratten, B., & Wilding, K. (2005). *Civil renewal and active citizenship—a guide to the debate*. NCVO. Retrieved Februar 1, 2017, from www.ncvo.org.uk.

Kákai, L. (2014). Az almához a körtét? Avagy a gazdasági válság hatása Nagy-Britannia és Magyarország nonprofit szektorára. (Apple to pear? Or the effect of economic crisis on the non-profit sectors of Great-Britain and Hungary.) *Civil Szemle, 11*(1), 59–80.

KSH (2016) A nonprofit szektor legfontosabb jellemzői, 2015. (The most important characteristics of non-profit sector, 2015.) *Statisztikai tükör*, 23 December 2016. Központi Statisztikai Hivatal, Budapest.

Kuti, É. (1998). *Hívjuk talán nonprofitnak*... (We should call it non-profit...) Nonprofit Kutatócsoport, Budapest.

Lévai, K. (1998). Néhány gondolat a civil szervezetekről. (A few thoughts about civil organizations.) In Lévai K (ed), *Civil a pályán*. Helyi Társadalomkutató Csoport, Budapest. pp. 9–12.

Nagy, Á., Nizák, P., & Vercseg, I. (2014). *Civil társadalom—nonprofit világ*. (Civil society—non-profit world.) Új Ifjúsági Szemle Alapítvány, Budapest.

Nárai, M. (2004). A civil szervezetek szerepe és jelentősége az egyének, közösségek, illetve a társadalom számára. (The role and importance of civil organizations for individuals, communities and the society.) *EDUCATIO, 4*, 616–634.

Nárai, M. (2008). A nonprofit szervezetek helye és szerepe a helyi társadalmak életében—A nyugat-dunántúli nonprofit szektor helyzetfeltárása. (The place and role of non-profit organizations in the life of local communities. The status analysis of non-profit sector in West-Transdanubia.) Doktori disszertáció, ELTE Társadalomtudományi Kar, Szociológiai Doktori Iskola, Győr–Budapest.

Nárai, M., & Reisinger, A. (2016). Társadalmi felelősségvállalás és részvétel. (Social responsibility and participation.) Dialóg Campus Kiadó, Pécs–Budapest.

Policy Paper on Citizenship Education. European Youth Forum. (2013). Retrieved January 20, 2017, from http://www.youthforum.org/policypaper/policy-paper-on-citizenship-education/.
Putnam, R. D. (1993). *Making democracy work: Civic traditions in modern Italy*. Princeton: Princeton University Press.
Putnam, R. D. (1995). Tuning in, tuning out: The strange disappearance of social capital in America. *Political Science and Polics, 28,* 664–683.
Putnam, R. D. (2000). *Bowling Alone*. New York: Simon and Schuster Paperbacks.
Sebestyén, I. (2015). *Az önkormányzatok és a nonprofit szervezetek kapcsolata, 2012*. (The relationship between local governments and non-profit organizations, 2012.) KSH, Budapest.
Szabó, M. (2004). *Globalizáció, regionalizmus, civil társadalom*. (Globalisation, regionalism, civil society.) Századvég Kiadó, Budapest.
Tocqueville, de A. (1993). *Az amerikai demokrácia*. (The Amerivan democracy) Európa, Budapest.

Chapter 9
Quo Vadis Romanian Marketing: The Future and Contribution of the Romanian Community

Nicolae Al. Pop

Abstract Marketing research in Romania faces a crucial question: where to turn its investigations and in what proportion it should turn to fundamental studies, in the field of meta-theory, respectively, to stimulate the applied researches, directly required by the business environment. The response to this dilemma requires a change of mentality among the decision-makers in the economy, in general, and among marketers, in particular. Civil society, through its requirements, including the field of marketing communication, can also play a significant role in solving this problem. After a brief overview of the beginnings of Romanian marketing, which it compares with its current status of development, the study marks the main orientation directions in the fundamental research, and in the applied marketing research. The study also presents, in the framework of fundamental research, the holistic approach of processes and market actors as well as the study of the surprise mechanisms and consumer behavior anticipation. The main directions in the applicative research focus on the essential characteristics of the contemporary marketer and its partnership orientation, to promote a vision, where the marketing is to be viewed as an investment rather than a cost, to explore ways to achieve excellence in the field.

Keywords Marketing · Holistic vision · Change of mentality
Partnership orientation · Marketing doctrine · Marketing excellence

9.1 Introduction

Civil society is a complex concept that plays a significant influence in the developed countries, both in the course of economic, social and political events on short term, as well as in the medium and long-term orientation of a country's historical course. By playing an important role in building the behavioral norms of a society, it fosters the involvement of individuals and communities in the governing body. Civil society

N. Al. Pop (✉)
The Bucharest University of Economic Studies, Bucharest, Romania
e-mail: nicolae_al_pop@yahoo.com

S. A. Văduva et al. (eds.), *Civil Society: The Engine for Economic and Social Well-Being*, Springer Proceedings in Business and Economics,
https://doi.org/10.1007/978-3-319-89872-8_9

advocates for improving the communication process between individuals, social groups and macroeconomic and policy decision makers. Above all, we believe that civil society plays an important role in the formation, development and change of the mentality among the population.

In an emerging country such as Romania, changing the mentality toward fundamental values that characterize the business world, in the spirit of ethical competitiveness such as labor discipline, precision in everything you do, performance orientation, fair-play in the inter-human relationships, partnership collaboration spirit, etc., is essential for long-term economic success. One of the basic elements of this approach is marketing theory and practice.

The multitude of environmental factors and their current developments determine significant paradigm changes in the contemporary marketing (Ferrell et al. 2015). Contrary trends in these factors manifestation, such as globalization versus localization, hyper competition versus classical competition, social media versus traditional media communication, behavioral changes, that balances between the group imitation to which it adheres versus the promotion of his own personality essentially contributes to these changes. We also mention the mutations in the marketing research physiognomy under the significant progress made in the process of the market information acquiring, under the empire of the spectacular evolution of information technology and of the achievements in the neuroscience field. Neuromarketing research (Thomas et al. 2017) ensures the penetration into the human subconscious by helping to decipher and anticipate the reactions of the demanded bearers to market signals.

The marketing research in Romania, as well as in other emerging countries, is facing a dilemma about its orientation between:

- fundamental studies deepening to ensure the strengthening of the scientific status of the field—meta-theoretical nature (Florescu 1987; Badot and Cova 1992; Ertel 2013);
- developing applicative research that offers a response to business world issues in a medium- and long-term vision using a holistic systemic approach (Kotler et al. 2002).

To answer this gnoseological dilemma, we will outline the main directions in which we consider the two stated tendencies should be directed. Before doing this is required a brief assessment of the stage of marketing development in Romania.

9.2 What is the State of the Art of the Romanian Marketing?

At this moment, the Romanian marketing presents itself as a clearly defined field of knowledge, both conceptually and operationally, fully integrated into the managerial sciences. It fully responds to the formulated definition, more than three decades ago, by the reputed German professor Heribert Meffert:

Marketing = enterprise leadership oriented on the market (Meffert 2000).This is understood both in the academic debate and in the optics of marketing transposition into practical work.

Any prospective approach to the Romanian marketing also calls for a brief retrospective approach, to know where it came from and who were its pioneers. Among the pioneers of the Romanian marketing, science is required to call for the contributions of three reputable teachers.

- Prof. Univ. Dr. C. Florescu (1928–2004) was the founder of the Marketing School in Bucharest and also the head of the first university department (established in September 1971) at The Bucharest University of Economic Studies. He had notable contributions in developing the theory of commodity demand and the action mechanism of its formative factors; has formulated—in an original manner—the marketing functions, made an own conceptualization of the market strategy, placing it in the core position of the marketing policies; has been concerned with the development of the enterprise market theory, namely the product (Pop 2011);
- Prof. Univ. Dr. P. Mâlcomete (1928–2016) was the founder of the Marketing School in Iasi and he established the first marketing department at the Technical University "Gh. Asachi" Iasi. Through the researches that he has coordinated, he has developed the marketing applications in the light industry, primarily in the textile one (Pop 2008). He initiated and conducted a cycle of scientific meetings at the national level involving academics and practitioners, at a time when the economy left little free space to the competition manifest, due to the action of the economic and social planning mechanism.
- Prof. Univ. Dr. M. Demetrescu (1919–2001) was an eminent cultured person and an encyclopedic scholar, a passionate of mathematical statistics applied in the economy. He published the first paper in Romanian language using the title "Marketing" (Marketing—market prospecting, Political Publishing House, Bucharest 1968). He was one of the founders of The Bucharest Commercial Research Institute, an institution called upon to develop a multitude of market researches, primarily in the consumer goods and services field (Pop 2008). He was a professor at The Bucharest University of Economic Studies and the University of Oradea.

In the nearly five decades since the marketing concept and theory introduction in Romania, it has evolved continuously. Currently, at the academic level, the Romanian higher education school has a rich list of study programs in the marketing field, as can be seen from the Table 9.1. Parallel to the marketing penetration and development in the academic environment, the economical practice has demanded and, at the same time, benefited from well-trained specialists in the field.

The most conclusive proof on this line is the fast insertion of the bachelor and master's studies graduates in the field of marketing on the labor market. The academic marketing programs are now found not only in the economical higher education, but also in the technical or even artistic faculties. The five doctoral schools from major universities have prepared an important number of doctors in the field. The academic marketing today is served by over 900 academics.

Table 9.1 Presentation of the Romanian academic marketing in the 2016–2017 academic year

Marketing studies in higher education in Romania

Bachelor education			
	Education with frequency	distance learning/ Education without frequency	
Public Universities	18	7	1
Private Universities	10	1	1
Master Education			
Public Universities other than economy)	42 (Of which 11 in faculties with a profile		
Doctoral education			
Public Universities	5 (Doctoral Marketing Schools)		
====== Source: Hotărârea de Guvern nr. 376/ 2016 privind aprobarea Nomenclatorului domeniilor şi al specializărilor/programelor de studii universitare şi a structurii instituţiilor de învăţământ superior pentru anul universitar 2016 - 2017			

Over 800 university teachers teaching marketing disciplines

Source: The Government Decision no. 376/2016 for approving the nomenclature of the university studies domains and specializations/programs and the structure of higher education institutions for the 2016-2017 academic year.

9.3 What to Do? Directions in Romanian Marketing Research

The answer to this question is based on the premise that *marketing is a social science*. The epistemology proves that the change dynamics in the social sciences field is much faster than that recorded by the natural sciences (Popper 1975; Dogan and Phare 1991; Kuhn 1996; Creswell 2008). This trend is also recorded in the marketing field, even more in some aspects, the economic practice in the field is significantly outpacing the theory (see in this sense the much faster behavioral changes under the information technology applications empire, which have not always found suitable answers in the marketing field theory (Woratschek 1998). The researchers have identified the need for theory to lead practice and the latter to stimulate the development of theory (Jaworski 2011), both played an essential role in generating marketing knowledge (Jaworski 2011; Lilien 2011). A graphic rendering of this relationship is presented in Fig. 9.1. This is marked by the systemical approach of the relationship between the two entities (theory and practice) specific to contemporary science. The marketing practice allows the formulation of some empirical generalizations, which indirectly contribute to the theoretical principles development, underlying new scientific constructions.

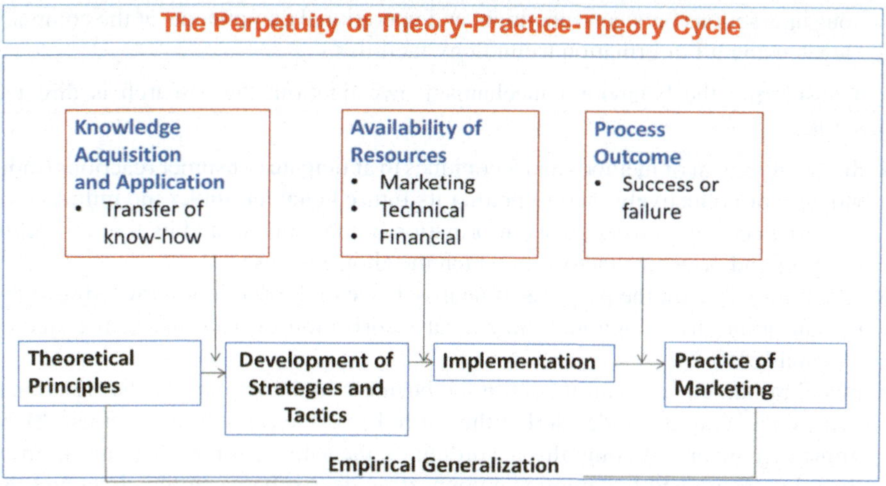

Fig. 9.1 The systemic approach of the theory–practice relationship. *Source* Kumar (2017)

9.4 What Would Fundamental Research Should Romanian Marketing Undertake?

The fundamental research aims to enlarge the scientific knowledge borders by substantiating, developing, and evaluating new theories and concepts. As a consequence, the marketing fundamental research aims to develop marketing models describing their content and mechanisms to lead to performance and excellence in the business world. It also combines the development of advanced data analysis methods with the design of early warning systems, called to anticipate major changes in market processes and phenomena. All this activity is part of the meta-theory. In the Romanian marketing, three decades ago, professor Florescu offered consistent arguments that such an approach is not premature (Florescu 1987) defining meta-marketing as "… the structure, the conceptual system, the methods" of the analyzed science (Florescu 1987).

We believe that the fundamental research field in Romanian marketing would require to address:

a. studying the mechanism of consumer behavior in an integrated view of all the impulses categories it faces until the actual manifestation of the demand;
b. concept foundation of holistic vision on the business environment in a systemic manner that integrates the economic, technological, environmental, legal, political, social, and cultural environment as well as all stakeholders involved in a business;
c. developing models of micro-, meso and macroeconomic organizational constructions that allow decision-making flexibility in marketing and engage continu-

ous interactions between functional and operational components at the company level, using all information technology facilities.

Considering the behavioral mechanism investigation, the research is directed towards:

- the development of methods and techniques to anticipate consumer reactions (individually or collectively) and to predict its future behavior, under the influence of new advances in knowledge, its information bombardment, and its limited ability to select and prioritize factors on which the choice is based;
- taking into account the progress of neuroscience in the depth of knowledge of the human brain physiology and the ethical valorization of neuromarketing studies (Thomas et al. 2017);
- modeling the client commitment in the business by integrating his/her relational experience with the bidder during the entire life cycle (Pansari and Kumar 2016) of the demander and doing this according to: the satisfaction level resulting from the relationship and the emotional connection degree between the client and the bidding company (Pansari and Kumar 2016).

These researches will also have effects in the applicative plan, in the company's marketing activity by better modeling the offer and addressing those to the most suitable customers, abandoning the invasive character of the sale act (Gamble et al. 2005).

Developing a holistic vision in any business understanding is another keystone for fundamental marketing research. This ensures understanding the market relationships in a systemic sense. So, each business will be perceived as the interaction result of all involved stakeholders, who are considered partners, not opponents. Using the information provided by Big Data Systems (Kumar et al. 2016), available to decision-makers in the company, the complex early warning systems. They will allow better grounding of future marketing decisions.

Finally, the fundamental research development in the organizational construction sphere will facilitate a better company structuring, with direct effects on the marketing decisions flexibility. At the same time, the creation of new organizational constructions will ensure wider applicability to the modeling processes, capable of sustaining the continuous interaction between the functional and the operative compartments of the company.

9.5 Directions in Marketing Applied Research

A key objective of the applicative research should be the mentality change among marketers. From the market orientation (Florescu et al. 2003), which involves the three subdirectories that became traditional (cost orientation, demand orientation, orientation after competition) requires a paradigm shift by moving to partnership orientation. This way, the contemporary marketer must have, in our opinion, three essential characteristics (Pop et al. 2015):

- empathetic thinking and action;
- rational creativity in conducting research-development-innovation activity (RDI);
- partnership spirit in all the actions it makes

Thought and empathic action allows the marketing specialist to call as accurately as possible, the needs, tastes, and preferences of the consumer, enabling them to shape their offer as close as possible to those requirements. The rational creativity will avoid unnecessary losses due to too high costs in RDI work and the transposition into a new benefit production (material product, service, right, idea) for which there is no effective demand, to justify this effort. The partnership spirit will allow the marketer to train the potential clients, from the RDI phase, to jointly making the new service. This partnership spirit is required to manifest itself both in external marketing, across all stakeholder groups involved in a business, as well as in internal marketing, towards all categories of employees in their own company.

Another key objective of the applied research concerns the vision change of the marketing action. The applied researches are required primarily focused on medium and long term, rather than to on short-term requirements solving. Such an action mode can be achieved if, at all the company's compartments levels (whether functional or operative), marketing will be perceived as an investment rather than a cost (Pop 2008). In this way, the marketing spends will no longer be reported to the extra immediate earnings, but will follow the return of investment mechanism (ROI).

Developing a marketing doctrine at the company level (Challangolla et al. 2014) is another significant object for applicative research. The marketing doctrine captures a sum of company-specific principles, resulting from the generalization of their own business experiences accumulated over time. Unlike the current marketing decision-making process, mainly based on a mechanical approach, with repetitive character, generating similar operating procedures, a company's marketing doctrine relies on the experience of this one, accumulated in time, and on their own values, generating unique principles in assessing the market relationships of each company. These principles aim to enhance the company "personality", by creating and developing a positive image, clearly outlined, and differentiated in relation to its competitors.

Among the main goals of the applied researches, we also mention those called to promote excellence in marketing. Studies on excellence should highlight four factors categories that interact to achieve this goal: the company's potential, the structures that configure the company, its human capital and the organization culture (Moorman and Day 2016). The company's potential is the result of the overtime accumulation of business knowledge and experiences, how to handle relationships with all stakeholder categories, but also functional capabilities related to marketing mix components, including brand management. Company configuration looks at its organizational structure evolution and its modeling tools. The most important role is played by the intellectual capital viewed from the point of view of its two parts: human and structural (Edvinsson 2006). The capital structure is constituted from organizational capital and customer capital (composed from: client databases, customer relations, clients potential). Ultimately, the business excellence can only be achieved in the presence of a solid organizational culture based on this value sets and

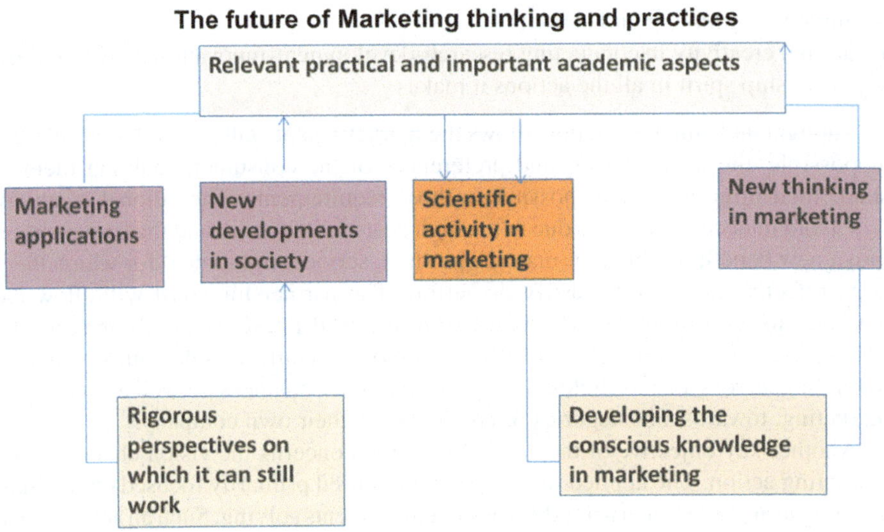

Fig. 9.2 How is the future of marketing of applied thinking and research applied? *Source* Kumar (2015, p. 7)

on the existence of a marketing doctrine. Research on business excellence requires a continuous concern for identifying and evaluating new market opportunities (Young et al. 2006), as well as developing an offensive attitude in marketing (Meyer and Davidson 2001).

The future of thinking and applied research in marketing is illustrated by the scheme proposed by reputed Professor V. Kumar (see Fig. 9.2).

In a simple, but suggestive manner, is marked the symbiosis between the theoretical and the applicative research, which is to carry forward the thinking and marketing action.

For the Romanian economy, the marketing research must meet this requirement of the theory–practice interpenetration. The mentality change among the marketers, which we have talked about, calls for the establishment of rigorous criteria for hierarchizing the macro- and microeconomic importance of the researches. The university and the business environment are required to cooperate much more closely, not on the basis of conjunctural or opportunity requirements, but by supporting a vision of the medium and long-term economic and social developments at national level.

References

Badot, O., & Cova, B. (1992). *Le néo-marketing*. Paris: ESF éditeur.

Challangolla, G., et al. (2014). Marketing doctrine: a principles—based approach to guiding marketing decision making in firm. *Journal of Marketing*, *78*(July), 4–20.

Creswell, J. W. (2008). *Educational research: Planning, conducting, and evaluating quantitative and qualitative research*. Boston, MA: Pearson.
Dogan, M., & Pahre, R. (1991). *L'Innovation dans les sciences sociales. "Sociologies"*. Paris: PUF coll.
Edvinsson, L. (2006). *Corporate longitude. What you need to know to navigate the knowledge economy*. Oxford: Book Hous Publishing.
Ertel, H. (2013). *Metamarketing*. Berlin: Scineo Verlag.
Ferrell, U. C., Hair Jr. J. F., Marshal, G. W., & Tamilia, R. D. (2015). Understanding the history of marketing education to improve classroom instruction. *Marketing Education Review, 25*(2), 159–175.
Florescu, C. (1987). *Strategii în conducerea activității întreprinderii, Reevaluări în teoria și practica Marketingului* (pp. 63–72). Editura Științifică și enciclopedică București.
Florescu, C., Mâlcomete, P., Pop, N. A. (Eds.). (2003). *Marketing. Dicționar explicativ.* București: Ed. Economică.
Gamble, P. R., Tapp, A. M., & Stone, M. (2005). *Marketing revolution. The radical new approach to transforming the business, the brand and bottom line*. London: Kogan Page Ltd..
Jaworski, J. B. (2011). On managerial relevance. *Journal of Marketing, 75*(July), 1224.
Kotler, P., Jain, D. C., & Maesince, S. (2002). *Marketing der Zukunft. Mit "Seuse and Response" zu mehr Wachstum und Gewinn* (pp. 50–53). Frankfurt/New York: Campus Verlag.
Kuhn, T. S. (1996). *The structure of scientific revolutions*. Chicago, IL: University of Chicago Press.
Kumar, V. (2015). Evolution of marketing as a discipline: What has happened and what to look out for. *Journal of Marketing, 79*(January), 1–9.
Kumar, V., Keller, K. L., & Lemon, K. N. (2016). Introduction to the special issue—mapping the boundaries of marketing. *Journal of Marketing, 80*(November), 1–5.
Kumar, V. (2017). Integrating theory and practice in marketing. *Journal of Marketing, 81*(March), 1–7.
Lilien, G. L. (2011). Bridging the academic—practitioner divide in marketing decision models. *Journal of Marketing, 75*(July), 50–53.
Meffert, H. (2000). *Marktorientierte Unternehmensführung*. Wiesbaden: Dr. Th. Gabler Verlag.
Meyer, A., & Davidson, J. H. (2001). *Ofensives marketing*. Freiburg, Berlin, München: Haufe mediagruppe.
Moorman, C., & Day, G. S. (2016). Organizing for marketing excellence. *Journal of Marketing, 80*(November), 6–35.
Pansari, A., & Kumar, V. (2016). Customer engagement: The construct, antecedents and consequences. *Journal of the Academy of Marketing Science* (published electronically June 11).
Pop, N. Al. (2008). Romanian academic marketing: Present and perspectives. *Management and Marketing, 3*(2 (10), Summer), 57–66.
Pop, N. Al. (2011). Professor C. Florescu–Founder of the Marketing School from Bucharest. *Amfiteatru Economic, XIII*(29 February), 322–330.
Popper, K. R. (1975). *The logic of scientific discovery, eight impression*. London: Hutchinson & Co (Publishers) Ltd.
Pop, N. Al., Todor, D. M., & Partenie, C. V. (2015). The marketing mentality within the organisation. A comparative study between Cpmpanies and non Profi organisations in Romania. *Annals of the University of Oradea, Economic Science Serie, 24,* 1260–1268.
Thomas, A. R., Pop, N. Al., Iorga, A. M., & Ducu, C. (Eds.). (2017). *Ethics and neuromarketing. Implications for market research and business practice.* Switzerland: Springer International.
Woratschek, H. (Ed.). (1998). *Perspektiven ökonomischen Denkens*. Frankfurt am Main: Deutscher Fachverlag.
Young, A. R., Weiss, A. M., & Stewart, D. (2006). *Marketing champions. Practical strategies for improving marketing's power, influence, and business impact*. Hoboken, New Jersey: Wiley.

Chapter 10
Online Research and Learning Environment to Facilitate the Elaboration of Bachelor's/Master's Theses in Multidisciplinary Teams

Mihai Florin Talos, Liciniu A. Kovács and Sebastian A. Văduva

Abstract Usually, the elaboration of a bachelor's/master's thesis is a solitary effort of the student, under the supervision of the coordinating professor. The thesis research idea is the result of the interaction between the same two actors, as such it is being limited by factors like: the student's research capacity; the professor's expertise; the financial and technological resources, etc. A possible solution for the above-mentioned problem is the development of a national or even international electronic research and learning environment, meant to facilitate the connection between all possible stakeholders in the elaboration of bachelor's/master's theses: students, professors, universities, entities interested in innovation/research and publishers. The paper presents an operation model tailored to some basic concepts of modern education, such as: multidisciplinary collaboration, the anchoring in the market's needs or the use of online tools. The online platform outlined in the paper aims to facilitate: establishing and saving research and learning objectives and documents; classic, video and holography conferencing; real-time support from coordinating professors; distance teaching or learning tasks' management. The paper might contribute to the development of new sets of methods, modes of operation, spaces and procedures for the research and learning alleged efforts to elaborate bachelor's/master's theses or even PhD theses.

Keywords Bachelor's/master's/PhD · Theses · Teamwork · Online platform
Higher education institutions (HEI) · Interdisciplinarity · Collaboration

---

M. F. Talos (✉) · S. A. Văduva
Emanuel University of Oradea, Oradea, Romania
e-mail: mihai.talpos@scoalainformala.ro

S. A. Văduva
e-mail: sebastian.vaduva@emanuel.ro

L. A. Kovács
Faculty of Business (Transylvania Business School – TBS), Babeş-Bolyai University, Cluj-Napoca, Romania
e-mail: liciniu.kovacs@tbs.ubbcluj.ro

S. A. Văduva et al. (eds.), *Civil Society: The Engine for Economic and Social Well-Being*, Springer Proceedings in Business and Economics,
https://doi.org/10.1007/978-3-319-89872-8_10

10.1 Introduction

Academia continues to keep open an important question regarding the most efficient way to elaborate a bachelor's/master's thesis: "*Should the effort of elaborating a bachelor's/master's thesis be a loner one or a team one?*" (Kovács and Talpoş 2013). In this sense, it was proposed a project (Kovács 2014).

The controversy deepens even more, under the pressure created by the rapidly changing knowledge-based economy, translated into an unprecedented need of the business environment to rapidly find adaptable, employable, highly qualified graduates (Moldovan 2011). After all, the most valuable resource that a company has is the human resources (Drambe 2014).

A pragmatic analysis of the phenomenon allows asserting that there are small chances of finding graduates with such attributes as the ones mentioned above, in higher education systems that encourage the elaboration of a bachelor's/master's thesis in a solitary effort of the student, under the "classic" supervision of the coordinating professor.

The chances of finding adaptable, employable, high qualified graduates increase significantly if the students are being engaged in a collaborative effort of elaborating their theses, by becoming a part of a multidisciplinary learning environment in which learners work collaboratively with active representatives of different environments (business environment, international academia, publishers, or even public authorities). Such a learning environment can ensure the real transfer of practical, applicable knowledge and skills toward the future employees or entrepreneurs.

A possible effect of the stimulation of the collaboration between higher education systems and the real economy (the working life) could be that the students become contributors (with their theses) in finding efficient and innovative solutions to different real-life or simulated problems (Moldovan 2011).

As such, how to design research and learning environment to facilitate the elaboration of bachelor's/master's theses in multidisciplinary teams, that lead to collaborative and experiential learning becomes the most difficult question to answer (Zitter et al. 2010).

The gap between the labor market and the educational curricula in Romania is considerable (Ţigănaş 2010). Given the fact that there is no institution (public or private) in charge of this issue (Ţigănaş 2010), even for our country, the only solution to ameliorate the gap between the labor market and the educational system would be to stimulate the cooperation between as many as possible of the stakeholders involved: universities, private companies, public institutions, publishers, grants offering entities, etc.

10.2 Requirements for a Research and Learning Environment

A modern research and learning environment for elaborating bachelor's/master's theses that would contribute to the amelioration of the disparities between the education system and the labor market should be:

(a) **International and cross-cultural**
Under the effects of the globalization process, an efficient research and learning environment should be, without doubt, international. Only such an environment could prepare the future employees or entrepreneurs for the challenges of interculturality. It is known the fact that the relations between different organizations, companies or even states involve the interference and interaction of different cultures (Cojocaru 2010). That is why, a modern research and learning environment should embrace a cross-cultural approach. In such a cross-cultural environment, the relationships between the three levels of collaboration: macro (national), meso (organizational), and micro (individual) should be formed on the strong interdependencies existing within them (Cojocaru 2010).

(b) **Internet based**
An efficient research and learning environment should benefit from the advantages of an online platform. In this way, the research and learning environment can succeed in: overcoming barriers of distance and time; making economies of scale and implementing novel instructional methods (Cook 2007). Another important attribute that derives from the Internet-based character of the research and learning environment is the scalability of the whole system. In order to ensure real scalability of the Internet-based research and learning environment, a decentralized approach to the development of the web-based applications is necessary. Such an approach will consist in creating a logical structuring of collaborating subsystems/applications and a geographically separated structure of replicated servers (Ezhilchelvan et al. 2001).

(c) **Multidisciplinary**
Increasingly less students elaborate bachelor's/master's thesis by addressing all of the current and emerging challenges from a singular disciplinary source (Jacob 2015). Multidisciplinary and interdisciplinary approaches to research and learning are essential underpinnings to best meet the dynamic needs of today's triad: graduates—higher education systems—labor market. As such, an Internet-based research and learning environment should be addressed to as many as possible industries and should work as an ideas' integrator.

(d) **Collaborative**
A modern research and learning environment should be, by definition, collaborative. Creating a collaborative environment is a key method of empowering students to thrive in the real world. Different curricular areas, cooperation, open-mindedness, discussion, different viewpoints, disagreement, higher order thinking skills, and debate are all elements that help students learn how to collaborate

Table 10.1 The main benefits of the stakeholders of a research and learning environment

Stakeholder	Possible benefit/benefits
Universities and other HEI's	• Better absorption rate of the graduates in the labor market
Students	• Better chances of finding a job, after graduation • Better application of the knowledge acquired
Business entities	• A wider recruitment pull and better prepared candidates • Reduced costs in terms of market research or innovation and launching new products and services
Grants offering entities	• A better disbursement rate for the educational grants • Dispersed and reduced risks, if the financing scheme of the research projects includes co-financing from the business entities
Public authorities	• Low rates of unemployment among young graduates
Publishers	• Interesting topics for print, with larger addressability to the public (including the business environment)

with others and thus become better prepared future employees or entrepreneurs (Hetherington 2013).

(e) **Based on incentives and tangible benefits**
The mission of the research and learning environment should include the wish to offer, to all stakeholders, attractive incentives/benefits (see Table 10.1), in a win–win collaboration model.

(f) **Familiar and easy to use**
An online research and learning environment should be developed on the most modern principles of usability and ergonomics and should thus require very little training to use. It should be an application with which, all users: students, coordinating professors, businessmen, publishers, etc., should be familiar.

10.3 Possible Structure of an Online Research and Learning Environment

A possible sitemap for an online research and learning environment to facilitate the elaboration of bachelor's/master's theses is presented in Fig. 10.1.

A possible structure of the online platform integrated in the online research and learning environment is presented in Fig. 10.2.

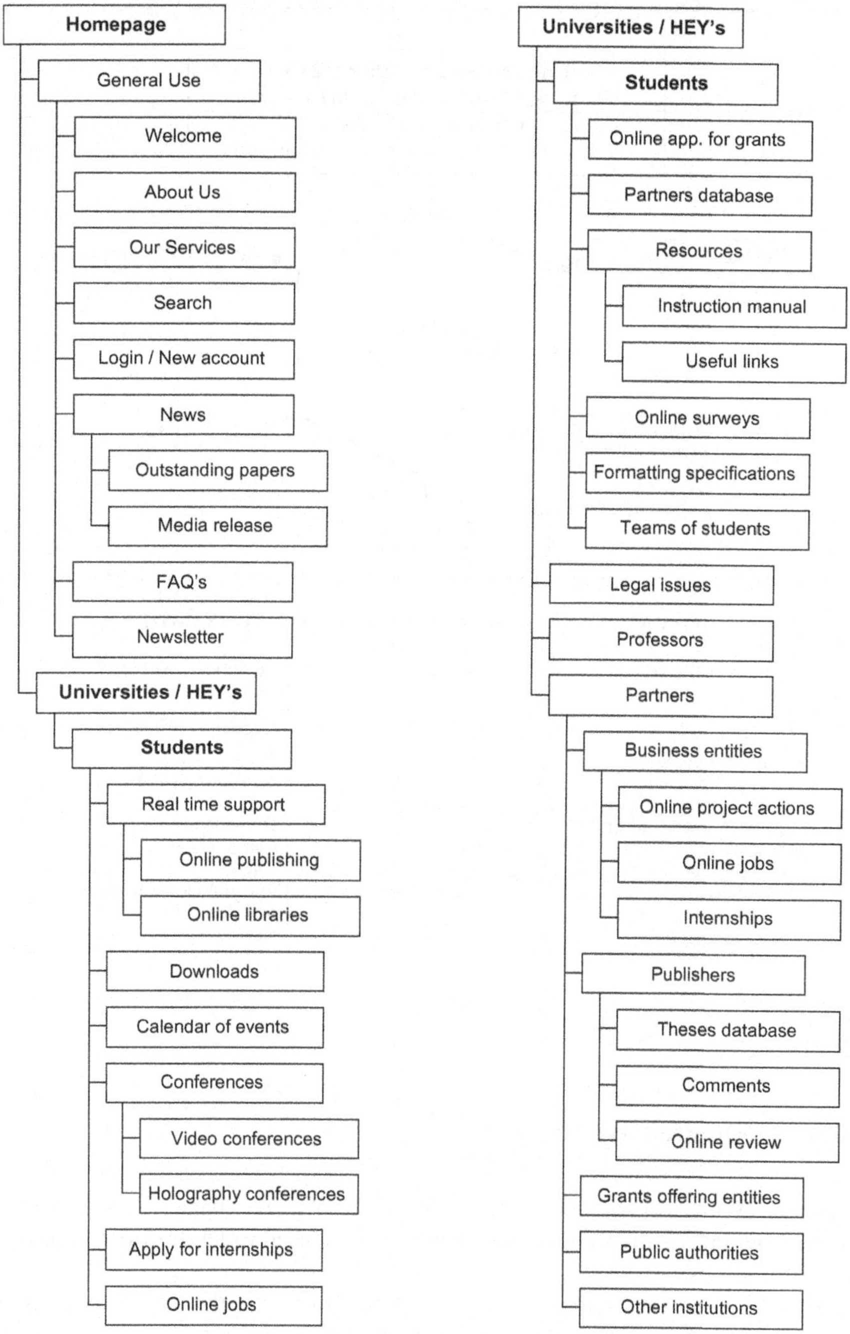

Fig. 10.1 A possible sitemap of an online research and learning environment

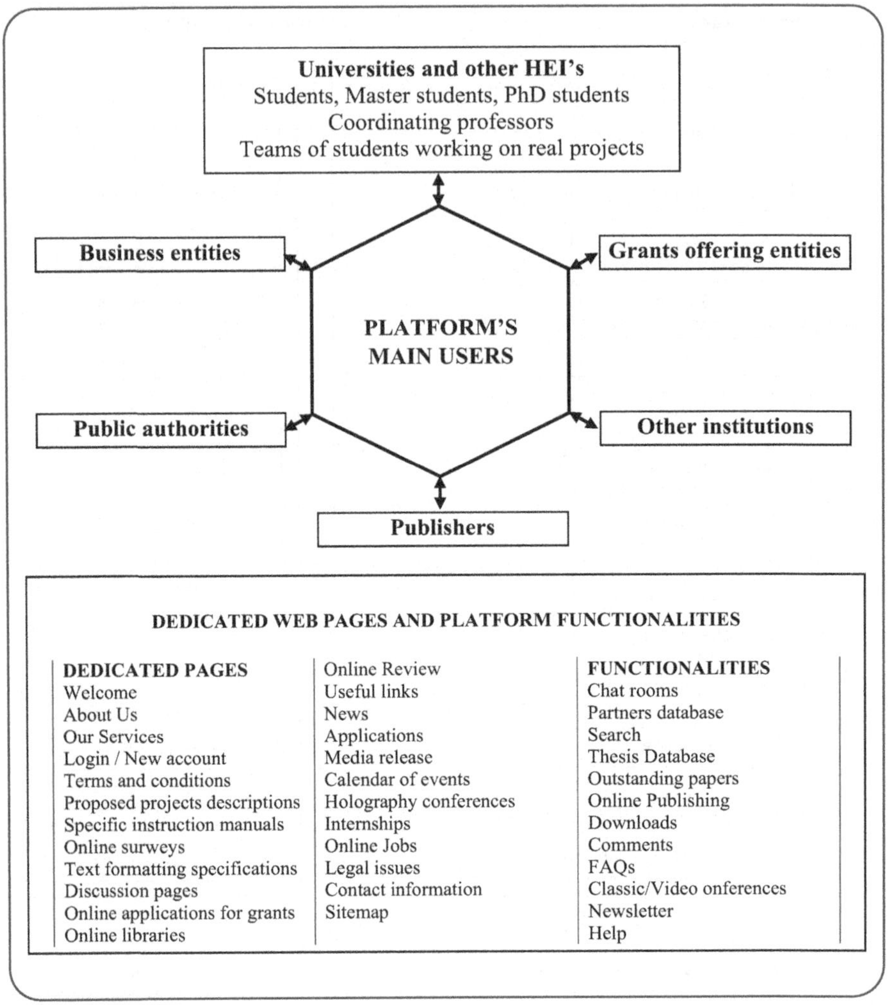

Fig. 10.2 A possible structure for the online platform

10.4 Dedicated Web Pages

Welcome: What will visitors/members find in the site? This page will describe site's structure and navigation philosophy. Links will be used to let the viewers navigate to other sections.

About Us: As this initiative overview, here will be briefly described the online research and learning environment's vision, goals, strengths, and strategies. Also, it will be described the initiative background, how did this initiative get started and what are its roots.

Our Services: This page will provide visitors/members a description of all the services. In addition, it will define each of the top sections and briefly describe what the user will find in each of these sections.

Login/New account: Here will be provided the procedure to get access to the system and the related applications/functionalities with a user ID and a password. If visitors are not registered, this will provide them with reasons to register with their name, affiliation, e-mail address, and other personal data.

Terms and conditions: This page will provide rules by which all registered users must agree in order to use the websites. This typically contains a definition of keywords and phrases, user rights and responsibilities, policy outlining the use of personal data, policy describing procedure for account termination, etc.

Proposed projects descriptions: This page will provide a brief overview of what users can expect to find in this section. There will be described, in separate linked pages, what users need to know about the current proposed projects. Also, will provide links to the archives to find projects that have been completed and to read summaries of each past project.

Specific instruction manuals: This page will provide links to detailed written guidelines informing how something should be done or operated in each specific proposed project.

Online surveys: This page will provide links to resources that facilitate to run online surveys in order to gain a deeper understanding of peoples' tastes and opinions about the online research and learning environment. Permission to associated reports to the surveys is granted by access policy.

Text formatting specifications: Here will be provided all the rules to be followed when formatting the text in a named and accepted wordprocessor.

Discussion Pages: This will allow to create threaded discussions. They are very useful for answering general/specific questions of the project, allowing team students to "meet" or having a discussion on a topic presented by the coordinating professor.

Online applications for grants: This is the page with or without links to specific pages where team of students can apply for grants, given by grants offering entities, to finance totally or partially their project.

Online libraries: This page provides links to electronic libraries or digital libraries, with a collection of resources (text, graphics, audio material, video material) and databases. This collection, stored as electronic media formats, is meant to support student's activities to conduct research or to consult information. The digital content may be stored on the main server, or accessed remotely to other suppliers via Internet environment.

Online Review: The online research and learning environment will provide a unique set of services and the partners will be either satisfied or dissatisfied. Partners may take their experience straight to the web. If the partner expresses a positive experience, the review can be amplified on the web and social media to encourage others. Negative reviews should be considered as opportunities to do better.

Useful links: This section of the website will contain links to some very useful resources and valuable information for writing theses. Links should be separated into different categories to make it easier to find what users/visitors are looking for.

News: This page will facilitate to put important announcements. Also, will specify what is the latest news that has value for the visitors/users. It will be a good idea to link this page to the Calendar of events and the Media Releases pages.

Applications: This page will provide links to some dedicated software applications or applications of another nature that help students to work in specific proposed project.

Media release: What are people/press/media saying about this initiative? This page will provide a short statement that describes the article/audio/video and use the data list on this page to link to separate descriptive pages.

Calendar of events: This page will provide short descriptions of each planned event.

Holography conferences: This page will provide a link to a partner that offers this new way of organize a conference.

Internships: This page will announce internships that offer students a period of practical experience in the industry relating to their field of study. In this sense, it is a good idea to encourage business entities to offer such internships, then to publish such opportunities on the website.

Online Jobs: This page will encourage all partners within the online research and learning environment to offer jobs to the students, then publish those opportunities on the website.

Legal issues: The activities within the online research and learning environment have to be legal. In this sense, after a pilot period of experimenting such activities, the partners have to contact the Ministry of Education with the proposal of having this way of elaborating bachelor's/master's theses as a permanent legal offer of the involved universities. The entire process is to be explained on this page.

Contact information: This page will contain the contact information of every active actor of the online platform with some more details for the key persons.

Sitemap: This page will help viewers find their way around and view the entire site at a glance. Users will click on the page titles to quickly navigate to the desired subject.

10.5 Functionalities

Chat Rooms: Chat rooms are great to connect all the team members with the coordinating professors and/or to get an immediate answer to a question.

Partners database: All registered individuals and their affiliation will be stored in this database. In addition to a basic directory, this will include brief biographies about key partners.

Search: This is a standard functionality every website should have and will provide a search button to quickly find information within the website.

Thesis Database: All the theses made in teams within the online research and learning environment's will be stored in this database. Permission is granted by the access policy.

Outstanding papers: All quality projects are to be awarded and/or published electronically or even in printed format. It is a very good way to disseminate the success of the online research and learning environment.

Online Publishing: Because electronic publishing has become very common in scientific publishing, this page will include links to the digital publication of the outstanding projects in e-books format. All other projects may be published in digital magazines format. At the same time, online publishing contributes to the development of online libraries.

Downloads: This section will allow partners, especially students, to take information from the main server and to store it to their computers for immediate access.

Comments: This page will provide the possibility that partners/visitors make written notes intended as explanations, new information, opinions, illustrations, conclusions, judgments, or criticism of any aspect found in the website and/or in the projects.

FAQs: This page will contain FAQs (Frequently Asked Questions) or Q&A (Questions and Answers), all supposed to be commonly asked in some context, and/or refer to a particular topic.

Classic/Video conferences: This functionality will facilitate the simultaneously meeting between stakeholders, either in a physical place or in the online environment.

Newsletter: This functionality will help to distribute regularly/periodically (via e-mail) a newsletter that is generally about one main topic of interest to site subscribers.

Help: This is a standard functionality which provides help/tutorials for each section of the online platform so that students will have what is necessary to accomplish every task of their project activity within a team.

10.6 Conclusions

- In a classical situation, the student might say: "I develop my thesis alone, on a given topic, because I have to graduate!"
- In this new, modern and legal approach the student might say: "I develop my thesis on a complex topic, within a team, because I love and I enjoy it!"
- Is this paper's approach possible? The only possible answer is: YES!

References

Cojocaru, M. (2010). Cultural diversity in international management. *Review of Management and Economic Engineering, 9/nr. 4*(38), 188, indexed in: ULRICH'S Periodicals Directory.

Cook, A. D. (2007). Web-based learning: pros, cons and controversies. *Clinical Medicine, 7*(1), 37, January/February 2007, Minnesota, USA. Retrieved April 19, 2017, from http://www.tau.ac.il/medicine/cme/pituach/240210/4.pdf.

Drambe, C. (2014). Depasirea crizei prin motivarea angajatilor. In S. Vaduva, & I. G. Pop (Eds.), *The crisis, an incentive for innovation*. 1st Griffiths School of Management Series (2nd ed., Oradea: Emanuel University Press, p. 95), ISBN: 978-606-8431-14-7.

Ezhilchelvan, P., Khayyambashi, M. R. R., & Morgan, G. (2001). Measuring the cost of scalability and reliability for Internet-based, server-centered applications. In *Object-oriented real-time dependable systems proceedings. sixth international workshop*. IEEE, ISSN: 1530-1443. Retrieved April 19, 2017, from http://ieeexplore.ieee.org/document/945114/.

Hetherington, P. (2013). 5 strategies for creating a collaborative classroom. Mimio Educator, Nov 4. Retrieved April 19, 2017, from http://blog.mimio.com/5-strategies-for-creating-a-collaborative-classroom.

Jacob, W. J. (2015). Interdisciplinary trends in higher education. *Palgrave Communications*, *1*, Article number: 15001. Retrieved April 19, 2017, from http://www.palgrave-journals.com/articles/palcomms20151.

Kovács, L. A., & Talpoş, M. F. (2013). Internet and transdisciplinary based teamwork formula for elaborating a bachelor's or a master's thesis. In K. Elleithy, T. Sobh (Eds.), *International Joint Conferences on Computer, Information, and Systems Sciences, and Engineering* (CISSE 13, December 12–14, 2013), University of Bridgeport, USA. Conference Proceedings published on DVD. The paper was also published in year 2015 in the volume *New Trends in Networking, Computing, E-learning, Systems Sciences, and Engineering* (pp. 445–452), ISBN: 978-1-4614-3534-1 (Print) 978-1-4614-3535-8 (Online) https://doi.org/10.1007/978-3-319-06764-3, Springer.

Kovács, L. A. (2014). Project for a model of teamwork formula for elaborating a bachelor's/master's thesis. In *Asia-Pacific E-Business and E-Government conference (APEE 2014)*, November 29–30, 2014, Shanghai, China. Proceedings published on DVD. The paper is indexed by ISTP(CPCI-SSH) and CNKI.

Moldovan, L. (2011). Innovative infrastructure and models for vocational training. In *International conference on quality and innovation in engineering and management* (p. 317). Cluj Napoca Technical University, ISBN: 978-973-662-614-2.

Ţigănaş, A. (2010). Investing in people. *Review of Management and Economic Engineering*, *9/nr. 4*(38), 125, indexed in: ULRICH'S Periodicals Directory.

Zitter, I., De Bruijn, E., & Simons, R. J., & Ten Cate, Th. J. (2010). Adding a design perspective to study learning environments in higher professional education. *The International Journal of Higher Education and Educational Planning*, Online First. Retrieved April 19, 2017, from https://www.researchgate.net/publication/225507740_Adding_a_design_perspective_to_study_learning_environments_in_higher_professional_education.

Chapter 11
Global Governance and the Role of Non-state Actors in Improving the Social and Economic Development of Growing Economies: A Conceptual Approach Using a Global Public Health Framework on Violence Prevention

Glendene Lemard-Marlow and Randolph Wilt

Abstract Small states and growing economies face a large number of challenges due to current and historical geopolitical forces and the various non-state actors that play a role in policymaking which have long-standing direct and indirect impacts on these societies' social and economic development. One underlying question is "on what level of governance—national, regional, local, or community level are non-state actors best equipped to support social and economic development?" This paper will seek to answer that question by examining the context in which non-state actors play a role in violence prevention—a key factor in the social and economic development of any nation—using a global public health approach. This paper will provide a conceptual framework utilizing the global ecological model of violence prevention and will analyze and discuss at what level of interaction can non-state actors in this arena best support the economic and social development of growing economies and small states that are prone to high rates of violence.

Keywords Violence prevention · Global public health · Small states
Growing economies · Global governance · Non-state actors

G. Lemard-Marlow (✉) · R. Wilt
Concordia University of Texas, Austin, TX 78726, USA
e-mail: glendene.lemard@concordia.edu; glemard@hsph.harvard.edu

R. Wilt
e-mail: Randolph.Wilt@concordia.edu

G. Lemard-Marlow
Harvard T.H. Chan School of Public Health, Boston, MA 02115, USA

S. A. Văduva et al. (eds.), *Civil Society: The Engine for Economic and Social Well-Being*, Springer Proceedings in Business and Economics,
https://doi.org/10.1007/978-3-319-89872-8_11

11.1 Introduction

Violence has been viewed as a global health challenge for over a decade. The seminal report by the World Health Organization published in 2002 detailed the different types of violence, their risk and protective factors, and steps that can be taken using an ecologic approach to prevent violence from occurring in the first place (Krug and World Health Organization 2002; Gamlin 2015; UN, World Health Organization 2014). This paper aims to shed light on the issue of violence using a global public health approach, in particular, how it affects the economic development of small and growing economies. The paper will also be using the ecologic model of violence prevention to address the question of, "on what level of global governance are non-state actors best suited to support civil society in its endeavor to create and sustain economic growth?" This paper is a concept paper drawing from a transdisciplinary lens in which violence, economics, politics, and the socioeconomic determinants of health interface with growing businesses, small states, international organizations, and nonprofit organizations. Furthermore, the paper will discuss the relevance of civil society and its importance in helping to reduce and prevent violence, and how a multilevel and multi-sectoral approach is not only recommended but also warranted, particularly if strides are to be made in reducing the negative impacts of violence from an economic development perspective.

First, this paper will outline a working definition of violence used by the World Health Organization (Krug and WHO 2002). Next, it will describe the different typologies of violence. It will further outline the economic impact of violence, especially in small growing economies and developing countries. Then follows a discussion on how the public health approach to violence is useful in understanding at what level of interaction are non-state actors best suited to deal with this problem. The paper will end with a holistic approach to the issue and a set of recommendations based on the utility of best practices currently established from a literature review from academic journals, as well as information gathered from nonprofit organizations, and country or regional reports from international organizations with member states that have reported on the issue of violence.

11.2 Violence: What Is It?

Theories on violence abound. From having a biological predisposition to being a perpetrator of violence to criminological perspectives on what constitutes deviance, violence has been studied in a variety of disciplines including biology (Masters and Gruter 1992; Koslowski 1999), criminology (Ellis and Walsh 2000), psychology (Walsh 2006), sociology (Sanderson 2001), and political science (Bloom and Dess 2003). The World Health Assembly in 1996 defined violence as, "the intentional use of physical force or power, threatened or actual, against oneself, another person, or against a group or community, that either results in or has a high likelihood of resulting in injury, death, psychological harm, maldevelopment, or deprivation" (Krug et al. 2002). In this realm, violence is about power and the abuse of power, as well as the intentional use of such power to the ill effects on an individual, family, community, whole societies, and nations. The key point being made is that violence is about intent and not whether the form of violence is considered **legal or illegal**. This is due to the fact that in some countries, certain forms of violence can be legal or normative, such as female genital mutilation (FGM), honor killings, corporal punishment, self-defense, and more (Abd 1997; Nayak 2016; Morag 2011). The legal status of violence in this paper matters less than the act of violence itself. The topic is more about the intentional use of force or power to the detriment of self, another, or a whole society.

Violence is further broken down into types of violence. These types can be self-directed, such as suicide or self-abuse, collective violence, such as civil war, gang warfare or other types of group violence typically stemming from sociological (including religious), economic or political motivations (Krug et al. 2002). The final typology of violence is interpersonal violence, which is the focus of this paper, and includes a variety of subsets such as youth violence, intimate partner violence, elder abuse, child abuse, violence in vulnerable populations, family violence, and more (Krug et al. 2002).

As scholars and practitioners have examined the issue of violence, evidence-based reports have established that the public health approach to violence offers a unique set of variables from which the underlying risk and protective factors related to violence can be determined. By doing so, programs can be created that delve into the root causes of the issue in order to reduce, control, or prevent violence from occurring in the first place (Krug et al. 2002). Violence may be fatal (homicide or suicide) or it may cause injury (physical, psychological, and emotional). The effects of violence on society—both fatal and nonfatal—have far-reaching economic implications, especially in small and growing economies.

11.3 The Public Health Approach to Violence Prevention

Violence similar to any other type of disease can be prevented. The public health approach is a systematic interdisciplinary approach which highlights the steps that can be taken to manage the issue of violence, especially since they can be caused by different factors (see Fig. 11.1). The first step in the approach is to define the problem and gather data on who is being a victim or a perpetrator of violence, what is being used when the act is being committed (brute force, guns, rope, etc.), where the violent act occurs, and when. By understanding these patterns using the tools of epidemiology, the problem is better defined and can be better understood (Surtees 2008; Mercy et al. 2003; Valenti et al. 2007). This requires systematic data collection and continued surveillance of violent activity. Next, the risk factors that promote an increase in violence, as well as the protective factors that allow for a decrease or prevention of violence also need to be identified. These factors will vary depending on the type of violence, country, demography of the population, levels of

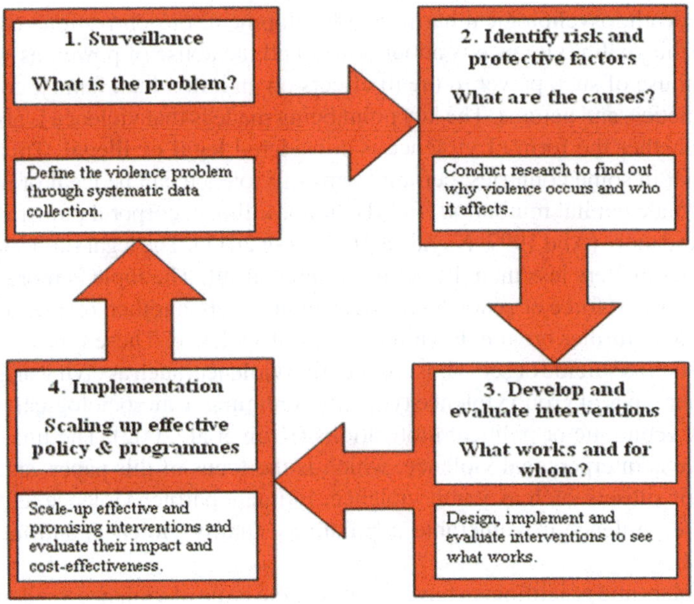

Fig. 11.1 The public health model on violence prevention (Mercy et al. 1993)

urbanization, and other factors including the quality of the data gathered (Meuleners et al. 2009; Patel and Burkle 2012; C. D. C. 2011). Once the risk and protective factors are identified, interventions can be designed and developed and then implemented. The expectation is that an effective program can be executed to affect policy change that can ultimately reduce and prevent violence. This requires continuous evaluation and re-evaluation of the problem.

The public health approach to violence reduction and prevention has been increasingly utilized. Studies have found that while some strategies are better than others, ultimately the public health approach is an effective approach to violence prevention (Spivak et al. 2014; McDaniel et al. 2014). When examining the issue in growing economies and developing countries with high rates of violence, the question becomes, at what point can non-state actors most effectively create positive change?

11.4 The Ecologic Model of Violence

The determinants of violence as noted above are gained from surveillance and understanding the risk and protective factors related to violence. Because there are different types of violence, the risk and protective factors may differ. However, as mentioned before, they are often interconnected if not intertwined. The ecologic model of violence presents another valuable and useful framework for understanding the determinants of violence and how best to prevent it. Later, another discussion on the role of

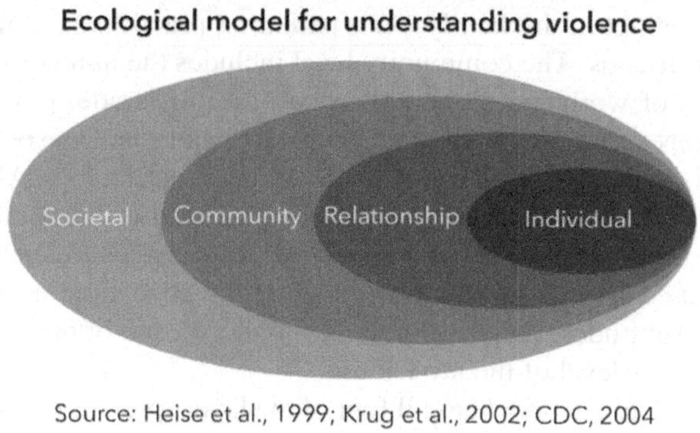

Fig. 11.2 Ecological model for understanding violence

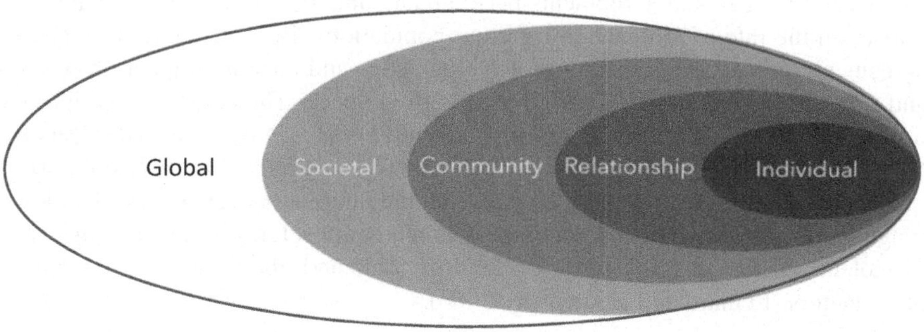

Fig. 11.3 The global ecological model for understanding violence. *Source* Lemard-Marlow

non-state actors and the use of this framework will provide insight on how violence can be prevented and the role of civil society in this process. Figure 11.2 illustrates the current ecologic model of violence. Figure 11.3 illustrates what Lemard-Marlow has coined the "global ecological model of violence", which adds an important layer to our understanding of how violence occurs and the factors that impact its risk and prevention.

This model for understanding the risk and protective factors related to violence is particularly useful when examining cases of interpersonal violence and self-directed violence. Interpersonal violence accounts for a large percentage of violence cases worldwide, compared with war and self-directed violence combined. Therefore, this figure is useful not just for collective violence or war, but for understanding how intertwined violent acts are within small and large communities. This figure shows four levels of violence and at each level, there are factors that influence violence victimization and/or perpetration. The individual level would include an individual's personal history, gender, age, income, level of education, psychological status, and whether or not there was any history of physical, emotional, or substance abuse. The relationship level includes family and peers and factors such as gender roles in a marriage, conflict in the family, poor parenting practices, and the influence of peer groups and friends. The community level includes the number of green spaces (for play), types of workplaces, the existence of a drug trade, poverty, transience of families, levels of employment, and whether or not there is social isolation or restricted versus unrestricted use of alcohol, among other factors. All of which, we conclude, impact the rate of violence. The societal level of the model features the larger systemic factors in society that have an impact on violence, such as the policies implemented on economic development, health, and education, as well as cultural norms and social attitudes. Policies that impact trade, the use of firearms, and alcohol all play a role at this level of the model, too.

The global ecological model has all four of the layers previously described. However, in addition to the societal level, Lemard-Marlow has added the global level to the model that incorporates such factors as the role of intergovernmental organizations and treaties and agreements between and among nation-states as having an impact on the rate of violence in different populations. Bilateral and multinational agreements influence the behavior of nation-states and have an impact on the risk and protective factors that are associated with violence. The actors on the international stage have had an influence on wars and violent crimes for decades, ranging from the Geneva Convention to the promotion of human rights for all. In our current globalizing world, the impact of decisions on the international stage have had long-ranging impacts on the state of violence within countries, for example, the high rates of violence in Jamaica as a result of the drug trade and illicit trade in guns among other factors (Lemard and Hemenway 2006).

11.5 Current State of Violence Worldwide

It has often been noted that more than 1.3 million people die every year as a result of violence in all the forms described above (Krug et al. 2002; UN WHO 2014). This number accounts for approximately 2.5% of global mortality. For people aged 15–44 years, violence is the fourth leading cause of death worldwide (UN WHO 2014). The report *Global Status Report on Violence Prevention 2014* which was commissioned by the World Health Organization, the United Nations Office on Drugs and Crime, and the United Nations Development Program provides information on 133 countries, which covers 6.1 billion people and represents about 88% of the world population. While response rates varied in different regions and countries, the report provides a snapshot of the current state of violence worldwide. An important note here is that non-state actors in different countries and regions also played a role in data collection to help with creating an understanding of this problem around the globe (UN WHO 2014).

Over the period 2000–2012, homicide due to violence was about 6.7 per 100, 000 population worldwide. Low- and middle-income countries had the highest rates of violence-related homicides with the region of the Americas having a rate of 28.5 homicides per 100,00 population, followed by the African region with a rate of 10.9

homicides per 100,00 population (UN WHO 2014). The lowest estimated rate of homicide worldwide is in low- and middle-income countries of the Western Pacific region with 2.1 homicides per 100,000 population. As of 2012, violence-related homicide was the third leading cause of death for males aged 15–44 years and accounted for 60% of the total cases of homicide in this demographic population (UN WHO 2014). As of 2014, one in every four children is physically abused, and one in every three women has been physically or sexually abused by an intimate partner in her lifetime (UN WHO 2014).

The reality, however, is that death from violence is only one aspect of the issue and is but a fraction of the health, social, and economic burdens to society that arise as a result of violence. According to the *Global Status Report on Violence Prevention 2014,* violence contributes to lifelong health burdens, especially for women and children, and can result in early death. Many of the leading causes of death, which include heart disease, stroke, and cancer, "are the result of victims of violence adopting behaviors such as smoking, the misuse of alcohol and other drugs, and in some instances, unsafe sex to cope with the effects of violence" (Catalá-Miñana et al. 2017). Concisely noted in the report, violence places a heavy strain on health and criminal justice systems. It places a strain on social and welfare services in society, and it negatively impacts the economic fabric of communities in general (UN WHO 2014).

The typologies of violence, while different, share underlying risk factors and inter-relationships that are important. Factors such as inadequate parenting, children suffering rejection, harsh physical or corporal punishment, sexual abuse, or those who witness violence at home are at greater risks of being victims and/or perpetrators of violence later in life. Yet, knowing the inter-relationships of the types of violence, only about 50% of countries who responded to the WHO survey (2016) reported having an integrated plan to address the multiple and interconnected types of violence. The synergies across types of violence create the need for non-state actors to be involved in different types of violence prevention activity at all levels of governance in order to address the issue as holistically and comprehensively as possible.

11.6 Violence, Economic Development, and Health

Violence has the ability to erode the economic fabric of society. Due to the negative health outcomes of violence, the economic development of small and growing economies can be severely hampered. Economic development and health were not always connected. During the 1970s and 1980s, economic growth was the primary focus of many countries and international actors. Structural adjustment programs were promising but failed to impact the growth and development of human capacity in society as the programs involved the reduction of subsidies and support for social and educational programs. Ultimately, the result was an indirect impact on the opportunities and freedoms that would enhance economic growth. The trickle-down effect did not work as well as anticipated. The 1990s focused more on health, or people-centered development, and having more involvement of civil society actors partaking in the decision-making regarding the needs of the country, the community, and families that may be vulnerable to poverty and other disadvantages.

Violence as any other disease, whether chronic or infectious, has a very strong negative impact on economic development. The WHO and the Centers for Disease Control and Prevention, along with other agencies and academics, have published reports and journal articles on the economic impact of violence. Small and growing economies and low- and middle-income countries suffer a greater economic burden of violence as they are typically grappling with the costs of infectious and chronic diseases as well. From a business point of view, violence is negative (though the growth of security forces and security guards may appear advantageous); the overall effect is vastly more destructive.

11.7 Non-state Actors and Global Governance

Traditionally, non-state actors including nonprofit organizations (NGOs), are typically expected to operate in the sectors of society that try to ameliorate problems such as homelessness, drug abuse, climate change, environmental pollution, natural and man-made disasters, and in some cases, domestic violence. However, similar to intergovernmental organizations (IGOs), NGOs are both pieces of governance and key actors in the international arena and the domestic arena playing a variety of roles (Karns and Mingst 2004). Global governance typically involves the role of IGOs as well as NGOs, which operate in a cooperative structure to deal with various issues and problems. NGOs and other non-state actors are typically private voluntary organizations with members that are either individuals or associations coming together for a common purpose (Karns and Mingst 2004). According to Karns, "NGOs are increasingly active today at all levels of human society and governance, from local or grassroots communities to national and international politics" (Karns and Mingst 2004, p. 8). She further notes that, "many national-level groups often called interest or pressure groups are now linked to counterpart groups in other countries through networks or federations" (Karns and Mingst 2004, p. 8). Likewise, international NGOs similar to IGOs may draw members from more than one country, they may be multifunctional or have a specific purpose, and they may be long-lasting and long-standing or formed on an ad hoc basis.

Non-state actors, especially NGOs, and their cooperative networks which have grown exponentially since the 1980s, have now become major factors in global governance at all levels all over the world with formal and informal networks and associations formed to deal with the subject matter(s) held in common. Karns states correctly that NGOs have become, "key sources of information and technical expertise on a wide variety of international issues," and they are, "key actors in raising awareness and helping to frame issues" (Karns and Mingst 2004, p.18). Another keynote from Karns is that NGOs can lobby for policy changes by states, IGOs, and multinational cooperation (Karns and Mingst 2004, p. 18). The ability to lobby for changes at the societal level shows the great value of international organizations in affecting change across the different sectors and levels of civil society. In violence prevention, this has been very useful as organizations such as the World Health Organization and the InterAmerican Development Bank have worked with governments and stakeholders in civil society to reduce the rate of violence especially in countries with small and growing economies (Alda et al. 2006; Jaitman and Compean 2015; Matzopoulos and Jabar 2017).

Other non-state actors include experts and epistemic communities from academia, think tanks, research institutes, private industries, and some from governmental agencies. Experts are often part of a transnational network or may be members of technical committees typically negotiating on behalf of an agenda or providing scientific evidence on an issue and helping to frame debates and discussions, and can propose specific solutions to issues raised.

The range of non-state actors include not only NGOs and experts, but social movements These can include informal coalitions, multi-stakeholder actors which are loose alliances made up of NGOs, IGOs, experts, professional associations, foundations, and even notable individuals. Multinational corporations have increased their role as non-state actors in global governance though they are private actors typically having a goal of making a profit. This departure from the typical perception of a non-state actor does not remove their relevance or importance in affecting the status of economic development, health, and the variety of issues that non-state actors are ordinarily involved in. Also, some non-state actors have more prominence than others depending on the types of budgets they have and their connections with other groups. Organizations such as the World Wildlife Fund, Save the Children, and Human Rights Watch are just a few of the easily recognizable non-state actors operating in the international arena.

What is of great value to consider is that there has been an exponential as well as accelerated growth of non-state actors and their influence on global governance since the 1970s. With increased globalization, access to information, integration of markets in different regions, and the breaking down of financial and national borders due to increased interdependence of nations, we have seen the growth of the power of non-state actors on state-level activities. Sovereign states are increasingly interacting with non-state actors, which can have both positive and negative impacts. Some of the more positive functions of non-state actors in global governance and other national governance functions include their ability to gather and publicize information, frame issues for public consumption, create and mobilize different networks, enhance public participation in different programs and projects, promote new norms, participate in global conferences in order to raise issues, and submit position papers or lobby for certain viewpoints or vulnerable populations.

The influence of non-state actors in global governance also has a range depending on the type and nature of the non-state actor in question. Many non-state actors lack the traditional type of influence in the international arena by virtue of not being sovereign states. They do not typically have military or police forces (though there are growing numbers of violent non-state actors affecting communities and whole nations in the twenty-first century). Unlike governments, they will have limited economic resources, and for many in the academic community, it is difficult to measure the effectiveness and the influence of NGOs and other non-state actors because of their large numbers, the diversity of the groups, and the overall lack of deliberate systematic steps at data collection on the activities of non-state actors. Even though it can be difficult to measure the influence and effectiveness of NGOs and other non-state actors as a group, this can still be done in targeted ways. For example, this can be achieved by examining the work of a non-state actor in its field of relevance and by analyzing its strategies and programs as well as evaluating the impact it has had in its area of service or research.

11.8 Non-state Actors and Violence Prevention

A typical perspective on non-state actors in the field of violence tends to deal with peace and security, collapsed states riddled by civil war, and intrastate conflict such as genocide and ethnic cleansing resulting in humanitarian crises such as famine and disease, hunger, and death. Many forms of collective violence from gangs and armed militia groups operate outside of state authority but can also operate with state authority. There has been a recent geopolitical shift in the political sphere that human security needs to take precedence over the security of governments and states. Because of the complexity of humanitarian crises and the use of weapons of mass destruction including chemical, biological, and nuclear warfare, as well as terrorism, IGOs have taken a strong role in trying to have member states become more proactive in their countries and regions to reduce violence. NGOs and non-state actors in the security and peace framework often work in tandem with IGOs. Peace operations become executed, multilateral agreements are made on countering terrorism, arms control, limiting the proliferation of nuclear weapons, improving collective security, creating sanctions with trade through multinational corporations and attempts at interventions to enforce peace and stabilize governments (Gentile 2011; Kellenberger 2009)

In a war-torn world, it would be easier to focus this paper on the types of operations of non-state actors in this particular sphere of violence. However, when we depart from the collective type of violence like war and genocide and civil conflict and examine types of violence such as interpersonal violence or suicide and use the lens of the public health approach, a different picture becomes formulated on the role of non-state actors in the area of violence prevention. Because of the health effects of violence and the pervasiveness of the less obvious types of violence such as gender-based violence or child abuse resulting in emotional and psychological effects, efforts to reduce, prevent, and mitigate the effects of violence must occur at all levels of society. The global ecological model for understanding violence (Fig. 11.3) allows us to frame the issue in a manner better suited to see how best non-state actors can assist in the prevention of violence altogether and help to promote human and economic development in societies with growing economies, or are small states with high rates of violence.

Non-state actors have already been playing a strong role in violence prevention worldwide. Important to note is that the rate of their growth as significant actors in this arena has been fast and continues to increase. The United Nations and its affiliates and the World Health Organization have partnered with non-state actors on all levels to create a network that is playing a key role in the advancements of effective violence prevention strategies in different countries worldwide. Partnership is key and this concept has been implemented in varying ways, depending on the country, region, opportunity, and timing, among other factors. Public private partnerships abound, multilevel and multi-stakeholder affiliations implement various types of programs, the Violence Prevention Alliance connects with NGOs, experts, think tanks, governments, civil society organizations, and other international organizations that have implemented programs on various levels in different countries for different types of violence prevention. While this paper has and will continue to make references to war, civil conflict, genocide, and other humanitarian crises, it will primarily focus on interpersonal violence which affects our productive members of society, occurs in non-failed democratic states, and has a destabilizing effect on the economic development of small and growing economies.

11.9 Non-state Actors and Global Governance: More to Be Done

It is known now that violence of all types whether self-directed, collective, or interpersonal are all strongly associated with social, economic, and political determinants such as poor rule of law, weak governments, gender and income inequality/inequity, unemployment, social change, norms, and limited educational opportunities. Because there are also crosscutting risk factors associated with the different types of violence, there needs to be a sustainable evidence-based approach if any violence prevention efforts are to be effective and long term. For any plan to be effective it is asserted here and reiterated in a variety of reports as cited above, that the plan or program under development must be based on the input of a wide range of actors, including governmental and nongovernmental. The mechanisms for violence control and prevention but be *coordinated* at the local and national levels so that collaboration between sectors can occur and be sustained allowing resources to be utilized more effectively.

11.10 Recommendations: Non-state Actors and Violence Prevention

The *Global Status Report on Violence Prevention 2014* details various ways in which non-state actors and the multiple stakeholders that they represent can help to reduce and prevent violence, particularly interpersonal violence. This section highlights the conclusion that non-state actors need to be involved in all levels of global governance—the regional level, the national level, the community level, the local level, the family level, and the individual level—if they are to be successful in reducing and preventing violence and helping promote the economic development of small and growing economies. As a reminder, these economies experience a negative impact as violence affects their prospects for economic growth and stability (UN WHO 2014).

The WHO and its affiliates, including international partners at the state and the non-state actor levels, have identified seven "best buy" strategies, six of which focus on preventing violence and one focused on response efforts (UN WHO 2014). The aim and expectation are that the strategies can reduce multiple types of violence and reduce the likelihood of both victimization and perpetration. The following is a list of these practices and the type of non-state actor involvement that would help to achieve these goals. Additionally, we see at what level of global governance this action would entail. The survey found that even with investments in prevention programs, countries that were doing so were not doing so at a level based on the needs, the scale, and/or the severity of the problem.

11.10.1 Data Collection (National, State, Local, and Individual Levels)

Violence prevention is evidence-based and so systematically collecting sound empirical data on violence from national registries, police departments, and creating passive and active surveillance systems is key. The data collected needs to be uniformed and compatible with other statistics (and the units that collect them) for comparative analysis reasons within and between countries. One recommendation is that data-collection systems need to be modified based on evaluation results (of program effectiveness). In particular, they note that entities involved must assess the cost-effectiveness of multiple stakeholders and ensure compliance with specific stakeholders' needs (UN WHO 2014). This includes using surveys, which can be implemented by non-state actors at the individual, local, community, and national levels of governance. Conducting an audit of policy and legal support for data collection and establishing an information working group using the non-state actor expert community among other stakeholders are also extremely useful for the development of successful violence prevention strategies.

11.10.2 Develop Safe and Stable and Nurturing Relationships Between Children and Their Parents and Caregivers (Individual, Family, and Community Levels)

This recommendation supports the importance of the family and the value placed on having strong and nurturing relationships that can increase the protective factors related to violence prevention. Programs targeting children and or parents, the family unit itself, or the community in which the family resides can all have an impact on reducing the rate of violence in the society overall. By improving the protective factors, children are more likely to have stability and thereby more resilience from becoming either victims or perpetrators of violence in the long run (UN WHO 2014).

11.10.3 Develop Life Skills in Children and Adolescents (Individual, Family, and Community Levels)

This recommendation highlights the importance of resilience in children and adolescents who can be prone to different types of risk for violent behavior or violent assault. Children and adolescents may be vulnerable to rates of violence due to their age and developmental status. Life skills are not only taught in homes but can be taught in schools and through community programs specifically targeting at-risk youth and adolescents. The importance of an intervention with this demographic population increases the potential of breaking the cycle of violence if it has already begun, depending on the home as well as increasing the protective factors that can lead to resilience against future perpetration of or victimization as a result of violence (UN WHO 2014).

11.10.4 Reduce the Availability of the Harmful Use of Alcohol (Global, Societal, and Community Levels)

The main approach to reducing the harmful use of alcohol may come in the forms of excise taxes, regulating the sale of alcohol to minors, and increasing regulations that can help to monitor the sale of alcohol. Other programs include providing support services for people and families already impacted by the use of violence. Regulations that can impact the availability of alcohol and are potential for misuse can arise at the international level with countries supporting international and global treaties to reduce the use and availability of alcohol especially to minors. Educating children and youth, families, and whole societies on the risk of alcohol use and abuse is important but more efforts are needed at the societal level and the need for the enforcement of the availability and potential use and abuse of alcoholic beverages (UN WHO 2014).

11.10.5 Reduce Access to Guns and Knives (Global, National, Community, and Family Levels)

While gun control efforts may be controversial in some countries, the current recommendation to reduce access to guns and knives occurs at all levels of society and can make a positive difference in the reduction of violence across the board. On a global scale, the international trade in small arms and the illicit trade in firearms and light weapons are areas of importance when aiming to impact the rate of violence. The United Nations and other international organizations work in this arena but more needs to be done. At the national level, countries still need to promote legislation that can reduce the illicit access to guns which have higher rates of fatality than other forms of weapons used in violent attacks. At the community and family levels, neighborhood watch and educating children on the risks of the use of guns and knives in altercations can provide some relief, but the easy access to guns and knives is a matter that still needs to be addressed at the national levels. The proliferation of guns in society and how to effectively address the use of guns in acts of violence is a question that we continue to grapple with across countries and remains on the international agenda on violence prevention and safety promotion (UN WHO 2014).

11.10.6 Promote Gender Equality to Prevent Violence Against Women (Global, National, Community, and Family Levels)

The need to protect women from acts of violence is not new. Women are a vulnerable population especially if they are pregnant, caretaking children, and dependent on a partner or spouse for income and support. As mentioned above, one in every three women has reported an act of violence occurring against them in the past 5 years and this type of violence can be underreported depending on the society and the rules that govern the actions of women. Efforts to promote gender equality are on the international agenda and in global health, this remains on the radar as we continue to systematically gather data and try to compare data on violence against women in different parts of the world. The promotion of gender equality also points to the need of more countries to implement regulations that can prevent discrimination against women in gaining employment, having a political say in government and having access to health services as needed. The investment in women carries intergenerational positive rewards and impacts the business community, the socioeconomic development of growing economies, and helps to break what is otherwise a cycle of violence, if violence is already occurring (UN WHO 2014).

11.10.7 Change Cultural and Social Norms that Support Violence (National, Community, and Family Levels)

The need to change cultural and social norms that support acts of violence is paramount. Lessons learned over the years have shown that if a culture supports the use of violence as a method of correction or a form of control, then violence can pervade the very fabric of society including at the family and the individual levels. Acts of violence become normative behavior even when other measures could be equally effective and certainly less harmful such as mediation. International organizations call for societies to develop programs aimed at reducing the values that support violence and increasing values and norms that promote peaceful means to conflict resolution. Conflicts will exist, but the manner in which they are addressed can be adjusted. This requires legislative efforts, community programs aimed at educating populations on peaceful options to end conflicts. Local governments will need to work to gain the trust of citizens and create programs that can keep victims and survivors safe, especially in violence-prone communities (UN WHO 2014).

11.10.8 Identify Victims and Have Strong Care and Support Programs (National, Community, Family, Individual Levels)

The survivors of violence need care and support. If shelters and other programs to help victims of violence are not in place, the return to violence would be imminent. Not all acts of violence go reported and so having hotlines and programs in place to screen for violence while having safe spaces if affected by violence are paramount. International organizations call governments to action. At the national level, investments in such programs need to be made. In areas where there is strong support for survivors of violence, the rate of recidivism can be lowered for perpetrators. As well, the likelihood of a survivor returning to a cycle of violence can be reduced as well. These levels of support occur at all levels of society (UN WHO 2014).

11.11 Conclusions

Ultimately, violence is an issue that pervades society in all forms. As noted above, it is valuable to utilize resources at all levels of society in order for any comprehensive effort at violence prevention to be successful. Violence weaves a complex web. The factors that influence the rise in the rate of violence occur at all levels of the ecologic model of violence including at the global level. The response to violence prevention, therefore, entails the need to incorporate actors at all levels of society. The ecologic model of violence shows that violence risk and perpetration occur at all levels. The organizations involved in violence reduction and prevention are addressing the issue at all levels of society. The global ecological model of violence prevention points out the need to incorporate actors in the international arena and their work over the years as having both a positive and a negative impact on violence, but must be included in the dialog on violence prevention.

To answer the question "on what level of global governance can non-state actors improve the social and economic development of growing economies" and using violence prevention as the conceptual approach to address this, we see that all levels of society are impacted by non-state actors and violence prevention efforts must take into account all the levels of the global ecological model of understanding violence in order to be effective. At the national level, there is the need to strengthen data collection in order to reveal the true nature of the extent of the problem with violence. National plans for violence must be data-driven and comprehensive. Integrating efforts on other platforms is also key. More than ever, it is also vital to enforce legislation that can protect survivors of violence and reduce the perpetration of violence.

At the regional and international levels, the global violence prevention agenda can be strengthened. Being able to set baseline targets and to track progress within and between countries would be very useful. Also, it becomes very important that we increase collaboration between international organizations, states, and agencies of civil society that donate funds to help with the issue of violence. The recommendations listed above are areas in which research has been done and still needs to continue in order to solidify our efforts at violence prevention across the globe. It is clear that the international community and non-state actors have worked hard and deliberately at trying to gather data from societies all over the world and to create consensus on the efforts that are needed in order to break the cycle of violence.

Violence is kaleidoscopic in how it can pervade society. The public health approach and the ecological model of violence are very helpful tools in helping to strategize violence prevention efforts. Violence prevention is more cost-effective than dealing with the effects of violence after the fact and small growing economies are in need of cost-effective solutions given limited resources. The global ecological model of violence illustrates the global level of interaction that can create both risks and protective factors on the rate of violence. It also illustrates that violence prevention must address all levels of society and that non-state actors, especially intergovernmental organizations; international nonprofit organizations must interact with all levels of civil society in any country or community in order to continue to reduce the rates of violence across the world. The recommendations listed above illustrate the need for action and future research on how to effectively integrate the strategies needed and how to get national governments and the other arms of civil society to work in a comprehensive manner to produce long-term positive results on this important topic.

Acknowledgements The authors would like to thank Rebecca Woolston, Lucy Krips, and Shelly Samuels for their assistance.

References

Abd el Hadi, A. (1997). A step forward for opponents of female genital mutilation in Egypt. *The Lancet* (London, England), *349*(9045), 129–130.

Alda, E., Buvini, M., & Lamas, J. (2006). Neighbourhood peacekeeping: The Inter-American development bank's violence reduction programs in Colombia and Uruguay. *Civil Wars, 8*(2), 197–214.

Bloom, R., & Dess, N. (Eds.). (2003). *Evolutionary psychology and violence: A primer for policymakers and public policy advocates*. Westport: Praeger.

Catalá-Miñana, A., Lila, M., Oliver, A., Vivo, J., Galiana, L., & Gracia, E. (2017). Contextual factors related to alcohol abuse among intimate partner violence offenders. *Substance Use and Misuse, 52*(3), 294–302.

Centers for Disease Control and Prevention. (2011). *Youth risk behavior surveillance system: Selected 2011 national health risk behaviors and health outcomes by sex*. n.p.: Centers for Disease Control and Prevention.

Ellis, L., & Walsh, A. (2000). *Criminology: A global perspective*. Boston: Allyn and Bacon.

Gamlin, J. (2015). Violence and homicide in Mexico: A global health issue. *The Lancet, 9968,* 605.

Gentile, P. (2011). Humanitarian organizations involved in protection activities: A story of soul-searching and professionalization. *International Review Of the Red Cross, 93*(884), 1165–1191.

Jaitman, L., & Compean, R. (2015). Promoting evidence-based crime prevention policies in Latin America and the Caribbean. *Translational Criminology, 9,* 14–19.

Karns, M. P., & Mingst, K. A. (2004). *International organizations: The politics and processes of global governance*. Boulder, Colo: Lynne Rienner Publishers.

Kellenberger, J. (2009). The ICRC's response to internal displacement: strengths, challenges and constraints. *International Review Of the Red Cross, 91*(875), 475–490.

Koslowski, P. (1999). *Sociobiology and bioeconomics: The theory of evolution in biological and economic theory*. Berlin: Springer.

Krug, E, & World Health Organization. (2002). *World report on violence and health*. Geneva: WHO.

Krug, E., Mercy, J., Dahlberg, L., & Zwi, A. (2002). The world report on violence and health. *Lancet*, *360*(9339), p. 1083. Psychology and Behavioral Sciences Collection.

Lemard, G., & Hemenway, D. (2006). Violence in Jamaica: An analysis of homicides 1998–2002. *Injury Prevention* 12(1), 15–18.

Masters, R., & Gruter, M. (1992). *The sense of justice: Biological foundations of law*. Newbury Park, CA: Sage.

Matzopoulos, R., & Jabar, A. (2017). Reducing the burden of injury in high-risk communities. *SA Crime Quarterly, 59,* 47–57.

McDaniel, D., Logan, J., & Schneiderman, J. (2014). Supporting gang violence prevention efforts: A public health approach for nurses. *Online Journal Of Issues In Nursing, 19*(1), 1.

Mercy, J., Krug, E., Dahlberg, L., & Zwi, A. (2003). Violence and health: The United States in a global perspective. *American Journal of Public Health, 93*(2), 256.

Mercy, J., et al. (1993). Public health policy for preventing violence. *Health Affairs, 12*(4), 7–29.

Meuleners, L., Lee, A., & Hendrie, D. (2009). Effects of demographic variables on mental illness admission for victims of interpersonal violence. *Journal Of Public Health, 31*(1), 162–167.

Morag, T. (2011). Religious tradition and the corporal punishment of children: A Comparison of the American and Israeli legal systems. *International Journal Of Law, Policy and the Family, 25*(3), 338–364.

Nayak, B. (2016). 'Honour killing' In Haryana: A socio-legal perspective. *International Journal Of Multidisciplinary Approach and Studies, 3*(5), 25–33.

Patel, R., & Burkle, F. (2012). Rapid urbanization and the growing threat of violence and conflict: a 21st century crisis. *Prehospital and Disaster Medicine, 27*(2), 194–197.

Sanderson, S. (2001). *The evolution of human sociality: A Darwinian conflict perspective*. Lanham, MD: Rowman & Littlefield Publishers.

Spivak, H., Jenkins, E., VanAudenhove, K., Kelly, M., Lee, D., & Iskander, J. (2014). CDC grand rounds: A public health approach to prevention of intimate partner violence. *MMWR Recommendations and Reports, 63*(2), 38–41.
Surtees, R. (2008). Traffickers and trafficking in Southern and Eastern Europe. *European Journal Of Criminology, 5*(1), 39–68.
UN World Health Organization (WHO). (2014). *Global status report on violence prevention 2014*. Geneva: World Health Organization.
Valenti, M., Ormhaug, C. M., Mtonga, R. E., & Loretz, J. (2007). Armed violence: A health problem, a public health approach. *Journal of Public Health Policy, 4*, 389.
Walsh, A. (2006). Evolutionary psychology and criminal behavior. In J. Barkow (Ed.), *Missing the revolution: Darwinism for social scientists*. Oxford: Oxford University Press.

Chapter 12
Romanian Hospitality Degree Graduates: Perceptions and Attitudes Among Industry Professionals

Joseph Takacs III, Sebastian A. Văduva and Robert Miklo

Abstract The customer experience is the lifeline of all hospitality providers and therefore requires special attention to the exact talent domains that are necessary for competitive existence in the highly fragmented marketplace. Robust training and continuing education are necessary elements to maintain employee readiness and competitiveness in most industries and business sectors. Understanding the most critical needs for operational improvement, aligned with the components that determine good and bad service, is critical touch point for hospitality managers.

Keywords Romanian hospitality · Hospitality training · Service sector
Customer service

12.1 Introduction

In business, we have come to prefer emails to phone calls, text messaging over personal sales calls and computer time to trade shows and travel. Emails and text messaging have become a necessity in our business and social lives. Hospitality service providers must be adept at leveraging the value and impact of these communication and data exchange tools, both those based on technology and those based on relationships, and understand when and where best to employ each. Those companies whose employees can deliver true customer service will capture the most market

J. Takacs III
University of Florida, Gainesville, FL, USA
e-mail: joetakacs@themvpservices.com

S. A. Văduva (✉)
Emanuel University of Oradea, Oradea, Romania
e-mail: sebastianvaduva@emanule.ro

R. Miklo
The Academy of Economic Studies in Bucharest, Bucharest, Romania
e-mail: robert.miklo@gmail.com

S. A. Văduva et al. (eds.), *Civil Society: The Engine for Economic and Social Well-Being*, Springer Proceedings in Business and Economics,
https://doi.org/10.1007/978-3-319-89872-8_12

share. The increasingly competitive service sector is always looking for employees who can do just that, perform well while providing a superior level of service quality.

Lashley (2007) suggested that, in the context of hospitality interaction, hosts (service providers) should understand and satisfy customer needs and expectations, using appropriate hosting performances and delivery transactions. This suggestion indicates elements of the experience between customers and host employees influence consumer perceptions of hospitality, despite the focus on the tangible product and service provided. In other words, what matters is equally about how the product, or service, is delivered, as it is about the product or service. The challenge, then, is how to understand and train hospitality service industry employees, based on the many varying perspectives and expectations of many different people from different cultures.

To meet new demands of customers' service expectations, practitioners must create an environment for and with employees that set up employees and the organization to perform successfully. Kini and Hobson (as cited in Whitney 2010) remarked that the quality of services depends on an employee's commitment, satisfaction, involvement and morale. One area of increasing concern is the ubiquity of technology and our dependence on it. While technology improves the availability of information and communication, it also makes it easier to distance oneself from the actual person. According to MacKay (as cited in Brudney 2007), a primary message repeated in many past articles has been concern over service providers being an entirely new generation of people and especially hospitality sales professionals and service providers who have mastered the art of technology-based selling, while forsaking the timeless skills required in relationship-based selling. 'Only a computer wants to do business with another computer. People respond to people' (MacKay, as cited in Brudney 2007, p. 76).

Service is about people. Employees are customers also, and there is a link between employee satisfaction and the service concept that has a direct impact on the customer satisfaction of consumers. This impact affects customer loyalty, which in turn influences revenue growth. Lastly, revenue growth fuels the internal service of the organization. Understanding an employee's level of satisfaction, commitment, involvement, and self-esteem, gives managers and strategists mean to create a favourable environment, where links in the service profit chain work to the advantage of the service provider (Crawford and Hubbard 2007).

12.2 Employees Training as a System to Improve Customer Service

Surveys of the hospitality industry have revealed that up to 75% of employees have received no job-related training since starting the job, just under 50% of small firms engaged their employees in training and 85% of hospitality employers surveyed provided some training for some employees. The variance in these figures might represent a wide and complex variety of practices and attitudes to training. Regardless of rationales used to justify not providing training, hospitality service leaders must realize that employees provide the service to the customers and must be equipped and prepared to do just that (Crawford and Hubbard 2007).

With tourism/hospitality being the number one rated industry around the world, regarding revenues, as well as employment, a question often asked is whether there exist hospitality-specific training programmes that allow employers to find new staff and train existing staff to possess competencies that the hospitality industry believes employees need. According to the World Travel and Tourism Council (WTTC) (2007), the United States' travel and tourism industry are expected to generate $524.5 billion dollars of economic activity. This growth is expected to add over 15 million new jobs in 2007 and $851.0 billion in revenue, with 16.1 million jobs by 2017 (World Travel and Tourism Council 2007).

At the same time, education and training fail because they are fewer than 1,000 secondary hospitality and tourism training (HTE) programmes located throughout the United States (Riegel and Dallas 2006). Because of the growth in these programmes the related revenue and employment opportunities, not just in the United States, but around the world, the tourism industry should enjoy a wide and diverse field of qualified applicants from which to choose. However, when it comes to formal institutional type training, one question is whether this institutional training is preparing the workforce and meeting needs of the industry.

In many cases, industry professionals claim what potential employees bring to the workforce is way behind (Goodman and Sprague 1991). Learning is changing more rapidly than ever and customers are constantly changing. Consequently, to sustain success, relevant competencies must also evolve. It is critical that institutional faculty and industry professionals work together to ensure what is being taught is relevant for future employees to enter the workforce and be a successful part thereof.

12.3 Training for the Right Competencies and with the Appropriate Impact

Competency by a specific profession or industry is determined by what the workplace and companies need (Council on Education for Public Health 2006). According to Tas (1988), the talents and skills needed to perform a given job are, in fact, called competencies. Brophy and Kiely (2002) expanded on this by including attitude as a competency. The United States Department of Education defines competencies as a set or group of skills and knowledge of the workforce; therefore, competencies should be what students and graduates possess as they leave institutions and enter the workforce.

Models and programmes designed around specific competencies are needed tools. Once industry insiders, managers and senior leaders determine the actual skills and abilities required to perform a specific job and once universities and educators understand required competencies, they can get them into groups, enabling employers to quickly assess where an individual excels, or fails, in a skill set.

In the U.S. dating back to the 1980s, the hospitality industry began to look for and define competencies and skills needed for college students once they graduate. As a result, a significant work and learning exists on this topic exists having been created and tested over the past 20 years. Most of the studies centred, however, on either the hotel industry by itself or the overall hospitality industry, with a few exceptions focusing solely on the food service industry (Horng and Lu 2006; Okeiyi et al. 1994).

The question in assessing training needs of the tourism and hospitality industry is understanding the viability of employability. Employability-linked training and learning are likely to continue to be subjected to simple outcomes, such as the percentage of college students that graduate and then get a full-time job, or the number of workers entering the workforce prepared with the skills needed, within a specified period, for example. In the United Kingdom, for example, 'first-destination returns' are tracked after only 6 months as key factors in determining employability. There is considerable pressure from government and funding circles to 'keep employability simple'. In effect, employability is being de facto equated with the gaining and retaining of fulfilling work (Hillage and Pollard 1998).

Two problems surface with such crude measures. First, the insistence that somehow the ability to or actual use of a graduate in the workforce is a measure of rate. Second, the tendency to slide into a view that employability is an *institutional* or somehow the schools resulting achievement rather than the propensity of the *individual* themselves actually look for and to get a job, meaning that job attainment is more than training in some cases and involves personality and other people-related skills that are on display at the time of hire.

However, the real question over the long term might well be whether more formal institutional training, as compared to on the job training, leads to better employees for the workplace and gives both the individual and the company a competitive advantage in the marketplace. Ultimately, it is employers who use to their advantage the skills of 'employability' into an actual job within the company that will better and more quickly find those employees that are ideally suited to a people-oriented industry. Employers' recruitment procedures on a formal or rational level will create a substantiation of the desired attributes, more than likely on a case-by-case basis. In this case, the quantitative employment rates of those with some form of hospitality-specific training may be seen as an indicator of employability and indirectly, or otherwise.

However, there exist a bevy of factors that are in play in the employment process, irrespective of training opportunities that might exist specific to hospitality (Harvey 2001). They include:

1. *Type of training platform and institution*. There is a definite 'pecking order' of institutions. Some institutions have higher employment rates, simply because of their reputation rather than how well students develop. However, in the long run, profitability and performance would tend to eliminate institutions that, in fact,

were not producing trained potential employees with the skills needed for the respective job.

2. *The mode of study*. Is there, for example, a differentiation of part-time and full-time students, wherein part-time students might be already working in the hospitality industry. Further, some training institutions offer on the job learning, as part of the curriculum.
3. *Where the training is and where the students live*. Not all employees, for various reasons, are mobile. Institutions also graduate far more students than the 'local' economy can employ; therefore, students often return to their homes. Some employers are wary, for various reasons, of employing graduates from parts of the country.
4. *The subject of study*. There are statistically proven variations: (i) in employment rates of trainees from different skill sets (Purcell et al. 1999), (ii) skill differences in training and employment, and (iii) differences in the type of job that is desirable. Many learners also undertake some form of entrepreneurship for at least part of their time (Blackwell and Harvey 1999).
5. *Previous work experience*. Prior experience is a major consideration and driver for many recruiters, especially smaller companies. Naturally, experience only exists as a result of previous work, whether a previous full-time job or on a part-time basis by potential employees while in some form of organized learning. An experience that is, often, independent of the institution of study or the training facility. However, companies and recruiters are increasingly drawn to potential employees wherein work experience was part of their curriculum of study (Harvey et al. 1997; Harvey et al. 1992).
6. *Age*. Potential employees face discrimination by recruiters based on their age (Harvey et al. 1997; Purcell et al. 1999).
7. *Race and ethnicity*. Although we are led to believe that in many circles, the level of discrimination against 'ethnic minorities' is reduced, some studies reveal direct bias in recruiting procedures, and it is unlikely that this is a negligible factor. This factor would also vary widely across cultures more so in an analysis of international hiring.
8. *Gender*. Females still face the 'glass ceiling' or cap on the level of seniority they can achieve and are underrepresented at senior levels in organizations. However, female recruitment is often in larger proportions than males in many organizations (Harvey et al. 1997).
9. *Social class*. The social class that one belongs to continues to alter employment opportunities, due largely to the entanglement of training opportunities, and experience and opportunities for extracurricular activity and social networks that develop (Brennan et al. 1996).

In the end, it might be that the 'employability' rate is a factor of the training afforded students to prepare them for on the job training. In other words, teaching them to learn how to learn. It is, at least, somewhat impossible and unrealistic to suggest that hospitality-specific training institutions can know and teach people-specific expertise across broad spectrums of companies, cultures and marketplace activities.

Rather, they should teach components of hospitality that in varying degrees, transcend all companies, such as attitude, finance and accounting, marketing principles, social responsibility, communication and human resource attributes needed regardless of the ultimate job.

12.4 The Training Needs of Romanian Hospitality Industry

In the post-communist economy of Romania, an examination of readiness levels of students entering the hospitality workforce is paramount to service providers seeking to compete on a global stage and in a now free market exchange. Prior studies examined management perceptions of innovation, the subsequent implication of technology and ultimate indicators of success. The value proposition perception among guests emerged as being one of the critical components when factoring in customer acquisition and retention (Iorgulescu and Ravar 2013).

Romania employment statistic, at 43% in the hospitality sector, lags far behind the European Union's percentage of 70%. Cultural influence plays a large role in the readiness level of individuals to apply new learning; therefore, further examination across age, gender, and levels of prior experience and education will provide insights into workforce training grouping.

A 2013 study of 31 European countries was conducted by Ernst and Young, on behalf of the Brewers of Europe, to determine an assessment of economic contribution from the hospitality sector. Romania was identified in this study as having seen strong growth between 2004 and 2008, because of accession into the EU, as well as maintaining lower tax assessments. However, from 2008 to 2010, an economic downturn and lower disposable income resulted in a tourism drop of 22%. The 2009 recession impacted gross domestic product in Romania (GDP) by 15% and increased the tax rate from 19 to 24%, further exacerbating limitations of growth, resulting in only 1% growth overall, from 2000 to 2010.

Restaurants and bars command the largest hospitality presence in Romania; however, hotels and canteens employ the largest percentage, which makes sense, because of the staff requirements of hotels and catering services. However, shifts within the labour code allow employers directly manage flexible demand; although, argued in the short term, might also increase unemployment and over the long term, economic recovery will create jobs. From 2000 to 2010, the Romanian hospitality sector outpaced GDP, the hospitality turnover index and the national and hospitality employment index.

Technology and political transformation continue to reshape the market and specific economies related to the hospitality industry. Adina (2009) recommended managers maintain a willingness to invest in digital technologies, as solid employee training is more likely to succeed in hospitality sectors. Western market hospitality firms have invested heavily in technology to maintain a competitive market position, including enticements towards Central and Eastern European citizens who are now able to travel freely. Before exiting communist rule, Romania entertained tourists from other communist countries but now, must compete for their continued patronage, as opportunities now exist for those travellers to experience Western attractions as well as competing for European destinations.

From a national perspective, improved customer experience supports retention of neighbouring post-communist travellers, while targeting Western travellers at a rate that outpaces potential losses; thus, potentially adding tourism, commerce and tax revenues to the national economy. Hospitality/tourism, as a contributor to local economies, varies from country to country and, in many cases, is also governed by local provinces, regions or municipalities. Those investing and marketing properly can secure enhanced tax revenues from outside visitation, allowing for job growth and commerce gains.

Policies play a major role in the creation of opportunities designed specifically to encourage tourism and hospitality trade, as was evident in the Romanian internal battle to construct Dracula Park, to capitalize on folklore and Western fascination with the 1897 Bram Stoker novel. Internal and external politics surfaced opposition from UNESCO, Green Peace and the European Parliament, for various and individual concerns, not too far removed from the authentic versus global debate (Light 2007). Alignment between policymakers and investor is essential and typically requires identifying mutual incentives. Economic growth with sufficient and reasonable tax coding can serve to incentivize both politicians and business investors and is incorporated into a national economic strategy, with policies in place to protect both.

Over the past 6 years, the hospitality industry, worldwide, when factoring in travel and tourism reached $7.60 trillion, with a compounded annual growth rate of 8.1%; thus, making this industry a solid investment and employment target (Statista 2017). Romania has experienced a 3-year consecutive drop in GDP, as well as employment; however, a segment shift of education from industrial, to service, has increased by 12%, respectively. Predominantly an agricultural industry, Romania's cultural influence placed a lower premium on service sector education before the 1989 communist exit; however, educators acknowledged the need for shifting focus and within the past 5 years, thus increasing the service curriculum.

12.5 Conclusions

Education is important, as it supports the development of the hospitality sector in Romania while helping to close the gap in economic contribution. Choi et al. (2000) identified other European countries as having only 7% of the total hotel rooms and employees, indicating a significant upside in growth, as Eastern European countries also hold only 6% of the world population. In a post-communist economy, open travel borders and aggressive tourism marketing, supported by abled service providers in Romania, support the need for additional market development and industry study to better compete with Western countries and competing for prior Eastern bloc countries.

As Romania seeks to achieve a stronger service sector role in the overall economy, preparedness for success should be measured, managed and maintained from the perspective of those operating within this industry and more specifically, within this geography. Tourism, hospitality and typical service sectors play a significant role in creating and developing the national economy. Like many of other countries within Central and Eastern Europe, Romania also struggled with transition pains from a somewhat divided citizenry. Even before communist influence, many Eastern European cultural and political elitist held closer nationalist aspirations that, after the 1989 Autumn of Nations, were quickly reasserted. This pre-communist conflict between the intelligentsia and national elitists clash over the post-communist redevelopment, in which international globalization and technology now play a more important role in the debate, was examined by Korkut (2006). Romania, like other CEE countries, needed to get it right if it was to compete on a global scale successfully. Education and educational reform have also been important areas of post-communism transition. The move from state employment, to privatization, is more difficult for unskilled and undereducated members of society. Additionally, in the first post-communist decade, Romania experienced an economic crisis, changes in social structures and a decrease in student population, from 24 to 20% (Tascu et al. 2002). Open borders and low pay created a vacuum of potential workforce as many Romanians left the country for employment in more developed countries offering increased pay.

References

Adina, B. C. (2009). The influence in Romanian hospitality industry of small medium-sized firms and their specific means to improve performance. *Annals of Faculty of Economics*, *4*(1), 576–580.

Blackwell, A., & Harvey, L. (1999). *Destinations and reflections: Careers of British art, craft and design graduates*. Birmingham: Centre for Research into Quality.

Brennan, J., Kogan, M., & Teichler, U. (Eds.). (1996). *Higher education and work*. London: Jessica Kingsley.

Brophy, M., & Kiely, T. (2002). Competencies: A new sector. *Journal of European Industrial Training, 26*(2), 156–176.

Brudney, D. (2007). Hotel owners and operators expecting higher yield from increases in more personalized, direct selling expenses.

Choi, J.-G., Woods, R. H., & Murrmann, S. K. (2000). International labor markets and the migration of labor forces as an alternative solution for labor shortages in the hospitality industry. *International Journal of Contemporary Hospitality Management, 12*(1), 61–67.

Council on Education for Public Health. (2006).

Crawford, A., & Hubbard, S. S. (2007). The impact of work-related goals on hospitality industry employee variables. *Tourism and Hospitality Research, 8*, 116–124.

Goodman, R., & Sprague, L. (1991). The future of hospitality education: Meeting the industry's needs. *The Cornell and Restaurant Administration Quarterly*, *32*(2), 66–70.

Harvey, L. (2001). Defining and measuring employability. *Quality in Higher Education*, *7*(2), 97–110. ISSN 1353-8322.

Harvey, L., Burrows, A., & Green, D. (1992). *Criteria of quality*. Birmingham, England: Quality in Higher Education.

Harvey, L., Moon, S., & Geall, V., Bower, R. (1997). *Graduates' work: Organisational change and students' attributes*. Birmingham: Centre for Research into Quality, University of Central England in Birmingham and Association of Graduate Recruiters.
Hillage, J., & Pollard, E. (1998). *Employability: Developing a framework for policyanalysis*. Department for Education and Employment (DfEE) Research report. No RR85. London: DfEE.
Horng, J., & Lu, H. (2006). Needs assessment of professional competencies of F&B/hospitality management students at college and university level. *Journal of Teaching in Travel and Tourism, 6*(3), 1–26.
Iorgulescu, M.-C., & Răvar, A. S. (2013). Measuring managers' perception of innovation in the romanian hospitality industry. *Procedia Economics and Finance, 6,* 512–522.
Korkut, U. (2006). Nationalism versus internationalism: The roles of political and cultural elites in interwar and communist Romania. *Nationalities Papers, 34*(2), 131–155.
Lashley, C. (2007). Discovering hospitality: Observations from recent research. *International Journal of Culture, Tourism and Hospitality Research, 1,* 214–226.
Light, D. (2007). Dracula tourism in Romania cultural identity and the state. *Annals of Tourism Research, 34*(3), 746–765.
Okeiyi, E., Finley, D., & Postel, R. T. (1994). Food and beverage management competencies: Educator, industry, and student perspectives. *Hospitality & Tourism Educator, 6*(4), 37–40.
Purcell, K., Pitcher, J., & Simm, C. (1999). *Working out? Graduates' early experience of the labour market*. Manchester: CSU.
Riegel, C., & Dallas, M. (2006). Hospitality and tourism: Careers in the world's largest industry. In *Guide to college programs in hospitality, tourism, & culinary arts. council on hotel, restaurant, and institutional education* (pp. 5–50).
Statista. (2017). Global hotel industry retail value from 2010 to 2018 (in billion U.S. dollars). Retrieved from https://www.statista.com/statistics/247264/total-revenue-of-the-global-hotel-industry/.
Tas, R. (1988). Teaching future managers. *Cornell Hotel and Restaurant Administration Quarterly, 29*(2), 41–43.
Tascu, M.-V., Noftsinger, J., & Bowers, S. (2002). The problem of post-communist education: The Romanian example. *The Journal of Social, Political, and Economic Studies, 27*(2), 203.
Whitney, L. (2010). High hopes in hospitality. Daily Mail. Retrieved May 6, 1999, from http://www.dailymail.co.uk.
World Travel and Tourism Concil. (2007). United States: The 2007 travel & tourism economic research.

The manufacturer's authorised representative in the EU is Springer Nature Customer Service Centre GmbH, Europaplatz 3, 69115 Heidelberg, Germany. If you have any concerns regarding our products, please contact ProductSafety@springernature.com

Printed and bound by CPI Group (UK) Ltd, Croydon, CR0 4YY
30/09/2026
02225263-0002